D1561508

PROFITABLE GRAIN TRADING

By

Ralph M. Ainsworth

with a new Introduction by
Edward D. Dobson

TRADERS PRESS, INC.
P.O. Box 10344
Greenville, S.C. 29603

Library of Congress Catalog Card Number: 80-53316
ISBN: 0-934380-04-X

Other publications of Traders Press, Inc.:

COMMODITY SPREADS: A HISTORICAL CHART PERSPECTIVE
COMMODITY SPREADS: VOLUME 2
THE TRADING RULE THAT CAN MAKE YOU RICH *
VIEWPOINTS OF A COMMODITY TRADER
COMMODITIES: A CHART ANTHOLOGY

Published October, 1980

TRADERS PRESS, INC.
P.O. Box 10344
Greenville, S.C. 29603

TABLE OF CONTENTS

THIS BOOK *is especially dedicated to those who, having the speculative spirit, have no actual knowledge of the fundamental principles of successful commodity trading; to those who have an excess of income over outgo, or surplus funds, the one essential for commodity trading, which, if properly handled, can change the station of the individual of moderate income to one of financial independence.*

Ralph M. Ainsworth
1884 — 1965

PROFITABLE GRAIN TRADING

INTRODUCTION

It is with great pride that Traders Press makes available this early classic on commodity speculation, which was first published by Ralph M. Ainsworth in 1933. This book, like the works of W.D. Gann, was out of print and virtually unobtainable for many years. My friend, Billy Jones of Lambert-Gann Publishing Company, performed a valuable service for the commodity world by making Gann's works available again. It is my hope that a similarly valuable service will be rendered by my providing renewed access to this early classic to today's trader.

The author, Ralph M Ainsworth, was born in Mason City, Illinois, in 1884. Ainsworth was a well known pioneer in the seed industry, author, grain trader, farmer, and a shrewd real estate speculator. He established Ainsworth's Financial Service, which published a weekly grain market forecasting letter for many years. This letter, which was widely read by grain farmers and speculators, was the largest in the country at the time it was published, primarily during the 1930's. Ainsworth was the best-known grain forecaster of his time. He discontinued his letter in 1941, because he felt that the government had become too involved in regulating the grain industry for him to continue to operate effectively as a forecaster.

Though he was primarily a fundamentalist, Ainsworth fully recognized the value of technical analysis. In fact, the reader will note that much of the material in PROFITABLE GRAIN TRADING, Ainsworth's best known work, is technical in nature. I am informed that the trading rules contained herein were largely the result of a contest sponsored by Ainsworth. He offered $500 cash prizes for the best trading rules submitted by his subscribers, and the ones he published in PROFITABLE GRAIN TRADING were the ones he felt were the best. Their efficiency in today's volatile markets has not been tested, to my knowledge. We would welcome comments from any readers who decide to test their effectiveness using more current data. It should be self-evident that many of the factors discussed in this book, such as the use of a two cent stop, should be adjusted substantially to be relevant in today's trading environment.

I would like to express my thanks to Chester Keltner, of Keltner Statistical Service of Kansas City, Missouri. Mr. Keltner needs no introduction to anyone who has been associated with commodity trading for any length of time. I am indebted to Mr. Keltner for furnishing me with much of the personal information I was able to obtain on Ralph Ainsworth, and for information concerning the origin and history of Ainsworths Financial Service. Readers might be interested to note that Chester Keltner worked with Ainsworth from 1934 through 1938, during which time he helped in the writing of Ainsworth's weekly market letter. In the early 1940's, Keltner began publishing his own market letter, which is still being published at this writing, and which, like Ainsworth's, concentrates on the grain markets and has become one of the best known of its time.

Greenville, S.C.
September, 1980

Edward D. Dobson

N. AMERICA
Wheat

1 Dot = 100000 bushels
Laurentian Shield
Western Cordillera

Where wheat is grown.

CHAPTER I

My Experience as a Grain Trader

KNOWING that no fortune is ever amassed, or any business conducted, without the element of risk, and believing investment to be the most difficult art of business, I determined, while a student of Economics at the University of Chicago, to acquire this art (and at that time I made my first ventures in speculative trading in grain futures). That was twenty-seven years ago. With this determination constantly in mind, and in connection with my own personal speculative activities, I have for the past twenty-seven years made a diligent and exhaustive study of investments and tradings in wheat, corn, cotton, stocks and bonds, with the result that I have proven conclusively to myself that intelligent commodity trading affords a maximum opportunity for profit, with a minimum assumption of risk. And I believe my own experience and long study enables me to prove this to others and valuably assist them in making profitable trades in grain futures.

That you may know the advice I offer is not an experiment but has been learned in the hard school of experience, I feel sure I may be pardoned when on subsequent pages I speak frankly of my personal financial efforts, and tabulate my profits and losses by years, as a concrete illustration of the subject.

It was not until I had spent six or seven years studying and trading, that I finally succeeded in overcoming the more serious pitfalls which confront every amateur speculator, although I admit I lost heavily in 1930–31 after having had twenty-five years experience. At first I was tempted to overtrade, overstay my market, sell too soon, take too small profits, trade too often, buy wheat when it should have been corn, or vice versa, or make my trades in Chicago when Winnipeg or Kansas City offered a better opportunity for profit, et cetera.

From the beginning, I have tried to be conservative, not putting all my "eggs in one basket," therefore, in the beginning (twenty-seven years ago) I worked out the following three-way financial plan for myself:

My capital, which at that time consisted of only Three Thousand Dollars ($3000.00), was divided into three funds:

FIRST: $1000.00 was to be straight savings and placed in a Savings Account and allowed to grow.

SECOND: $1000.00 was to be used in the buying of bonds of the investment class. These were railroad bonds which later declined to less than 50 cents on the dollar.

THIRD: $1000.00 was to be used as Margin Money in buying and selling of grain, cotton, sugar, and other commodities, with the understanding that all trades would be limited and should not exceed in commodity value four times the amount of available margin.

All profits accruing from the investment of each fund were to be left in that particular account. I was to look to my cash grain business for my livelihood.

As the years passed and I observed that my Grain Account was faring so much better than the Savings and Bond Investment Accounts, I became impatient to use the latter funds in more profitable lines of investment.

Fortunes are never made in a savings account. They are only conserved and protected there after first being made. If you have a fortune in a savings bank, you put it there, or some one put it there for you. It did not grow there. Therefore, my Savings Account was changed to Farm Land Investment Account and my Bond Investment Account was made to include Stocks as well as Bonds.

Altogether I have purchased six farms and sold four.

Notwithstanding the fact that these four farms, aggregating four hundred and sixty acres, were sold at war peak prices, I made less than Twenty-five Thousand Dollars on the four trades. And in these trades I had assumed Nineteen Thousand Dollars in mortgages which was later

The above trade was the result of a correct forecast of damage due to winter killing in the spring of 1928.

paid. In my other Accounts, no indebtedness was assumed at any time. In 1933 I bought two more farms from profits made in the grain market. As I write this book in 1933 I have a lot of land, no debts, and not very much cash. My fortune, such as it is, was made in the grain market. I have never inherited a dollar.

The $7,731.25 which I had in the Grain Account in 1915, (as shown in statement on page 23 has grown in twelve years to $115,124.32. In addition the interest I have received from this account would amount to fully $20,000.00 more. The grain buying has been mostly May corn, May wheat, July corn, and September wheat. During all these years very few scalping trades (frequent small profit trades) have been made. Most of the trades were allowed to run open several weeks and sometimes months and in no case was more than half of the capital required for margin. While this Account has been by far the most profitable, it has actually been less hazardous than the Farm Land Investment Account or the Bond Account, and in my opinion, it always will be.

Until 1912 I depended, to a certain extent, on a successful grain trader for market advice. He told me of certain rules to which all the big traders adhered. He also stated that the big traders were seldom short on the market. Mention was made of one in particular, who had made millions in grain and cotton and who had never been short the market. I disagree with this now and take the short side with just as much confidence as I take the long side.

I owe more, in a financial way, to this friend, who was a student of practical economics, than I do to any other person. He helped me get started in the right direction twenty years ago. I only wish I might here give him the credit that is due him.

This friend once said: "The Dream of Speculation is to invest a dollar and have it double within a year. This doubling process, if carried on for thirty years, would, if successful, make the trader the richest man in the world, but it has never yet been done. The continuity is always broken and no one will succeed who follows a 'risk all' program."

The year of 1929 was the most memorable year in my experience as a grain trader, although 1933 was the most satisfactory because I had learned by that time that grain is not always a bargain when it is selling at less than the cost of production.

In 1929, about half of my profits were loaned to two large brokerage houses. The invoice on page 10 shows $47,145.64, which I loaned to Lamson Brothers and for which they paid me 8¼ per cent interest. In one month this income amounted to $366.76. As this book goes to press, brokers are not paying 8¼ per cent interest on substantial balances. As a matter of fact, they are paying only about one per cent a year for the use of my money.

A profitable short sale made in a time of public excitement.

Since 1931 I have been very happy to trade in five thousand bushel units and find I can be more nearly right on a five thousand bushel unit in cash grain than I was on a fifty thousand bushel trade in 1928.

Over-trading will make a coward of any man and so warp his judgment that he cannot hope to succeed. It was not until the last two years when I traded in smaller quantities that I realized the fullest pleasure from trading. As

I have just said 1933 has been my most successful year as a grain trader. In that year, my profits on all trades, showing a gain, totalled $1.74¾ per bushel against losses on all loss trades of 14⅜ cents. My net gains over all losses amounted to $1.60⅜ per bushel. (See itemized trades on page 192.)

What follows in this book is not theory, it is the result

FORM 12 25M 1-33			CHICAGO, 10-30-33 19					
ACCOUNT PURCHASE AND SALE OF 5000 Bu / Corn								
BY **LAMSON BROS. & CO.** 2200 BOARD OF TRADE BUILDING								
FOR ACCOUNT AND RISK OF								
LEDGER 1			Rm Ainsworth			N° 34831		
No. K553								
DATE	BOUGHT	SOLD	DELIVERY	PRICE				
10 16	5		July	48 1/4	2 41 2 50			
30		5	—	55 1/4		2 76 2 50		
			A LONG POSITION					
							3 50	
LAMSON BROS. & CO.				TAX	1 40			
PER			COMMISSION		1 7 50		13 90	
E & O E			TO YOUR				3 36 10	

A short swing trade in corn. Not a single loss was taken on a corn trade in over a year.

of my own personal experience as a trader in grain futures.

No apology is offered for the manner in which the subject matter in this book is treated. This book has been six years in the making. Most of the material appeared currently in a weekly publication issued by Ainsworth's Financial Service. Therefore, I hope the reader will overlook some slight repetitions. The better rules have all been checked with actual markets in order to show just what performance may be expected, as well as the amount of margin required when the application of these rules carry the trader into heavy paper losses. Most of these trading rules are checked only to 1928 or 1929 because those were the years when they were first published.

I trust my readers will pardon the personal references made in this chapter to my own experiences as a trader. I have what I consider a good reason for making personal allusions to my own trades. My library is full of financial books, mostly written in 1929 by economists and theorists. These books were careful to suggest how a fortune might easily be made through proper investments in good stocks and bonds, but not one book told what the author did with his own funds—assuming that he had any funds to invest. This is not that kind of a book since it portrays the past record of an individual trader in times when he was wrong as well as times when he was right.

It is because I have made more money and with less risk in grain trading than in any other line of business, that I offer to my readers all the more important grain trading rules used by prominent traders in arriving at their buying and selling prices. The book is complete in that it shows just how much capital is required to trade under the various rules without too much danger of being pushed out before the objective is reached.

On the following pages I am giving my profits and losses by years to show that the profits have been consistent and that the element of luck has not been a factor in the building of my estate.

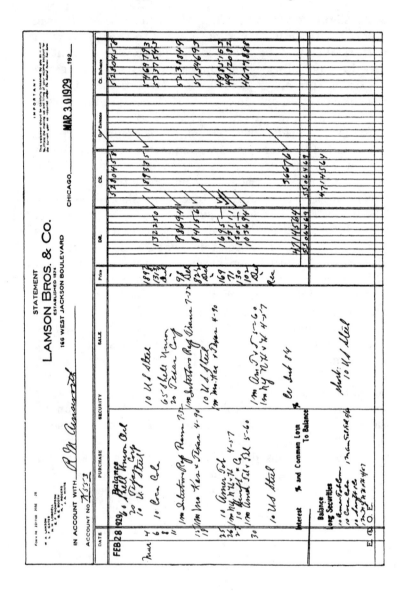

CHAPTER II

Why a Futures Market?

THE excuse for the institution of futures trading can be found by making a study of the technique of organized markets. I shall only be able to cover in the very briefest manner the technique of futures trading in grains and other commodities. This subject is of such vital importance to the orderly marketing of grain that dozens of books have been written on futures trading. In my opinion, the three outstanding books on this subject are: "Future Trading on Organized Commodity Markets", by G. Wright Hoffman; "The Value of Organized Speculation", by Harrison H. Brace; and "Risk and Risk Bearing", by Charles O. Hardy.

Those who are about to read my book will probably be interested to know that the author has yet to see a book on the subject that condemns the institution of futures trading as conducted by the Chicago Board of Trade and other exchanges. While many books have been written on the technique of futures trading, I believe this is the only book ever published that includes all of the more popular trading rules used by veteran traders, millers, and others who are engaged in the cash grain business. The above mentioned books do not attempt to explain the art of grain speculation but deal only with mechanics of organized markets and their economic merit. I consider what follows in this chapter as extremely important to those who trade in grain futures.

The average man is apt to think of grain trading as a tug of war between a group of bulls who want higher prices on the one hand, and a group of bears who want lower prices on the other hand. I wish to say emphatically that this is not the case. As a matter of fact, there are very few speculators and grain merchants who really want grain to decline, unless it is for the purpose of reinstating lines that were closed out at a higher price.

In its simplest form, here is how the system works. First, let it be known, that the *long interest* is always exactly equal to the *short interest;* it could not be otherwise.

FORM 18 23M 5-23			CHICAGO, 10-30-23 19					
ACCOUNT PURCHASE AND SALE OF 10 M Bu Wheat								
BY LAMSON BROS. & CO. 2200 BOARD OF TRADE BUILDING								
FOR ACCOUNT AND RISK OF								
LEDGER 1 No. K553		R M Ainsworth				N? 34832		
DATE	BOUGHT	SOLD	DELIVERY	PRICE				
10 18	5		may	81⅝	4 0 81 25			
21	5			85	4 25 0			
					8 33 1 25			
20		10	—	92¾		9 27 5		
			A LONG POSITION			9 43 25		
LAMSON BROS. & CO.				TAX	4 70			
PER				COMMISSION	25		29 70	
E & O E			TO YOUR				9 14 05	

Taking profits at the top of a good advance in a major bear market then switching to the short side as shown in invoice on page 13.

But this does not mean that the *speculative* short account is equal to the *speculative* long account. Under any or all market situations, the *speculative* short account is only a small fraction of the *speculative* long account. The short account is mostly a hedging account against the actual holdings of cash grain.

We will now get back to the farmer who grows the grain. He is long grain because he raises it and has it to

sell, just the same as I am long grain when I buy a May or
July future. The price he receives is the Chicago cash
price minus the freight and handling charges which include some exceedingly small profits for those who are
engaged in the cash grain business. These profits are so
small that it can be said without fear of contradiction that

This trade and the one on page 12 were made by combining "The
Year Around Trading Plan," "Rule Eighteen" and "A Study of
Bear Markets." This was the last trade made before this book
went to press. The above trade is a short sale.

the farmer markets his wheat and corn at a lower marketing cost than is found in any other commodity with the
possible exception of cotton.

The cash buyer in Chicago buys the grain as it arrives
in carload lots and in competition with hundreds of other
buyers. The price he is willing to pay is determined
largely by the price of the futures. When the cash dealer

buys the grain, thanks to the futures market, he is not required to sell it immediately to the ultimate consumer. In
fact he is never required to sell it to a consumer; frequently none can be found. Furthermore, he will not want
to sell the grain he has just purchased if he can sell and
deliver into one of the delivery months at a higher price.
He will sell to his best advantage whether it be to consum-

A purchase made on cheapness of price alone and sold at price
midway between extreme price range for season.

ers or to speculators who are buying the futures with the
intention of seldom if ever taking delivery.

I hope I have made it clear that under normal marketing
conditions, those who have taken the short side of the
market are not, as a rule, speculators, but more often are
cash handlers of grain. In some cases they may be farmers, who, being satisfied with the price, sell the futures

short before their crop is harvested. Such trades are what
are called hedging or merchandising trades and are far
less speculative in character than is the case of a merchant
who lays in a stock of goods.

Remember, these merchandising short sales (hedging
sales) need never be bought in if a grain merchant has the
grain in Chicago to deliver on his contract. All that is
necessary for the cash handler to do is deliver his cash
grain on his short sale contract and his contract is closed.
In the case of a farmer selling short he must of course buy
in his short sale of grain unless he can actually make delivery in car lots in Chicago.

Under normal conditions, about eighty per cent of the
short side of the grain market represents merchandising
sales which situation is an important part of the machinery of marketing grain. The remaining twenty per cent
may be speculative short sales by that very small minor-
ity who, of course, desire a lower market in order to realize
profits.

When you understand this large speculative long interest and very small speculative short interest that does not
offset, it puts a new light on market action.

This lopsided interest produces a number of market situations that otherwise would never take place. It explains
why grain often advances rapidly in the midst of the crop
marketing season when receipts are tremendous and the
demand poor. This is because new speculative buyers are
continually being added to a bull market, which gives the
cash grain trade an opportunity to dispose of receipts that
sometimes run twenty times the current consumptive
needs. It explains why bear markets are frequently of
very long duration, whereas, bull markets seldom last
over 30 days. When a market starts to decline and a group
of traders become discouraged and desire to unload their
holdings of long grain, it is invariably sold to other traders who are willing to take the long side at the lower
figure. In other words, it is *new longs* who are buying the

grain that is being liquidated. For twelve months in the year speculators throw the grain back and forth at each other and this is what makes a market.

The cash handler has already completed his trade, when he sold the future short since the grain he has purchased has been conditioned and warehoused and is now being stored to deliver on his short sale as soon as the delivery month arrives. The delivery month may be May, September, July or December.

Just keep in mind that there is seldom a tug of war between longs and shorts as is popularly supposed. In the majority of cases, it cannot be said that a short seller makes five thousand dollars when one who is long loses five thousand dollars. If I make five thousand dollars on the long side of the grain market, I never know just who lost the five thousand dollars and I am glad I don't know. But I do know that in four cases out of five the loss was assumed by some trader who got long at the wrong time and wrong price.

Who loses what the more skillful speculators make? There can be only one answer. It must be other speculators who are less skillful. It can be said positively, that over a period of years the money that is made in grain speculation is not lost by the cash grain handlers as a group; neither is it lost by farmers as a group. This loss, which is a part of the hazards of risk bearing, is lost by a very large group of inexperienced speculators.

You can answer this question to your own satisfaction if you will first ask yourself a question. "How many people do you know of who have lost a large sum of money over a period of years on the short side of the grain market? How many speculators do you know of who sold corn and wheat short in the summer of 1933?" Your friends were either out of the market or else they were long. As is usually the case they left the short side to the cash grain trade who actually held cash grain and were short the futures.

The following item appeared in the Chicago Tribune on October 12, 1933:

"Cash interests were good buyers of December corn yesterday against sales of the May delivery, and were understood to be changing over hedges into the deferred future. The bulk of the changing was around 6¾ cents a bushel premium for the May delivery, which was regarded as a satisfactory carrying charge."

This illustrates a process that is in continuous operation. In this particular case cash interests could not get enough spot corn so they were buying the December to take delivery in December and sold the May to deliver the grain at a higher price in May. No matter what course the market takes these cash handlers will receive 6¾ cents for storing corn and keeping it in condition for four months under conditions as shown in the above clipping. This shows why the speculative short interest is so exceedingly small compared to the long interest.

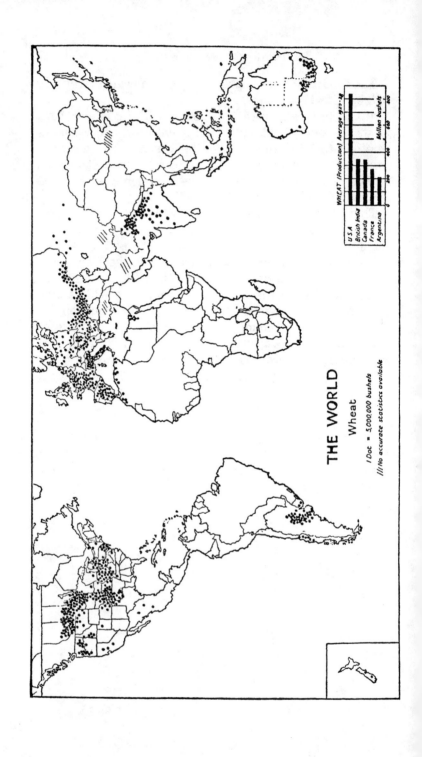

THE WORLD

Wheat

1 Dot = 5,000,000 bushels

/// No accurate statistics available

WHEAT (Production) Average 1923-'28

U.S.A
British India
Canada
France
Argentina

Million bushels
0   200   400   600   800

CHAPTER III

Trading Terms Explained

INEXPERIENCED traders will need to study this chapter carefully and familiarize themselves with certain trade phrases in order to fully understand the contents of this book.

HIGH AND LOW: Throughout this book and particularly in the chapter referring to the "Year Around Trading Plan," we use the terms the "low" of August, the "low" of the month before, the "high" of the season, etc. These terms are abbreviations for the lowest price reached in the period referred to or else they mean the highest price reached in the period referred to.

I would not consider it necessary to mention the above interpretation except that in previous writings, some inexperienced traders have been confused by these terms.

BEAR: This term refers to one who seeks or desires lower prices.

BULL: A person who believes in higher prices or one who buys grain futures, stocks or bonds and holds for higher prices. Bulling the market means trying to advance prices.

LONG: A man who has bought grain futures and who is holding these futures in expectation of higher profits is long the market.

SHORT: A person who sells something with the hope of buying it later at a lower price and thereby securing a profit is short the market.

HEDGING: Those who sell short against the actual holdings of cash grain are indifferent regarding the future course of the market. They would just as soon have the market go up as down or vice versa. The hedger likes especially to have the more distant futures sell at the full carrying charge above the cash.

CARRYING CHARGE: Carrying charges always refer to cash grain and include only storage rates in terminal warehouses, interest and insurance on grain and other commodities.

STOP OR STOP ORDER: This is an order to close a trade for a certain price through limiting the loss or profit as the case may be. For example, if the trader has bought wheat for May delivery at 85 cents and wishes to limit his loss at 3 cents a bushel, he places a stop loss order at 82 cents.

VISIBLE SUPPLY: By visible supply is meant the stocks of grain in public elevators in large cities and afloat on canals, lakes and rivers.

COMMISSIONS: Commissions are a nominal charge which usually amounts to $12.50 on 5,000 bushels of grain. It is charged by brokers for the buying and selling of the property.

SHORT INTEREST: This usually refers to that small percentage of the open short interest that has taken the short side of the market in the hope of securing a speculative profit and not as a hedge against the actual holding of cash grain. This explains why the short interest is sometimes stated as being very small or very large. After a major decline, a large short interest is bullish because it will want to buy and take profits at some point. A small short interest after a major decline is bearish since the number of traders who buy in their grain, close their contracts and take profits is too small to be a major market force. In the great market decline of July to October 1933 the speculative short interest was very small. Therefore when traders were forced to close out long lines it was necessary to find other traders who were willing to take a long position. There were no speculative shorts to buy in take profits and support the market.

CHAPTER IV

Successful Grain Speculation

THE man who is a successful grain speculator may be compared with the expert at checkers, contract bridge, or poker. He must know the rules of the game; but, on the other hand, he must not be completely bound down by these rules. There are times when independent judgment should be substituted for even the best of rules.

The expert in checkers who walks along a table and plays ten men at a time and beats them all has over 10,000 possible plays committed to memory. He has the board numbered. He has read all the authorities. When his opponent makes a certain play, he knows instantly what play to make because he knows thousands of best positions. The expert at checkers is a rule-and-thumb player. He is mechanical. He uses little independent judgment or thought.

With the expert at contract bridge, three-fourths of the skill consists of knowing the rules of bidding and of play, and one-fourth is probably independent judgment in which the expert learns where all the cards lie by the manner in which they are played by the opponents.

The expert at poker knows the relative value of every hand, yet his skill as a winner depends as much on bluff as it does on his knowledge of the rules of the game. The poker player must continually fool his opponents into thinking his hand is less valuable or more valuable than it really is. Therefore, he occasionally makes small, absurd bets to mislead his opponents deliberately.

The expert in grain speculation does not depend on thousands of mechanical rules to the extent witnessed in a championship checker game; and, on the other hand, he does not use the bluff that is used in poker. He is more

21

like the expert at bridge. He knows a hundred rules for conservative trading practice. They are his stock in trade and they guide him in all his operations. Yet they do not blind him to independent judgment.

Technical Knowledge

The mental furniture of the expert grain speculator includes a knowledge of seasonal trends: The months of the year when wheat normally sells at its highest and lowest points; average daily, monthly, and yearly price swings expressed in per cent—not in cents. Tables and charts are available to show the extent of these swings.

Many of the older traders have charts of grain price movements on their office walls. Patten depended more upon tables arranged in book form.

In periods of congestion, scalping methods are used, and at other times long pull methods are used. Resistance points are shown by the "Head and Shoulder Method" and "stops" are sometimes placed just above and below these points. Trades are always made with a proper regard to the amount of margin which the trader can furnish or which he is willing to risk.

The value of a five or ten per cent reduction or increase in world production is expressed in terms of the per cent that should be taken from or added to the value of a bushel of wheat. The difference in the price of cash wheat and the price of the more distant futures has some effect on the market opinion of the seasoned trader in grain futures. His judgment is also influenced more or less by the size of the open interest, daily volume of trading, advertising effect of the crop damage reports that make the front pages of daily papers, and a hundred other factors. All of this knowledge (most of which is made available in charts and tables) is obtained from a study of past markets.

No speculator has ever learned all that tables, charts, and the history of past markets has to offer. It is estimated that twenty years of study is required to have a good working knowledge of all the hundreds of factors that make grain prices. If it takes twenty years to learn to be an expert at bridge, it should take twenty years to learn the basic underlying principles of successful grain speculation. The bridge player has his text books, and the grain trader has his *Market Service* to aid him in this work.

My Grain Profits and Losses for Seventeen Years

Year	Quantity Bushels	Net Gain or Loss for Yr.	Capital at End of Yr.	Maximum Margin Required
1912........	10,000	1,025.00	2,025.00	630
1913........	10,000	506.25	2,531.25	1,000
1914........	10,000	200.00	2,731.25	800
Added $5,000.00 to trading capital				
1915........	30,000	1,552.50	9,283.75	4,000
1916........	40,000	6,987.55	16,271.30	3,500
1917........	30,000	5,891,00	22,162.30	2,500
1918........	50,000	8,790.00	30,952.30	8,980
1919........	100,000	32,025.00	62,977.30	6,000
1920........	100,000	16,181.25	79,158.55	12,000
1921........	100,000	*11,650.85	67,507.70	35,000
1922........	120,000	12,968.50	80,476.20	11,000
1923........	80,000	6,193.25	86,669.45	16,000
1924........	120,000	10,726.52	97,395.97	6,000
1925........	135,000	1,756.54	99,152.51	22,000
1926........	120,000	*4,062.03	95,090.48	16,000
1927........	120,000	5,408.84	100,499.32	16,500
1928........	120,000	20,625.00	121,124.32	15,300

Less Original Capital....6,000.00

115,124.32

The asterisk (*) shows the two years when losses were taken.

When I started as a grain speculator in 1912, all I knew was to sell on major bulges (without the aid of stops) in the season of the year when grain normally sold highest, and to buy on breaks at the season of the year when grain normally sold lowest. I also knew that I was willing to risk just $1,000 on the venture.

I had been told that James A. Patten was a long pull trader and used his knowledge of seasonal and monthly swings to good advantage. Therefore, I arranged the May

Wheat futures in tables of monthly highs and lows to give me the monthly extreme price range, starting with 1897; and, three years later, I added July Wheat, May Corn and July Corn to my table.

The tables, charts, comments, and rules cover 306 typewritten pages. From this *very limited field* of market study, I succeeded in making my original capital of $1,000 in 1912 grow to $115,124.32 by August, 1928—as shown in the preceding table of profits and losses, and also as itemized in "Investment Buying." Since I was financed on two occasions by others I had to pay a part of the profits to two other traders. Now I trade only for my own account. I don't care to divide with partners.

I shall now give the rules for making long pull commitments in grain speculation, as brought out in the "Year Around Trading Plan." These profits were actually obtained without the aid of either that most remarkable of all scalping rules, "Trading Rule Number Eleven," or "Trading Rule Number Eighteen," which helps to find the end of a bull market; and without any of the splendid help which is obtained from the other factors I have enumerated above.

I want to present one thing at a time to the readers of this book. You will now get the buying and selling rules which made me a fortune in grain trading in the earlier days of my trading experience.

CHAPTER V

The Year Around Trading Plan

T HIS is called the "Year Around Trading Plan" because the trading in one future overlaps with that of a more distant future. With the possible exception of a short period in September or October, the trader is long grain the year around. In theory the rule can not fail to show a profit when applied to any ten-year period. It is based on what some traders claim is the one and only axiom in successful speculation, which is: "The sum total of all the yearly, monthly, weekly, and daily *highs* of wheat or corn is a larger figure than the sum total of all the yearly, monthly, weekly, and daily *lows*."

If it were possible to recognize the daily *lows* when they come, and buy at these *lows*, then recognize the daily *highs* and sell at these *highs*—a trader with $1,000 to start with could have $1,000,000 before the end of the year. But no trader can recognize these daily *highs* and *lows* until after the market has closed. Therefore, he does the best he can in finding the approximate daily *highs* and *lows* by following *"Trading Rule Number Eleven"* which is carefully explained and checked with nine months of daily markets on pages 92 to 101.

A long pull trading plan attempts to use to advantage the monthly price range as well as the seasonal price range. In a normal ten-year period, wheat averages selling lowest in November and highest in June, with July coming second. If only a trader could buy May Wheat at the lowest price reached in November and sell it at the highest price reached in March, April, or May—he could, in a period of five or ten years, make his $1,000 of margin grow into $1,000,000. If wheat could be bought on the *low day* in November and could be sold on the *high day* in

25

May, the trader would often take advantage of the full season's price swing. But, since the monthly and seasonal lows are never known until after they are passed, the trader who tries to catch only the major swings often *feels his way* by applying the rules of the *"Year Around Trading Plan."*

He wants to take on a line of May Wheat and May Corn on some major break in the fall months. Then, in order to *average out* he will undertake to buy July Corn in the period between December 1 and May 30, and he will later try to add September Wheat on some market break in the period of March 1 to July 30. If he can not buy on breaks he will not buy. He is willing to be long 10,000 bushels each of May Wheat, May Corn, July Corn, and September Wheat—all at the same time, although it seldom works this way.

Starting his plan in August, he attempts to buy both May Wheat and May Corn. Let us assume that our long pull trader considers 10,000 bushels of May Wheat his *line* and 5,000 bushels a unit for trading. The same applies to May Corn.

The Buying of May Wheat and May Corn

In September he places an order to buy 10,000 bushels of May Wheat and 10,000 of May Corn at the lowest price reached in August, and three years out of four he gets his lines of wheat and corn in September at the *low* of August. Failing to secure his wheat and corn in September at the August low, he places an order in October at the September low. Should he fail to secure his wheat and corn in October at the September low, the effort is repeated in November to buy at the October low. Should he fail, he again attempts to buy in December at the November low. Nine times out of ten he will secure his wheat and corn at the low of some previous month before the first of January.

But this trader wants to average out. He wants to carry

his plan the year around. He wants to "average out" the purchase of wheat against the purchase of corn. He is like the banker who knows that it takes some of the profit from good loans to make up for the loss on bad loans. In a year's trading this investment buyer of grain futures is determined that his profits will more than offset certain inevitable losses. He is determined to average out, so he proceeds as follows. (See a more detailed explanation for the buying and selling of May Wheat on page 39.)

The Buying of July Corn

In December, regardless of whether he has a big paper profit or big paper loss in his wheat deal, he undertakes to buy July Corn. Therefore, he places an order in December to buy 10,000 bushels of July Corn which is exactly equal to his line of May Wheat. He endeavors to buy his 10,000 bushels of July Corn at the lowest price reached in November. If not secured, the order is placed in January to buy at the lowest price reached in December. Each month he attempts to buy at the low of the month before, until his July Corn is obtained.

If he fails to obtain his July Corn at the low of some previous month, he gives up the effort in June.

The Buying of September Wheat

But this trader wants a still better opportunity to average out. So, regardless of how great his paper profits or losses may be on May Wheat and July Corn, he makes an effort to buy 10,000 bushels of September Wheat on a major reaction. But, he makes no attempt to buy September Wheat until sometime in March. And even then, he will not buy at the lowest price reached in February, because his experience has taught him that September Wheat often reaches its lowest price of the season in March, after the spring rains have discounted most of the hazards of winter killing. He is, therefore, very conservative at the start and will not buy his September Wheat unless he can obtain it at 2 cents below the lowest price reached in February. Should he fail to get his wheat in March at 2 cents below the February low, he places an order in April to buy at the low in March. If not secured, an order is placed in May to buy at the April low. And so on, until the wheat is secured.

Bear in mind that the 2 cents discount is used only for the March buying order. Thus, the trader may find himself, sometime in April, with four lines of grain, all of which may show a paper profit or a paper loss, or some may show a paper profit and some a paper loss. But, he does not become unduly excited. He tries to get out of his trades just as systematically as he got in.

Regardless of how fortunate or unfortunate his position may be in the market, he has the happy satisfaction of knowing that each of his four purchases was made on a fair-sized decline from the season's high. Certainly the average of his four purchases is well below the average of the season's high, since he made his purchases at three and possibly four different periods of the year and each time on a decline. Always he bought against the trend, but never did he try to average down. When he got his 10,000 bushels of each future he was through buying until some was sold.

But, he will not undertake to dispose of a full line at any one time. Therefore, he uses the following selling plan for each of his four futures—which are May Wheat, May Corn, July Corn, and September Wheat.

Closing Out His Line of May Corn

In disposing of the 10,000 bushels of May Corn, exactly the same method is used as with wheat. In some cases the sales will be made on the same day as wheat, but more often not.

Closing Out His Line of July Corn

While the trader's 10,000 bushels of July Corn was purchased at one time and price, he will not close out all of his

July Corn at any one time or price. He proceeds as follows:—

5,000 bushels of July Corn is offered for sale at 8 cents above the purchase price, and if sold is repurchased on a 4 cent decline from the sale; resold on an 8 cent advance from the last purchase, and so on as many times as are possible.

5,000 bushels is offered for sale at 10 cents above the purchase price and bought back on a 5 cent break and resold on a 10 cent advance as many times as are possible.

All corn not disposed of under any of these selling plans is carried to the 25th of the delivery month of July and sold at the market, and profits or losses taken. If you are afraid to take delivery switch to September on June 25th and close out what September wheat may be left on July 25th.

Closing Out His Line of September Wheat

5,000 bushels of September Wheat is offered for sale at the first opportunity to secure a gross profit of 10 per cent. When and if sold, the grain is repurchased on a five per cent break, if the opportunity offers itself. Assuming that the grain can be repurchased on a five per cent break after taking a 10 per cent profit, it is again sold on a 10 per cent profit from the last purchase, and so on as many times as the opportunity offers.

5,000 bushels of September Wheat is held until August, regardless of how big the profits may have been in the meantime. It is then offered for sale in August at the highest price reached in July.

In the event that the trader is unable to dispose of his September Wheat under either of these two plans, the wheat is carried until the 25th day of September and sold at the market, in which case we will assume, for purposes of checking, that the carrying charge for 25 days will amount to approximately 2 cents. Experience has taught me that delivery is made only about half the time up to and including the 25th day of the delivery month.

Capital Required

In any mechanical plan of trading, the successful operator must know at the very start just what the maximum requirements are to carry the plan through to its objective.

In looking at the table on page 23 the trader will perhaps be very much surprised, as well as disappointed, to see that in 1921 it was necessary on one particular day for me to have a margin of $35,000 to margin 100,000 bushels of grain. This is equivalent to 35 cents a bushel. As a matter of fact, my actual margin requirement was somewhat less than $30,000, but my broker was given $35,000 because that was the amount he asked for. In all the other years, 20 cents a bushel was sufficient and in some years 5 cents was all that was ever required.

I also call your attention to the fact that in 1931 I had a loss and also in 1926, as shown by the asterisks in front of the amount. While my margin requirements were heavy at times, it is comforting to know that all of this margin had been made in the market. I was only using a part of what I had previously made, and after the first year it was never necessary for me to use as margin more than half of my profits. The trader who wishes to follow this plan literally and trade in as much as 40,000 bushels should feel that $6,000 in margin will carry him through any paper loss as long as wheat is selling close to $1.00 a bushel. In making this recommendation it is right in line with my own experience. It is possible, of course, that $6,000 might not be enough.

Profits to Be Expected

A glance at the table on page 23 will show that I averaged making 100 per cent each year on my margin money, which compares very favorably with certain very hazardous businesses. Home finance corporations that make a practice of lending $300 and less to individuals average getting an interest return of 22 per cent; but, after allowing for losses and overhead, their net profit is somewhat less than 10 per cent. The most successful of pawn brokers cannot hope for a gross profit of over 50 per cent on his capital. He does well if he has a net of 25 per cent.

I consider both of these enterprises more risky than systematic, mechanical speculation in grain futures. Neither are they so pleasant.

The Theory of Long Pull Mechanical Trading

The Year Around Trading Plan is like a circle; it has no end after the start has once been made.

Assuming that the trader has a big paper loss on his May Wheat and May Corn at the time when he is ready to take on his 10,000 bushels of July Corn, it naturally follows that his July Corn will be purchased on a drastic decline. After the purchase of July Corn, we will assume that the market continues to decline until March, when the trader is ready to buy September Wheat at the low of some previous month. After the purchase of September Wheat the market continues to decline for the rest of the season, in which case the trader has a loss for his year of trading. But, such a situation is not likely to happen more than one year in six, at the most.

In theory as well as in actual practice, this trading rule yields a fair profit when the price at the end of the year is about equal to the price at the beginning of the year. If, each year, grain sells at a higher price level—as occurred from 1914 to 1920—the profits each year are tremendous.

I Follow No Mechanical Plan Literally

To me it is always an indication of weakness for a trader to become wedded to some particular mechanical trading plan. It looks like he is trying to substitute a rule for independent thinking. Yet, that does not mean that rules should be disregarded. Every successful operator in wheat and other commodities has his rules which guide him in his trading. They help him to recognize a fair and worthwhile profit and also a proper decline in which to enter the market.

In giving my readers the Year Around Trading Plan, I have given them the most logical and workable of all long pull trading plans for operating in grain. There has never been a five-year period when this rule would not have shown a handsome return on the margin invested.

Checked With Thirty-Five Years

The Year Around Trading Plan is actually checked with 35 years in which each individual purchase and sale is shown. Capital to start with $30,000.00.

Gains and Losses By Years

By following literally the Year Around Trading Plan.

1897

May Wheat	20000 Bu.	Gain	$	4,164.99
Sept. Wheat	20000 Bu.	Gain		2,499.50
July Corn	20000 Bu.	Gain		325.00
May Corn	20000 Bu.	Loss		950.00
Net gain for year				6,038.50
Balance bro't. forward				36,038.50
Maximum margin required	$ 7,900			

1898

May Wheat	25000 Bu.	Gain	$	5,289.00
Sept. Wheat	25000 Bu.	Loss		3,787.50
July Corn	25000 Bu.	Gain		468.75
May Corn	25000 Bu.	Loss		93.75
Net gain for year				2,876.50
Balance bro't. forward				38,915.00
Maximum margin required	$ 12,000			

1899

May Wheat	30000 Bu.	Gain	$	4.037.50
Sept. Wheat	30000 Bu.	Loss		1,237.50
July Corn	30000 Bu.	Loss		2,287.50
May Corn	30000 Bu.	Gain		225.00
Net gain for year				737.50
Balance bro't. forward				39,652.50
Maximum margin required	$ 12,000			

Gains and Losses By Years

1900

May Wheat	35000 Bu.	Loss	$	3,423.45
Sept. Wheat	35000 Bu.	Gain		3,193.75
July Corn	35000 Bu.	Gain		3,143.75
May Corn	35000 Bu.	Gain		3,563.50

Net gain for year		6,477.55
Balance bro't. forward		46,130.05
Maximum margin required	$ 14,150	

1901

May Wheat	40000 Bu.	Loss	$	1,325.80
Sept. Wheat	40000 Bu.	Loss		594.90
July Corn	40000 Bu.	Gain		4,837.50
May Corn	40000 Bu.	Gain		5,625.00

Net gain for year		8,541.80
Balance bro't. forward		54,671.85
Maximum margin required	$ 16,800	

1902

May Wheat	45000 Bu.	Loss	$	193.55
Sept. Wheat	45000 Bu.	Gain		3,881.25
July Corn	45000 Bu.	Gain		5,175.00
May Corn	45000 Bu.	Gain		1,912.50

Net gain for year		10,775.20
Balance bro't. forward		65,447.05
Maximum margin required	$ 25,300	

1903

May Wheat	50000 Bu.	Loss	$	1,217.90
Sept. Wheat	50000 Bu.	Gain		8,318.20
July Corn	50000 Bu.	No trades possible.		
May Corn	50000 Bu.	Gain		1,187.50

Net gain for year		8,287.80
Balance bro't. forward		73,734.85
Maximum margin required	$ 18,300	

1904

May Wheat	55000 Bu.	Gain	$	6,565.65
Sept. Wheat	55000 Bu.	Gain		10,690.65
July Corn	55000 Bu.	Loss		550.00
May Corn	55000 Bu.	Loss		843.75

Net gain for year		15,862.55
Balance bro't. forward		89,597.40
Maximum margin required	$ 21,150	

Gains and Losses By Years

1905

May Wheat	60000 Bu.	Loss	$	2,853.50
Sept. Wheat	60000 Bu.	Loss		4,800.00
July Corn	60000 Bu.	Gain		6,175.00
May Corn	60000 Bu.	Gain		1,450.00

Net loss for year 28.50

Balance bro't. forward 89,568.90
Maximum margin required $ 32,175

1906

May Wheat	65000 Bu.	Loss	$	4,293.90
Sept. Wheat	65000 Bu.	Loss		5,278.95
July Corn	65000 Bu.	Gain		3,256.25
May Corn	65000 Bu.	Gain		2,437.50

Net loss for year 3,879.10

Balance bro't. forward 85,689.80
Maximum margin required $ 32,175

1907

May Wheat	70000 Bu.	Gain	$	3,382.15
Sept. Wheat	70000 Bu.	Gain		6,142.50
July Corn	70000 Bu.	Gain		6,106.25
May Corn	70000 Bu.	Gain		3,512.50

Net gain for year 19,143.40

Balance bro't. forward 104,833.20
Maximum margin required $ 28,700

1908

May Wheat	75000 Bu.	Gain	$	333.55
Sept. Wheat	75000 Bu.	Gain		7,921.90
July Corn	75000 Bu.	Gain		8,125.00
May Corn	75000 Bu.	Gain		9,093.75

Net gain for year 25,474.20

Balance bro't. forward 130,307.40
Maximum margin required $ 48,610

1909

May Wheat	80000 Bu.	Gain	$	11,853.75
Sept. Wheat	80000 Bu.	Gain		3,122.50
July Corn	80000 Bu.	Gain		6,212.50
May Corn	80000 Bu.	Gain		6,918.75

Net gain for year 28,107.50

Balance bro't. forward 158,444.90
Maximum margin required $ 50,400

Gains and Losses By Years

1910

May Wheat	85000 Bu.	Loss	$ 817.05
Sept. Wheat	85000 Bu.	Loss	5,185.60
July Corn	85000 Bu.	Loss	3,293.75
May Corn	85000 Bu.	Gain	2,362.60

Net gain for year   6,933.90

Balance bro't. forward   151,511.00
Maximum margin required $ 55,350

1911

May Wheat	90000 Bu.	Loss	$ 7,995.00
Sept. Wheat	90000 Bu.	Gain	5,061.20
July Corn	90000 Bu.	Gain	7,875.00
May Corn	90000 Bu.	Loss	7,987.50

Net loss for year   3,046.30

Balance bro't. forward   148,464.70
Maximum margin required $ 70,200

1912

May Wheat	95000 Bu.	Gain	$ 7,644.55
Sept. Wheat	95000 Bu.	Loss (Error)	6,862.50
July Corn	95000 Bu.	Gain	7,875.00
May Corn	95000 Bu.	Gain	11,300.00

Net gain for year   24,957.05

Balance bro't. forward   173,421.75
Maximum margin required $ 53,250

1913

May Wheat	100000 Bu.	Loss	$ 4,878.75
Sept. Wheat	100000 Bu.	Loss	1,613.10
July Corn	100000 Bu.	No trades this year.	
May Corn	100000 Bu.	Gain	1,056.25

Net loss for year   5,435.60

Balance bro't. forward   168,986.15
Maximum margin required $ 46,000

1914

May Wheat	105000 Bu.	Gain	$ 1,523.20
Sept. Wheat	105000 Bu.	Gain	20,146.90
July Corn	105000 Bu.	Gain	3,412.50
May Corn	105000 Bu.	Loss	262.50

Net gain for year   24,820.10

Balance bro't. forward   193,806.25
Maximum margin required $ 73,950

Gains and Losses By Years

1915

May Wheat	110000 Bu.	No trades this year	
Sept. Wheat	110000 Bu.	Loss	$ 4,537.50
July Corn	110000 Bu.	Gain	13,562.50
May Corn	110000 Bu.	Gain	6,500.00

Net gain for year	15,525.00

Balance bro't. forward	209,331.25
Maximum margin required $ 67,100	

1916

May Wheat	115000 Bu.	Gain	$ 19,500.00
Sept. Wheat	115000 Bu.	Gain	31,013.90
July Corn	115000 Bu.	Gain	7,650.00
May Corn	115000 Bu.	Gain	11,712.50

Net gain for year	69,876.40

Balance bro't. forward	279,207.65
Maximum margin required $ 74,750	

1917

May Wheat	120000 Bu.	Gain	$ 43,430.00
Sept. Wheat	120000 Bu.	Gain	15,480.00
Note: Plan 6 not used in Sept.			
July Corn	120000 Bu.	No trades possible.	
May Corn	120000 Bu.	No trades possible.	

Net gain for year	58,910.00

Balance bro't. forward	338,117.65
Maximum margin required $ 72,800	

1918

May Wheat	125000 Bu.	Wheat trading discontinued	
Sept. Wheat	125000 Bu.	by order of Chicago Board of Trade.	
July Corn	125000 Bu.	Gain	$ 14,825.00
May Corn	125000 Bu.	Gain	20,125.00

Net gain for year	43,950.00

Balance bro't. forward	382,067.65
Maximum margin required $ 44,900	

1919

May Wheat	130000 Bu.	Wheat trading discontinued	
Sept. Wheat	130000 Bu.	by order of Chicago Board of Trade.	
July Corn	130000 Bu.	Gain	$ 43,612.50
May Corn	130000 Bu.	Gain	52,462.50

Net gain for year	96,075.00

Balance bro't. forward	478,142.65
Maximum margin required $ 41,700	

Gains and Losses By Years

1920

May Wheat	135000 Bu.	Wheat trading discontinued	
Sept. Wheat	135000 Bu.	by order of Chicago Board of Trade.	
July Corn	135000 Bu.	Gain	$ 8,831.25
May Corn	135000 Bu.	Gain	39,712.50

Net gain for year	48,543.75

Balance bro't. forward	526,686.40
Maximum margin required	$ 51,050

1921

May Corn	140000 Bu.	Gain	$ 1,444.00
Sept. Wheat	140000 Bu.	No trades possible	
July Corn	140000 Bu.	Loss	11,725.00
May Wheat	140000 Bu.	Loss	70,000.00

Net loss for year	80,281.00

Balance bro't. forward	446,405.40
Maximum margin required	$215,600

1922

May Wheat	145000 Bu.	Gain	$ 22,198.00
Sept. Wheat	145000 Bu.	No trades possible account no figures available.	
July Corn	145000 Bu.	Gain	9,262.50
May Corn	145000 Bu.	Gain	10,237.50

Net gain for year	41,698.00

Balance bro't. forward	488,103.40
Maximum margin required	$ 38,100

1923

May Wheat	150000 Bu.	Gain	$ 21,338.00
Sept. Wheat	150000 Bu.	Loss	17,060.00
July Corn	150000 Bu.	Gain	14,725.00
May Corn	150000 Bu.	No trades possible	

Net gain for year	19,003.00

Balance bro't. forward	507,106.40
Maximum margin required	$ 70,500

1924

May Wheat	155000 Bu.	Loss	$ 7,846.00
Sept. Wheat	155000 Bu.	Gain	31,756.00
July Corn	155000 Bu.	Gain	18,793.75
May Corn	150000 Bu.	Loss	5,350.00

Net gain for year	37,353.75

Balance bro't. forward	544,460.15
Maximum margin required	$ 91,550.00

Gains and Losses By Years

1925

May Wheat	160000 Bu.	Gain	$ 26,206.00
Sept. Wheat	160000 Bu.	Gain	22,400.00
July Corn	160000 Bu.	Loss	35,400.00
May Corn	155000 Bu.	Loss	18,212.00

Net loss for year   5,006.00

Balance bro't. forward   539,454.15
Maximum margin required $196,000

1926

May Wheat	165000 Bu.	Gain	$ 12,776.00
Sept. Wheat	165000 Bu.	Gain	5,720.00
July Corn	165000 Bu.	Loss	16,706.25
May Corn	160000 Bu.	Loss	29,792.00

Net loss for year   28,002.25

Balance bro't. forward   511,451.70
Maximum margin required $150,000

1927

May Wheat	170000 Bu.	Gain	$ 21,361.00
Sept. Wheat	170000 Bu.	Gain	3,541.00
July Corn	170000 Bu.	Gain	19,555.00
May Corn	165000 Bu.	Gain	11,842.50

Net gain for year   56,299.50

Balance bro't. forward   567,751.20
Maximum margin required $123,550

1928

May Wheat	175000 Bu.	Gain	$ 20,615.00
Sept. Wheat	175000 Bu.	Loss	58,187.00
July Corn	175000 Bu.	Gain	17,062.00
May Corn	170000 Bu.	Gain	11,087.50

Net loss for year   9,422.50

Balance bro't. forward   558,328.70
Maximum margin required $141,000

1929

May Wheat	180000 Bu.	Loss	$ 28,025.00
Sept. Wheat	180000 Bu.		11,475.00
July Corn	180000 Bu.	Gain	3,825.00
May Corn	175000 Bu.	Loss	40,200.00

Net loss for year   52,925.00

Balance bro't. forward   505,373.60
Maximum margin required $174,000

Buying and Selling May Wheat According to a Definite Plan

It was impossible to place all of my selling prices for May Wheat in the table on page 44. I have shown the month and price at which purchase was made and also the average price on May 25th. From the monthly range of prices shown in the table on page 43, it will be possible for every trader to check up on any year's profits or losses. Like the plan shown in September Wheat and July Corn, the buying is done at the low of the preceding month.

Buying Plan

An order is placed to buy *May Wheat* in September at the low reached in August. If not secured in September, the order is placed in October to buy at the September low and so on each month until the line of wheat is secured. I hope I have made it clear that the buying is all done at one time; there is no averaging up or averaging down. Nine years out of ten, the low of the month before comes nearer representing complete liquidation than most traders are able to forecast. This method offers a far firmer footing for buying than do the fickle promises of a fall supply or demand, which frequently change over night.

Now, let us assume that the trader has undertaken each month to get his May Wheat at the *low* of the month before. If the wheat is not secured by January 7th, the order is placed in the second week in January to buy at the low of the first week. If not secured, the order is placed in the third week to buy at the low of the second week. If not secured by this time, the order is placed in the fourth week to buy at the low of the third week. If all this effort fails to secure the wheat, the idea is abandoned for the season. It is interesting to note that on the table on page 44 there was only one year in the whole period in which this plan failed to secure the wheat on a good reaction of a few cents to as much as forty cents under the high price of the previous month.

Selling Plan No. 1

One-fourth of the line is offered for sale in April at the high price reached in March. If not sold, this one-fourth portion is sold the last day of April, regardless of price.

Selling Plan No. 2

Another fourth of the line of wheat is offered for sale on exactly the same terms as Plan No. 1 except that in the event of the trader being unable to get rid of his wheat in April at the highest price in March, he does not close out his trade on April 30th and take a loss, but carries his trade into the delivery month of May until he can secure a price, which, after including storage and commission, lets him out of the trade at just what he paid. Obviously this plan is more profitable than the first plan, when considered over a period of years. Naturally there is some reward for taking delivery or delivery would never be taken by any trader.

Selling Plan No. 3

One-fourth of the line is carried into the month of May and offered at a price that is 2 cents above the highest price reached by the May future between the period of August 1st to April 30th, inclusive. If the price cannot be secured, the trade is carried until the 25th of May and sold at the market. In all cases where grain is carried into the delivery month, a charge of $2\frac{3}{4}$ cents is assumed as right for storage, interest, commission and insurance. This is a generous allowance, since in fully half the cases, delivery is not made until after the 25th of the delivery month, although it is frequently made on the first day.

Selling Plan No. 4

The last one-fourth of the line is offered for sale on the

following basis: at the first opportunity to secure 10 cents gross profit, a sale is made and an order is immediately placed to re-purchase this one-fourth line on a 5 cent break from the sale price. After having repurchased, the trader again holds out for 10 cents profit. While no purchases are made after the first day of May, any grain left on hand is carried to the 25th of the delivery month, unless in the meantime 10 cents gross profit can be secured on the last sale. Since we cannot clearly show all trades on a table, we will now give an example.

Plan No. 1

Under Plan No. 1 the trader bought 500,000 bushels of Chicago May Wheat on October 18th, 1927, at $1.38⅝ which was the low price reached in the previous September. The trader will now proceed to sell 125,000 bushels under each of four different plans.

Under Plan No. 1 he carries his trade into April and waits until a high of $1.44¾ is reached. This price is secured on April 4th. His gross profit is 10¾ cents, leaving a net profit, commission paid, of 10½ cents. 125,000 bushels of wheat, yielding a net profit of 10½ cents a bushel amounts to $13,125.00.

Plan No. 2

Under Plan No. 2 he gets exactly the same, since a sale is also made on April 4th and net profits are also $13,125.00.

Plan No. 3

Plan No. 3 calls for carrying the grain into the delivery month until the high price of the season is reached. The high in April was $1.71½, but since this price is never reached in May, the trader holds on patiently until May 25th and sells his wheat at the average price of the day, which proved to be $1.50¼. This leaves a gross profit of 16⅝ cents or a net profit of 16⅜ cents. On 125,000 bushels this yields a profit of $20,462.50. I have purposely not subtracted 2¾ cents for carrying charges in the delivery month, since it so happened that I carried wheat from May 1st to May 25th in 1928 on which delivery was not made.

Plan No. 4

Plan No. 4 calls for selling on the first 10 cent advance and buying back on the first 5 cent break. A price of $1.43⅝ was secured on April 2nd, giving a gross profit of 10 cents and a net profit of 9¾ cents. Since it was impossible to buy this wheat back on any 5 cent break, the profit under this plan is $12,187.50 or 9¾ cents a bushel on 125,000 bushels. The total profit secured for the whole 500,000 bushels is the sum of these four totals, or $58,900.00 as shown on page 45.

Margin Requirements

Now we will look at margin requirements for the year 1928. It was necessary to carry this trade thru a loss of approximately 7 cents. Adding 10 cents for margin makes 17 cents. Seventeen cents a bushel on 500,000 bushels is $85,000.00.

The Monthly Price Range of May Wheat

The Year Around Trading Plan depends for its successful operation on the monthly price range and also on seasonal trends.

Undoubtedly more money has been made in the grain market through a careful study of monthly price fluctuations than has been made by any single method including the "Head and Shoulder" and all other graph methods.

As long as forty years ago, keen students of market action observed that,

FIRST: The extreme monthly price range of wheat averages about ten per cent of the market price of the grain.

SECOND: Wheat usually sells much cheaper sometime in

(*Continued on page 46*)

MONTHLY RANGE OF PRICES OF WHEAT FOR MAY DELIVERY AT CHICAGO

	In Sept.	In Oct.	In Nov.	In Dec.	In Jan.	In Feb.	In March	In April
1929–30..	141⅞@155⅞	124½@148	121¾@140½	125½@143¼	118½@138	102¾@124½		
1928–29..	119¼@127⅞	119¾@127½	120⅝@125⅜	117¾@124¼	115¾@130½	126⅜@133⅝	118 @131⅞	111 @124¼
1927–28..	133⅝@144½	126¾@137¾	129⅞@136½	128¼@135⅜	128¾@133¼	128⅛@135⅜	133⅞@144⅜	142 @171½
1926–27..	138 @146⅝	141⅜@150⅝	136½@147½	137½@142¼	136¼@143	138⅛@143½	131½@142⅜	130¾@138
1925–26..	138¾@158½	133 @149¼	142⅛@164	158½@185½	166¾@183¼	160⅞@178½	152⅜@166¾	154 @170½
1924–25..	132½@148⅝	144¾@157	144½@164¼	158¾@183⅞	173½@205¾	177½@202¼	140½@202	136½@162¼
1923–24..	106⅞@113½	109 @114⅝	107 @112¾	105⅜@111¾	107¼@111½	109½@113¾	100¼@112⅛	100⅞@105¼
1922–23..	104½@113⅝	107 @114⅝	111⅝@118¾	114½@126¾	115¼@122½	116¼@124⅞	116¼@123⅛	119½@127¼
1921–22..	123¾@142¾	107¼@125¾	103¼@118¼	110⅜@119	107½@119⅞	118½@149⅞	128½@148	128¾@149⅛
1920–21..	Trading	Suspended	....	150½@164¾	148 @175½	140¾@165½	137½@164¼	119½@140½
1917–19..	....	....	....	....	....	....	....	....
1916–17..	144¾@158¼	154 @188½	170¾@195¾	153½@182⅜	170¼@191	154½@182⅛	175¾@198⅞	195½@279¾
1915–16..	93 @101⅜	96¾@110½	102¼@108⅞	107¼@129	121⅞@138⅛	108 @136	105⅞@116¼	111⅜@121½
1914–15..	110¼@132	111¼@122⅞	117⅛@124½	119½@131½	129⅞@152	146 @167	135¾@160	151 @165½
1913–14..	91½@ 97⅞	86¾@ 92¾	88¾@ 92	89⅝@ 92⅝	90⅞@ 94⅜	92½@ 95½	90⅝@ 94⅜	90⅛@ 93¼
1912–13..	94¼@ 96⅞	95 @100½	89⅜@ 96⅛	88½@ 92¼	91⅛@ 95⅜	92 @ 94⅝	88⅛@ 93	89½@ 93⅜
1911–12..	100⅜@105½	102 @107¼	98¼@102⅜	96¼@100½	98⅛@103⅞	99½@104¾	100⅝@105⅝	101 @116⅜
1910–11..	102 @109¾	96 @105¼	95⅝@ 98	95⅛@ 97⅝	95⅝@102⅝	88⅝@ 97⅛	85¾@ 92⅛	84⅜@ 91½
1909–10..	97 @103¾	101¾@107¾	101⅝@107¼	105⅛@114¼	107⅞@115	108⅝@116	110⅛@115¾	105 @115¼
1908–09..	98⅝@105⅛	100¾@105	102¾@109⅛	104⅜@111	104 @108¾	107½@119	112⅜@119½	118 @129¼
1907–08..	102⅝@108⅛	102⅛@112⅝	99 @101¾	99⅛@108	95¼@108½	90¾@ 99⅞	92 @101⅛	89 @ 99¾
1906–07..	75½@ 79⅞	77⅛@ 80⅜	77½@ 79½	76⅝@ 79½	79⅝@ 99⅝	76⅝@ 80⅞	74⅝@ 78½	75½@ 81
1905–06..	83⅞@ 88	85¼@ 92⅞	85¾@ 91⅜	86½@ 90¼	84¼@ 89⅛	81¼@ 85⅝	76¼@ 81⅜	77 @ 82¼
1904–05..	107⅜@118⅞	107¾@115⅛	108 @114½	108½@115⅝	113½@118¼	113½@121½	109 @116¼	86½@118¾
1903–04..	77⅝@ 85	77¼@ 89¼	76 @ 81⅝	80¼@ 84⅞	84¾@ 92⅝	89⅜@109	89¾@102⅞	85½@ 96⅜

A BUYING AND SELLING PLAN APPLIED TO MAY WHEAT

(ORIGINAL CAPITAL $23,812.00)

Year	Month when purchased and price	Average Price May 25th	No. bushels traded in	Gain or Loss in $ per year	Greatest margin requirements at any one time	Original capital Plus gains or Minus losses
1896–97	Sep. $.62½	$ .82	95,000	$19,781.25	$ 4,800.00	$ 27,612.00
1897–98	Oct. .87⅝	1.63	110,000	23,675.00	13,000.00	51,287.00
1898–99	Sep. .63	.75½	125,000	16,150.00	6,250.00	67,437.00
1899–00	Sep. .74	.66	140,000	13,693.75*	14,000.00	53,743.25
1900–01	Nov. .75½	.73½	155,000	5,150.00*	12,400.00	48,593.25
1901–02	Oct. .73⅜	.72⅜	170,000	731.25*	13,600.00	47,863.00
1902–03	Jan. .77⅞	.76	185,000	4,506.25*	20,350.00	43,356.75
1903–04	Sep. .81	.96¼	200,000	23,875.00	18,000.00	67,231.75
1904–05	Jan. 1.15	1.07	215,000	10,225.00*	18,000.00	57,006.75
1905–06	Jan. .86⅞	.86¼	230,000	15,193.75*	34,500.00	41,813.00
1906–07	Sep. .76¾	.90	245,000	11,837.50	17,150.00	53,650.00
1907–08	Oct. 1.02⅝	1.02	260,000	1,156.25	46,800.00	54,806.75
1908–09	Jan. 1.06⅝	1.33	275,000	40,743.75	13,500.00	95,550.50
1909–10	Nov. 1.01¾	1.09	290,000	2,787.50*	14,250.00	92,763.00
1910–11	Sep. 1.07	.99	305,000	26,650.00*	64,000.00	66,113.00
1911–12	Nov. 1.02	1.14	320,000	25,750.00	28,350.00	91,863.00
1912–13	Sep. .95¼	.92	335,000	16,343.75*	43,550.00	75,519.25
1913–14	Sep. .93¾	.97¾	350,000	5,331.25	59,000.00	80,850.00
1914–15		No trades possible in this year.				
1915–16	Sep. .95¾	1.09	365,000	63,825.00	43,800.00	144,675.50
1916–17	Dec. 1.70¾	3.22	380,000	137.525.00	108,000.00	282,200.50

Year	Month when purchased and price		Average Price May 25th	No. bushels traded in	Gain or Loss in $ per year	Greatest margin requirements at any one time	Original capital Plus gains or Minus losses
1917–18	Trading suspended by order Chicago Board of Trade.						
1918–19	Trading suspended by order Chicago Board of Trade.						
1919–20	Trading suspended by order Chicago Board of Trade.						
1920–21	Jan.	1.50½	$1.78	395,000	$ 4,325.00	$164,000.00	$286,525.50
1921–22	Oct.	1.23¾	1.28	410,000	60,675.00	120,000.00	347,200.00
1922–23	Sep.	1.04¾	1.19	425,000	60,453.00	42,500.00	407,653.00
1923–24	Nov.	1.09	1.05⅞	440,000	22,275.00*	88,000.00	385,378.00
1924–25	Nov.	1.44¾	1.71	455,000	74,525.00	81,900.00	459,903.00
1925–26	Sep.	1.54½	1.60	470,000	36,394.50	145,700.00	496,297.50
1926–27	Sep.	1.39½	1.52	485,000	60,891.00	82,450.00	557,188.50
1927–28	Sep.	1.33⅝	1.50¼	500,000	58,900.00	85,000.00	616,088.50

EXPLANATION.—All items in "Gain or Loss" Column followed by the asterisk (*) represent losses.

Lack of time made it impossible to compile a new table showing monthly highs and lows for August and May. We give below the August lows for the fall months in which May Wheat was purchased in September at the August low.

AUGUST LOWS WHEN SEPTEMBER PURCHASES WERE MADE

1896, 62½; 1898, 63; 1899, 74; 1903, 81; 1906, 76¾; 1910, 1.07; 1912, 95¼; 1913, 93¾; 1915, 95¾; 1922, 1.04¾; 1925, 1.54½; 1926, 1.39½; 1927, 1.33⅝; 1929, 1.47¼.

Complete tables showing the high and low for May Wheat in the delivery month of May may be found in the Chicago Board of Trade Year Books. Complete checking data may also be found in Bartels' Red Books for thirty-three years. There is one book for each year.

October and November than it does in the crop scare
months of June and July.

THIRD: Until 1928 May wheat frequently showed a
broad advance from the October or November low to
the highest prices made in April or May.

FOURTH: September wheat should, and frequently does
sell in March at a big discount under the May. This is
due to the fact that May is an old crop month and
carries heavy storage charges, whereas September
is a new crop month in which heavy deliveries are
often made out of a bountiful harvest.

All of the above-mentioned observations were brought
together in 1912 by one of the most successful grain traders in the United States and later synchronized under that
most remarkable of all long pull trading rules. I call this
rule the "Year Around Trading Plan" for want of a better
name. As I have already stated, this rule calls for attempting to buy at the low of the month before and in the season
of the year when the futures usually sell lowest; then
patiently holding into the season of the year when these
same futures frequently sell at the highest price of the
season. After holding the trade open for two to six months
an attempt is then made to sell at the highest price made in
a previous month.

Those who have followed this rule have often succeeded
in buying at practically the season's low and selling at not
far from the season's high. Since the average seasonal
fluctuation in May wheat is 40 cents (see table on page
48) the profits secured by these long pull traders with
ample capital, have been tremendous.

The "Year Around Trading Plan" worked beautifully
for 40 years and was especially good from 1912 to 1928.
Then in 1929 something happened that tended to iron out
the natural seasonal price trend of grains. The Farm
Board was organized for the purpose of giving a better
market to the farmer. After the summer price advance

which usually came in June or July to be followed by a major decline in the fall months, this government financed grain board would buy wheat in the fall months, thereby checking the decline. This buying was done in order to give a better market to spring wheat growers whose crop was harvested too late to market at the higher summer prices. Having bought the wheat it was necessary to sell it later, with the result that it was pressed on the market in May and June when the milling demand was about the poorest of the year.

A 20-Year May Wheat Average

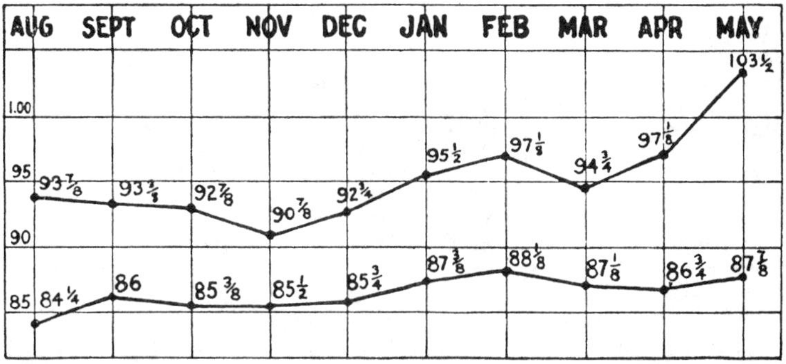
AUG
SEPT
OCT
NOV
DEC
JAN
FEB
MAR
APR
MAY
1.00
95
90
85
93 7/8
93 3/8
92 7/8
90 7/8
92 3/4
95 1/2
97 1/8
94 3/4
97 1/8
103 1/2
84 1/4
86
85 3/8
85 1/2
85 3/4
87 3/8
88 1/8
87 1/8
86 3/4
87 7/8

The top line in the above chart shows the 20-year (1909-28) average of the monthly "highs" made in the life of the May Wheat Future. The bottom line is the 20-year average of the "lows". The area between the lines represents the average monthly price range of May Wheat. Note the seasonal price advance prior to 1928.

This spring selling of fall-purchased wheat by the Farm Board caused a slump in the season of the year that was farthest from the harvest and when grain should bring more money. Apparently the buying and selling of the Farm Board actually increased the monthly price range, although it tended to reverse the seasonal trend. The cash grain trade that normally buys the farmer's grain in the fall season of heavy deliveries and holds until it is needed by mills and importers, became so discouraged as a result of heavy losses sustained in holding cash grain off the

A Table Showing the Five-Year Average Monthly Price Range for Chicago May Wheat

Months	1928	1929	1930	1931	1932	5-Year Average	Average Monthly Range
August Low...	1.18	1.47½	97⅛	54	56	94½	
August High...	1.29¼	1.63¼	1.14	59¾	64½	1.06⅛	11⅝
Sept. Low.....	1.19¼	1.41⅞	82⅝	50¼	56⅞	90⅛	
Sept. High....	1.27⅞	1.55⅞	99⅝	56⅛	65	1.00⅞	10¾
October Low..	1.19¾	1.24½	81½	48¾	48⅝	84⅝	
October High..	1.27½	1.48	91	66½	59½	98½	13⅞
Nov. Low.....	1.20⅝	1.21¾	73	54¾	46⅜	83⅜	
Nov. High....	1.25⅝	1.40½	83¼	73	52¼	94⅞	11½
Dec. Low.....	1.17¾	1.25½	78¾	53¾	43¼	83⅞	
Dec. High.....	1.24¼	1.43¼	83	60½	49⅜	92⅛	8¼
	1929	1930	1931	1932	1933		
Jan. Low......	1.15¾	1.18½	81	55⅛	44½	82⅞	
Jan. High.....	1.30½	1.38	86⅛	61¾	51¾	93⅝	10¾
Feb. Low.....	1.26⅜	1.02¾	81⅛	56⅝	46	82⅝	
Feb. High.....	1.33⅝	1.24½	84⅛	63	49⅛	90⅞	7¼
March Low....	1.18	1.05¾	81¼	52	46½	80⅝	
March High...	1.31⅞	1.16⅝	84⅝	62⅛	56½	90⅜	9¾
April Low.....	1.11	1.01⅛	81¼	52⅞	53⅝	79⅞	
April High....	1.24¼	1.16¾	84½	62	71	91⅝	11¾
May Low.....	93¼	1.00	81¼	52¼	66½	78⅝	
May High.....	1.14⅞	1.08½	86¼	60⅜	74½	88⅞	10¼
Yearly Price Range.........	39¾c	63¼c	35¼c	24¼c	30c		

A 5-Year May Wheat Average

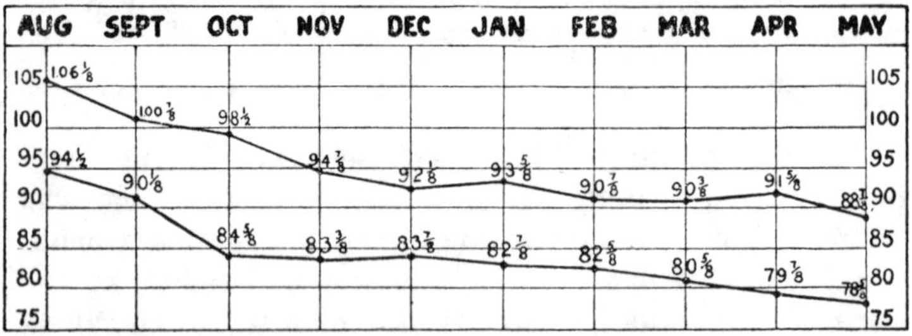

The top line in the above chart shows the 5-year (1928-33) average of the monthly "highs" made in the life of the May Wheat Future. The bottom line is the 5-year average of the "lows". The price area between the lines represents the average monthly price range of May Wheat. Note the seasonal price decline since 1928 which was due to Farm Board buying in the fall months and Farm Board selling in the spring months.

market that many of them quit the business. Undoubtedly this lack of buying by the grain trade together with a lack of capital contributed to the low prices of 1932. The chart on page 47 shows a twenty year composite of monthly price swings as well as the seasonal trend of May wheat for the years 1909 to 1928. This chart shows a natural and orderly seasonal advance. Under such conditions it paid well to store grain in public warehouses for the higher spring prices. In the past five years it has paid to dump it at harvest time.

In those years prior to 1928, wheat often sold at the highest price of the year when Kansas and Illinois farmers were selling their new crop and millers were bidding briskly for choice new wheat. The lowest price of the year was often made in October just as the last of the North Dakota crop was delivered to the county elevator and when the market had to absorb all of the off-grade, weather damaged wheat that stood in the shock through the fall equinoctial rains.

On the opposite page is a five year chart that was made from the average of the monthly highs and lows, using the May future for the years 1928–33, inclusive. Note how different this chart looks from the first chart. Furthermore, these two charts have a direct bearing on the successful operation of the "Year Around Trading Plan".

If the seasonal trends are to be as pronounced in the next twenty years as they were from 1908 to 1928, then any man can start with $5,000 and trade in quantities small enough to permit a 50 per cent margin and have his capital grow to $125,000 in twenty years. This does not include at least $20,000 that his broker would pay him in interest on idle funds of $10,000 and more. (See Lamson's statement on page 10.)

If the trader is clever and can buy at lower prices than the rule indicates and sell at higher prices than the rule indicates his profits in twenty years should far exceed $125,000 from a $5,000 start, or $25,000 from a $1,000 start. I have always averaged better than the rule and use it only as a guide in buying cheap and selling high.

On the other hand, if the grain market in the next twenty years shows no more of a seasonal trend than it has shown in the past five years, the trader will not do quite as well by using this rule. But the fact must not be overlooked that any factors that tend to depress the May future in the spring months give an even better opportunity to buy September wheat in March or April at a bargain price. The contemplated purchase of September wheat is a necessary part of the "Year Around Trading Plan".

I think I have made it clear that the big gains from following the "Year Around Trading Plan" are in years when the trader can use the rule to buy at near the lowest price reached in the fall season of low prices and sell at near the high price in the spring and early summer season of high prices. The "Year Around Trading Plan" with all its shortcomings is the foundation stone of successful investment buying of grain futures. It is to the grain trade what the Dow-Jones theory is to the stock market.

The successful grain trader studies the increase and decrease in the visible compared with other years. He studies the monthly price range and seasonal trends in past years as well as the market action following short crops; and, last but not least, he remembers that 75 cents (in gold dollars of $20.67 to the ounce) is a cheap price for wheat and $1.50 is likewise a high price. These fundamental facts and many others are like a trading alphabet to the grain speculator. They are the elementary part of his trading technique.

The grain trader is not bothered with the earnings of corporations, too much plant expansion, dishonesty of management, too large salaries to executives, stock bonuses to employees, inventions or changes in public taste that affect adversely the earnings of the companies in which he might want to buy common stocks. The grain trader is buying and selling the most necessary of all articles that enter into human diet. Wheat will always be needed and it will always fluctuate in price in an effort to slow down the ebb and flow of supply and demand.

I have strong reasons for believing that the Roosevelt administration is in favor of leaving the actual marketing of grain to private capital. I, for one, think a broad speculative public interest is necessary to higher prices; government buying kills this interest. The Roosevelt administration has made a big stride forward through a planned reduction in acreage as well as by cheapening the dollar. Along these lines the government can render a real service in creating higher prices that are based on scarcity. In the next four years, I look for the old seasonal trends again to appear and encourage investment buying of cash grain by private capital.

Until the carryover of July 1st of each year gets below 200 million bushels, I believe "The Year Around Trading Plan" should be used as often in the making of short sales as in taking a long position. The five year average chart certainly gives this indication.

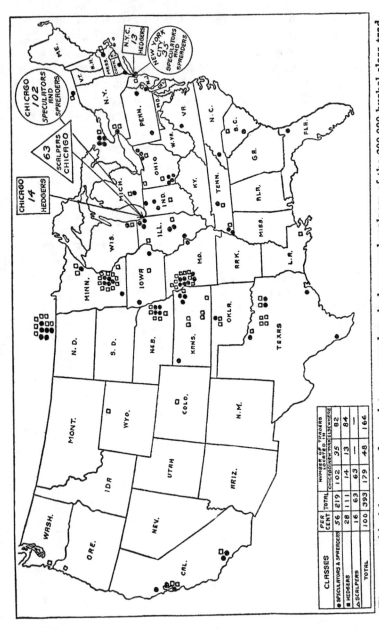

The geographical location of speculators, spreaders, hedgers, and scalpers of the 200,000-bushel class trading in Chicago wheat futures during the period from Jan. 3, 1927, to Oct. 31, 1927

CLASSES	PER CENT	TOTAL	NUMBER OF TRADERS LOCATED IN		
			CHICAGO	NEW YORK	ELSEWHERE
● SPECULATORS & SPREADERS	56	219	102	35	82
■ HEDGERS	28	111	14	13	84
△ SCALPERS	16	63	63	—	—
TOTAL	100	393	179	48	166

CHAPTER VI

The Man Who Traded Only in Corn

I CONSIDER what follows as the most remarkable case of calendar trading I have ever known.

In the past five years so many traders have asked for additional copies of the calendar trading dates used by a New York surgeon in which he made a very large fortune in trading in July Corn, that I am again publishing the table. When I published this table the first time, I offered $100.00 to anyone who could show a calendar trading table covering any other commodity or any other corn future in which the profits equal those earned by Dr. X's July Corn calendar trading table.

In theory, at least, there are more sound reasons why July Corn should advance in price in the spring and summer months than there are reasons for expecting a year in and year out advance in any other commodity over any seasonal period.

Now I do not advise a close adherence to any calendar dates. I also grant that to have followed Dr. X's calendar in 1929 and 1930 would have resulted in losses. But the calendar trading table given below is interesting in that it shows how fortunes can be made by careful traders who start with a right idea, even though it is nothing but a few calendar dates.

The calendar shown below made Dr. X $2,730,286.10 in twenty-eight trading years. I think the very best way to explain this calendar is to quote from Dr. X's letter, which follows:

"Dear Mr. Ainsworth:

"I promised you that when I quit trading I would send you the grain trading calendar which to me, at least, has been the 'Goose that Laid the Golden Egg'. You are welcome to the calendar, but under no circumstances are you to mention my name. There are some others who know what I have done; in fact, I have had quite a following at times, which of course didn't hurt anything. My operations, as you know, were confined exclusively to the long side of the July Corn future.

"I am sending all invoices and ledger statements since 1908. You may keep these a week and return, carefully sealed and registered and marked 'personal'. The calendar shows about $2,400,000 more than I actually made. I will explain: After 1914 I had to give so much of my profits to the Government (income tax) that I did not have the capital for margin that the calendar indicates. Another thing: I was always afraid I could not get rid of so much corn the last of the delivery month, so I would often unload part of my line on hard spots in June. You will agree with me that the market in July Corn is quite often mighty thin by July 25th.

"I hope the calendar is clear. The purchases are made in equal amounts at three different times, and (in theory at least) all sold on July 25th. Up to and including 1922 I traded in quantities slightly under four times my capital profits at the time. After that I spent most of my time traveling and therefore, bought only double the bushels of corn that I had dollars in capital, since I wanted to feel safe while away from home.

"You can see there was only 25 cents margin between my trades and failure until 1922, when I decided to trade in half the quantities, which, of course, made it possible to margin all corn 50 cents if it should have become necessary.

"*Of course,* I have been worried at times. On the last day of May, 1918, I had a private wire run into my office (a foolish thing to do) but it gave me some comfort. On June 3rd, July Corn sold at $1.30⅜ and my paper loss was 18¼ cents, which called for 23 cents a bushel to margin the account. This was the greatest paper loss I ever had up to that time. I then made up my mind to cut loose at $1.28, in which case I would have lost all I had made in previous years, except about $200,000 in interest. The next day corn advanced.

"In May of 1925, I left with my wife and son's family for the interior of China, with orders to my broker not to notify me of any losses. I was blissfully ignorant of what happened until August 1st, when I arrived in Japan and saw a paper. From June 25th to July 3rd an armful of securities was transferred each day from my safekeeping account in bank, to broker's account. Of all this I knew nothing until I returned to New York.

"In conclusion, I want to say that no calendar has any merit that is not based on sound logic.

"Over a period of years, July Corn will follow a pronounced seasonal trend upward. Briefly, this is due to a number of factors, which, while known by the trade, are not fully discounted in the market until June or July.

"The purchases are made just after the heavy winter marketing, and before the corn has found its way into consumptive channels. Corn shrinks tremendously in weight in June and July, and wet corn spoils. While sound corn may gain some in grade as the moisture leaves it, the summer loss in weight is more than what is just needed to make the best grade of corn. July 25th comes when farmers are marketing wheat and have no time to market corn. This date often synchronizes with crop scares due to drought. Corn sells for more in July than it does in May because it is worth more. The average difference over a period of years should be several times the carrying charges.

"With best wishes for your continued success, I remain,
"Sincerely yours,
"Dr. X.

"P.S.—While I made no trades in 1900, 1902 or 1907, I would have been better off had I traded in those three years."

Dr. X's Calendar

JULY CORN CALENDAR, ORIGINAL CAPITAL, $20,000

Year	Price Mar. 1st	Price April 1st	Price May 1st	March April, May Av.	Price July 25th						
1897	.25⅜	.26¼	.25½	.25¾	.27½	gain	.01¾	Gain	$ 1,200	Capital	$ 21,200
1898	.31⅞	.30½	.34½	.32¼	.35½	gain	.03¼	Gain	2,600	Capital	23,800
1899	.37½	.36⅝	.35¼	.36½	.32¼	loss	.04¼	Loss	3,400	Capital	20,200
1901	.40⅞	.44½	.46	.43¾	.55¾	gain	.12	Gain	9,600	Capital	29,800
1903	.45¼	.43⅞	.45¼	.44⅞	.51½	gain	.06⅝	Gain	4,950	Capital	34,750
1904	.54⅞	.54	.48¾	.52½	.49¾	loss	.02¾	Loss	3,850	Capital	30,900
1905	.48⅜	.47¾	.46⅝	.47½	.57¼	gain	.09¾	Not delivered, gain	11,700	Capital	42,600
1906	.43¾	.44⅝	.46½	.44⅞	.51¾	gain	.06⅞	Not delivered, gain	10,800	Capital	53,400
1908	.60⅛	.64¼	.64½	.62⅞	.78	gain	.15⅛	Delivered July 4, gain	31,350	Capital	84,750
1909	.65¾	.66½	.68⅞	.67⅛	.71½	gain	.04⅜	Delivered July 1, gain	14,856	Capital	99,616
1910	.67⅞	.64½	.63¼	.65¼	.65½	gain	.00¼	Delivered July 5, loss	630	Capital	98,986
1911	.49	.49⅛	.53	.50⅜	.62	gain	.11⅝	Delivered July 19, gain	45,480	Capital	144,466
1912	.70¾	.75¼	.78⅝	.74⅞	.73	loss	.01⅞	Not delivered, loss	11,200	Capital	133,260
1913	.54½	.55⅝	.56½	.55½	.61	gain	.05½	Delivered July 17, gain	29,480	Capital	162,740
1914	.67¼	.65	.65	.65⅜	.69¼	gain	.03⅞	Not delivered, gain	23,168	Capital	185,908
1915	.75⅝	.75⅝	.81	.77⅜	.80½	gain	.03⅛	Delivered, gain	21,600	Capital	206,908
1916	.75	.76½	.77½	.76¼	.84	gain	.07¾	Delivered, gain	41,000	Capital	247,980
1917	1.02¼	1.20⅞	1.44¼	1.22⅜	2.23½	gain	1.01⅛	Not delivered, gain	800,000	Capital	1,047,980
1918			1.48¾	1.48¾	1.54⅛	gain	.05⅝	Delivered, gain	124,757	Capital	1,172,637
1919	1.22	1.46¼	1.63½	1.43⅞	1.96¾	gain	.52⅞	Not delivered, gain	2,158,000	Capital	3,330,637
1920	1.31⅝	1.54¾	1.77½	1.54⅝	1.50¾	loss	.03⅞	Delivered, loss	560,000	Capital	2,770,637
1921	.71¾	.64¼	.62⅞	.66⅝	.64⅜	loss	.02¼	Delivered, loss	252,230	Capital	2,518,407
1922	.70	.61⅜	.65¾	.65⅝	.62	loss	.03⅝	Not delivered, loss	250,000	Capital	2,268,407
1923	.76½	.77	.82½	.78⅝	.87¼	gain	.08⅞	Not delivered, gain	374,000	Capital	2,642,407
1924	.82⅛	.78¾	.78⅜	.79¾	1.09	gain	.29¼	Not delivered, gain	1,508,000	Capital	4,150,407
1925	1.38¼	1.10¾	1.12½	1.20½	1.03¼	loss	.17¼	Not delivered, loss	1,440,000	Capital	3,710,407
1926	.83½	.77½	.77	.79⅜	.77⅝	loss	.01¾	Not delivered, loss	128,000	Capital	3,582,407
1927	.82¾	.77⅜	.79¾	.80	1.01¾	gain	.21¾	Delivered, gain	1,540,435	Capital	5,122,842
1928	1.00⅛	1.03	1.13	1.05⅛	1.06⅞	gain	.01¾	Not delivered, gain	153,685	Capital	5,276,527

In 1917 I sold at 80½ cents profit per bushel. Would have gotten $1.01⅛ if held to July 25th.

In 1919 I sold June 17th to 24th at $1.80.

Each year gains were added to capital. Capital gains or losses do not always check with cents per bushel on account of carrying charges on delivered grain.

CHAPTER VII

Seasonal Trends

WHEN considered over a period of years, there are fairly well defined seasonal trends in the price of grain futures, although they are not all comparable in scope or regularity with those in the cash grain markets. Since grain futures do not have the wide fluctuations that the cash has, one can naturally conclude that the speculator is rendering a service by ironing out to a large extent the seasonal tendencies in grain.

I have compiled the following table which shows the seasonal trend of May Wheat for twenty-three years:

TABLE NO. 1

Average of lows in August for 23 years............	84.2	cents
Average of lows in September for 23 years...........	86	cents
Average of lows in October for 24 years...........	85.3	cents
Average of lows in November for 24 years...........	85.4	cents
Average of lows in December for 24 years...........	85.7	cents
Average of lows in January for 24 years...........	87.3	cents
Average of lows in February for 24 years...........	88.1	cents
Average of lows in March for 24 years...........	87.1	cents
Average of lows in April for 24 years...........	86.6	cents
Average of lows in May for 24 years...........	87.7	cents

AVERAGE OF THE LOWS FOR 24 YEARS........ 86.34 cents

Average of highs in August for 23 years..........	93.9	cents
Average of highs in September for 23 years..........	93.3	cents
Average of highs in October for 24 years..........	92.9	cents
Average of highs in November for 24 years..........	90.7	cents
Average of highs in December for 24 years..........	92.6	cents
Average of highs in January for 24 years..........	95.5	cents
Average of highs in February for 24 years..........	97.1	cents
Average of highs in March for 24 years..........	94.6	cents
Average of highs in April for 24 years..........	97.1	cents
Average of highs in May for 24 years..........	103.5	cents

AVERAGE OF THE HIGHS FOR 24 YEARS....... 95.12 cents
SUBTRACTING THE AVERAGE LOW OF LOWS.... 86.34 cents

AVERAGE MONTHLY FLUCTUATION............. 8.78 cents

The chart on page 47 was made from the above table.

Spreads Between Cash Grain and Futures

In the old crop futures one usually expects the future to be enough above the cash to express the full carrying charge. Where grain is selling very low, or below the cost of production, this invariably is the case, which means that the future quotation is tending to hold up the cash. The spread between the cash and the future in the old crop months cannot exceed the carrying charge, or investors with plenty of capital would buy the cash grain, store it and sell the more distant position. The trade is closed by selling the cash and buying the future in the delivery month.

This proves conclusively the value of a futures market when grain prices are low. Only when the price level is very high, do we expect the cash to sell higher than the futures in the old crop months.

A Popular Grain Trading Calendar

Buy Wheat Feb. 22nd. Follows the bearish effect of the first Argentine run.

Buy Wheat July 1st. On likely deterioration following a period of good prospects.

Buy Wheat Nov. 28th. Before time to hear of crop damage from Southern Hemisphere.

Sell Wheat Jan. 10th. Just because it is apt to have overshot its mark.

Sell Wheat May 10th. This is the last of the winter kill scare.

Sell Wheat Sept. 10th. Follows the black rust scare.

Buy Corn March 1st. Follows heavy run to meet taxes or to change farms.

Buy Corn June 25th. Corn has been green and looks well. Hot weather is approaching.

Sell Corn May 10th. Corn delivered on May contracts is usually less than the trade expects.

Sell Corn Aug. 10th. Crop scares at height and before old corn movement becomes heavy.

CHAPTER VIII

Valuable Grain Trading Rules

THE foundation or back log of the professional grain trader's market technique (call it skill if you prefer) is made up of trading rules which are just as important as knowledge of Culbertson is to the expert bridge player.

Speculators can never be sure of a profit on any individual trade. If profits could be guaranteed on every trade then big profits would be impossible since they would be reduced to a banking six or eight per cent return on the margin invested. It is the very uncertainty of speculation that makes skillful grain trading over a period of years very profitable.

Now, there are times when even the most experienced trader is very much in doubt regarding the next broad market move. He knows that if the market has had a recent broad advance it has probably already discounted most if not all of the bullish news. This was the case on July 17, 1933. Under such circumstances the trader finds a great comfort in applying certain time-honored rules as a supplement to what he already knows of the action of past markets. From this knowledge he makes his forecast, being careful not to be influenced too much by such obvious market factors as crop damage, big milling demand, etc.

In addition to trading rules a good memory of just what happened in every past bull and bear market for twenty years back is exceedingly valuable.

Now let us get back to our illustration of the bridge expert which I consider very apt. A man may know his Culbertson by heart; but, if, in addition to his technical skill he can remember every card that has been played

he is far better at bridge than the man who knows only
the rules of the game.

One job of forecasting is to refresh the memory on
what conditions prevailed when certain past bull markets
turned into bear markets and vice versa. For this knowledge I depend on charts that show the daily price range
of wheat and corn since 1921. The walls of my office are
lined with these charts that can be read ten feet away.
Back of 1921 I have tables. Then I also have bound copies
of Howard Bartel's Daily Trade Bulletins that give the
history of past markets where I can refresh my memory
on details. For example, I had to read up regarding the
great bear market that followed the all-time record short
wheat crop of 1893 since I was only nine years old when
that market occurred. I tell the story of that market collapse on page 165. The knowledge of how a certain past
market performed when conditions were almost identical
to a certain present market is the most valuable of all
market knowledge to the professional grain trader. It is
more important than a working knowledge of all grain
trading rules. Yet, trading rules are so important that I
could not possibly get along without them.

Now that I have made clear to my readers the relative
merit of grain trading rules, memory and experience, I
shall describe the more important rules in detail and tell
how and when they are used. This will help traders to do
a major part of their own forecasting. I have no market
secrets and look with distrust on those who claim their
methods are better than methods which have been accepted by the grain trade for the past twenty years.

Going With the Trend

The man who is determined to trade in large quantities
on very limited margin must *go with the trend* right from
the start or else be forced out of the market. Two rules
that help to determine the trend and show just where to
enter the market after the trend is established are the

Head and Shoulder Formation and *Trading Rule Number Eighteen.*

The title of Chapter IX which follows is somewhat misleading. In Chapter IX Mr. George W. Cole describes briefly the Head and Shoulder Formation. Then immediately following this explanation I describe very briefly all of the more popular trading rules including those that are discussed in detail in previous and subsequent chapters. In other words Chapter IX states all the trading rules that are described at length in this book.

CHAPTER IX

The Head and Shoulder Formation

I SHALL now give George W. Cole's explanation of the *Head and Shoulder Formation*. Mr. Cole has spent a lifetime in the cash grain business and is a member of the Chicago Board of Trade.

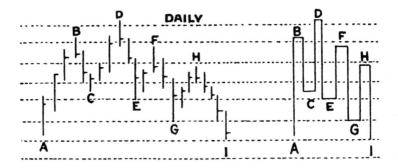

There are a number of different top and bottom formations in a market movement; there are weak ones and strong ones. We list them as follows: Head and shoulder, the broadening formation, double spread, coiling, declining and inclining formations. We have listed these as to their importance according to our experience, others have them arranged a little differently. We cannot describe each of these in detail, but the head and shoulder formation is illustrated in the above graph.

The above illustration outlines a daily graph of the highs and lows of the market and along side of it you will find the block method showing the "two day or more movement" graph showing only highs and lows of the minor trends. From the low at A advanced four days to B, then declined to C, then advanced to D, then declined to E,

which you will note is lower than C, then advanced to F
and then declined again passing E to G. The same letter
reference refers to the block graph also. This is an illustration of a perfect head and shoulder formation (D head,
B and F left and right shoulders) and the top is completed and made definite when it passes the low at E.
Sometimes the advances and declines in making a head
and shoulder formation will have a combination of coils
and congestions and small broadening movements in each
of the movements, for instance from A to B, B to C, C to
D, or D to E, etc., not illustrated in this graph. When this
occurs it makes the top (or the bottom which is just the
reverse of the above graph) that much stronger.

As to trends, there is a principal and minor trend. The
principal trend is the general direction of the market and
will take too long an explanation for this book. It is
very apparent in the formations, but the minor trend is
just what the word implies, the immediate or small movements. The principal trend is made up of minor trends
each succeeding the other. Now when the market advanced from C to D passing the high at B, the minor
trend changed up and when it declined from F to G it
confirmed the minor trend and started the principal trend
down. When the market after making the above formation passes the low at E sales should be made immediately
with stops above the high at F. If the market should reverse up to H not passing the high at F and declines again
passing its last low at G, then the stop should be placed
above the last high at H. For instance supposing the
market after making the low at G reversed and advanced
for a day or two, then turned around and sold down again
below the low at G, you would reduce the stop on your
short sales placing above the high made after G, continu-
ing to lower stops on each reverse until stops are caught
or profits taken. Operating over a bottom would be just
the opposite. Turn the graph upside down and a bottom
formation is shown.

Trading Rule Number Eighteen

This rule undertakes to do for the practical trader what the *head and shoulder formation* does for the chart trader who knows the *right shoulder* when he sees it. Few see it until too late.

Revised Trading Rule Number Eighteen

After the market hesitates, having had a major advance like occurred from June 18 to July 17 of 1933 and then closes lower than the previous day's close; and then if, just before the close of the day following the first lower close, the market is again about to close lower (making two lower closes in succession) sell 5,000 bushels short just before the close and protect with a one-cent stop if you cannot afford a ten cent loss.

In making such a trade speculators should realize that it is possible that a high opening the following morning might result in a three to five per cent loss, regardless of whether a one or two cent stop is used.

After the market hesitates, having had a major decline that has extended over a period of at least thirty days and then closes higher than the previous day's close; and then if just before the close of the day following the first higher close the market is again about to close higher (making two higher closes in succession) buy 5,000 bushels just before the close and protect with a one or two-cent stop if you must limit your losses.

The above rule is based on a time-honored trading rule used by professional traders in the Winnipeg market.

Grain Scalping Rules

All successful grain scalping rules call for buying and selling *against* the trend and not *with* the trend, as shown in the above rules. Furthermore, only a rather choppy, *sideways* market can be successfully scalped. To scalp a market and make money week in and week out depends on a successful forecast of a sideways trend. It is absurd to attempt to scalp a bull or bear market since the trader would naturally want to stay and get the larger profits.

A Simple Scalping Rule

Until 1932 the rule that follows was the most widely used of all scalping rules. The weakest parts of the rule are indefiniteness and the fact that it can only be applied occasionally. I sometimes use this rule for taking a long position on a Monday's market in which I give a definite buying price. This is the rule:

If the market sells off quickly after the opening, then the market is a Buy at the lower quotations for a scalp of at least one-half cent, in most cases for a cent or more, depending upon the activity of the market. The trade is always closed on the current day.

Scalping Rule Number Eleven

I shall now give what I consider the most technically perfect of all scalping rules. This rule assures a *maximum of profits* and a *minimum of losses* in any sideways market having no definite trend, and that is all that can be expected in any grain scalping rule. I don't believe in scalping a grain market except when a sideways market is a reasonably safe forecast. But for traders who are determined to scalp, this is the best of all scalping rules.

Whenever possible *sell* 5,000 bushels of May Wheat at one-half cent *above* the *high* of the previous day, and whenever possible *buy* 5,000 bushels of May Wheat at one-half cent *below* the *low* of the previous day.

Each day just *one buying* and *one selling* order is placed, good only for that *one day*. Before the opening of the market, regardless of whether you are *out* or *long* or *short*, you enter an order (good only for the day) to sell 5,000 bushels at one-half cent above the highest price reached on the previous day, and you enter an order to buy 5,000 bushels at one-half cent below the lowest price reached on the previous day.

The literal application of this rule gave 46 profit trades showing 75⅛ cents profit and 19 loss trades showing 34½ cents loss from January 14 to October 5, 1932. In our comment, we consider 5,000 bushels a unit or line. Cub traders trade in "jobs" of 1,000 bushels each.

See pages 92 to 101 for a detailed description and check up with ten months of markets.

A Long Pull Trading Plan

This plan called the Year Around Trading Plan has been checked with actual markets for a period of 35 years. I have two typewritten books of 306 pages which are devoted entirely to describing this plan and checking it with actual markets.

Stated in the briefest manner possible, the plan undertakes to *buy* May Wheat, May Corn, September Wheat, and July Corn at the *lowest price reached* in a preceding month in the early life of the above-mentioned futures and to *sell* one to three months before the futures expire at the *highest price reached* in a preceding month. This rule was described in detail in chapter V.

Trading Rules Used by Others

I am giving a few trading rules which are used by other forecasters. While I have not checked all of these rules with actual markets, they contain considerable merit.

When, after the market (having made a new high) drops back past the previous close, many traders endeavor to get out on the theory that a major decline is about to take place.

If there has been a narrow price range for a week or two and the market breaks out on the up side, *buy* about a point and a half above the narrow range; or, after it breaks out on the down side, *sell* at about a point and a half below the narrow range.

If a secondary advance continues on actively and reaches about two points above the first high point made, then the up swing has not been completed. This rule is obtained from observing head and shoulder formations, as has been explained in this chapter.

When an advancing market reverses and declines below the bottom point of the top day by a half point, the market is considered a *sale*. When a declining market reverses and advances above the high point of the bottom day by a half point, the market indicates a *purchase*.

Every double top does not indicate a final top, and every double bottom does not indicate a final bottom. But they frequently indicate the preparation for a big reversal.

CHAPTER X

Trading Rule Number Eighteen

THE literal application of this rule causes the trader to enter the market after the trend has been established. If the trend is reversed, the trader is pushed out through stops. The best that can be said for this Canadian rule is that it calls for a minimum of margin and frequently shows tremendous profits. I never use this rule except to find the turning point in a major bull or bear market. For this purpose it has no equal.

I simply call this a successful trading plan because this Winnipeg trader appears to have attained a fair degree of success by his use of the head and shoulders method of *buying* and *selling* indications. I have seen the invoices of his trades and they show mostly profits. The man who gave me this rule in 1930 is a heavy trader in the Winnipeg market. In my opinion the plan lacks all of those definite indications that are to be found in successful *trading tables* like I have shown on pages 75 and 77.

A Canadian Trading Rule

"On any extended decline a purchase of wheat should be made just before the close on the first day that the market having made another new low, stops, turns and advances to a point higher than the close of the previous day.

"Immediately upon making this purchase a stop loss selling order is placed at a figure 2½ cents lower than the low of that day. The trade is then kept open until either the stop is caught and a loss taken or the market advances to show a profit. Profits should be taken, just before the close on the first day after an advance when the market having made a new high, stops, declines and is about to close at a figure lower than the close of the previous day.

68

A short sale is then made at the same point with a stop loss buying order, 2½ cents over the high of that day and the trade kept open until either the stop is caught or a buying indication appears when profits are taken on the short sale and a long position taken as before. When a stop is caught the trader is then out of the market and stands aside until the next indication appears."

A Modification of the Above Rule

In giving this modification we will quote literally from the author's letter. "In my original formula which I sent you, I stipulated that the trade should be at the close of the buying and selling days. However, I have revised this somewhat and now stipulate that the trade should not be put on till the market on some subsequent day, *passes one cent over the high of the buying day* or *one cent under the low of the selling day.*

"I have done this in order to keep my trades more of the long pull variety and to keep from being reversed too frequently, which is quite possible in narrow markets.

"I fully realize that this will detract several cents from the profit trades and add several cents to the loss trades, but, on the other hand, it prevents a large number of stop loss trades and keeps the trades in the general trend of the market. In other words, I feel that the market, after having given a buying or selling indication and having the power to go one cent further in the direction to which it points, that is, *one cent over the high of the buying day* or *one cent under the low of the selling day*, is almost absolute proof that it is headed considerably further in that direction and it will compensate the trader for the loss of one cent either way."

Buying and selling prices, dates, profits and losses taken from this plan are shown on pages 70 to 74 and cover practically five years of trading. A large number of these trades have actually been made by the author of the above letter.

Canadian Trading Rule Checked with Chicago Wheat 1925

MAY WHEAT			Price	Stop	Date		Price	Profit	Loss
1	Jan. 7	Buy	1.80	1.71	Feb. 10	Sell	1.88¾	+ 8¾	
2	Feb. 10	Sell	1.88¾	1.96¾	Feb. 14	Buy	1.85½	+ 3¼	
3	Feb. 14	Buy	1.85½	1.75	Feb. 17	Sell	1.82		− 3½
4	Feb. 17	Sell	1.82	1.90	Feb. 18	Buy	1.85¾		− 3¾
5	Feb. 18	Buy	1.85¾	1.77¼	Mar. 9	Sell	1.95½	+ 9¾	
6	Mar. 4	Sell	1.95½	2.04½	Mar. 16	Buy	1.72¼	+ 23¼	
7	Mar. 16	Buy	1.72¼	1.59½	Mar. 17	Sell	1.59½	Stopped	−12¾
8	Mar. 23	Sell	1.65½	1.73¾	April 6	Buy	1.44¾	+ 20¾	
9	April 6	Buy	1.44¾	1.34½	April 14	Sell	1.55½	+ 11	
10	April 14	Sell	1.56¾	1.64¾	April 22	Buy	1.52½	+ 4¼	
SEPT. WHEAT									
11	April 22	Buy	1.33		June 2	Sell	1.56	+ 23	
12	June 2	Sell	1.56	1.65	June 3	Buy	1.60½		− 4½
13	June 3	Buy	1.60½	1.53	June 12	Sell	1.58½		− 2
14	June 12	Sell	1.58½	1.69½	July 13	Buy	1.50	+ 8½	
15	July 13	Buy	1.50	1.40	July 16	Sell	1.50¾	+ ¾	
16	July 16	Sell	1.50¾	1.58¼	July 17	Buy	1.56		− 5¼
17	July 17	Buy	1.56	1.47¼	July 20	Sell	1.54¾		− 1¼
18	July 18	Sell	1.54¾	1.61¼	Aug. 1	Buy	1.53	+ 1¾	
19	Aug. 1	Buy	1.53	1.43½	Aug. 11	Sell	1.62½	+ 9½	
20	Aug. 11	Sell	1.62½	1.70	Aug. 20	Buy	1.61¾	+ ¾	
21	Aug. 20	Buy	1.61¾	1.53	Aug. 25	Sell	1.58¾		− 3
MAY WHEAT									
22	Aug. 25	Sell	1.62½	1.69¾	Sept. 16	Buy	1.54¼	+ 8¼	
23	Sept. 16	Buy	1.54¼	1.48¼	Sept. 23	Sell	1.52½		− 2
24	Sept. 23	Sell	1.52¼	1.57½	Oct. 24	Buy	1.41	+ 11¼	
25	Oct. 24	Buy	1.41	1.34½	Dec. 5	Sell	1.66	+ 25	
26	Dec. 5	Sell	1.66	1.74¾	Dec. 15	Buy	1.65¾	+ ¼	
27	Dec. 15	Buy	1.65¾	1.58	Dec. 18	Sell	1.64¾		− 1
28	Dec. 18	Sell	1.64¾	1.71½	Dec. 23	Buy	1.65½		− ¾

Profits (cents) per bushel	+170
Losses (cents) per bushel	39¾
Gross gains (cents)	130¼
Less Commissions (28 Trades × ¼c)	7
NET PROFIT per bushel (cents)	123¼

493% ON MONEY INVESTED
On Basis of 25c per Bu. Margin

Canadian Trading Rule Checked with Chicago Wheat 1926

MAY WHEAT			Price	Stop	Date		Price	Profit	Loss
1	Dec. 23	Buy	1.65½	1.56	Dec. 31	Sell	1.77	+ 11½	
2	Dec. 31	Sell	1.77	1.84½	Jan. 19	Buy	1.73¾	+ 3¼	
3	Jan. 19	Buy	1.73¾	1.67¾	Jan. 22	Sell	1.67¾	Stopped	– 6
4	Jan. 26	Buy	1.71¾	1.64¼	Feb. 5	Sell	1.72½	+ 1¼	
5	Feb. 5	Sell	1.72½	1.78½	Feb. 23	Buy	1.67¾	+ 4¾	
6	Feb. 23	Buy	1.67¾	1.60¾	Feb. 24	Sell	1.66¾		– 1
7	Feb. 24	Sell	1.66¾	1.73	Mar. 10	Buy	1.58½	+ 8¼	
8	Mar. 10	Buy	1.58½	1.52½	April 1	Sell	1.56		– 2½
9	April 1	Sell	1.56	1.63	April 14	Buy	1.63	Stopped	–7
MAY WHEAT									
15	Aug. 19	Buy	1.46½	1.41	Oct. 4	Sell	1.44¼		– 2¼
16	Oct. 4	Sell	1.44¼	1.49¼	Oct. 14	Buy	1.43½	+ ¾	
17	Oct. 14	Buy	1.43½	1.39	Oct. 26	Sell	1.47¾	+ 4¼	
18	Oct. 26	Sell	1.47¾	1.53¼	Nov. 23	Buy	1.39	+ 8¾	
19	Nov. 23	Buy	1.39	1.34	Dec. 8	Sell	1.40	+ 1	
20	Dec. 8	Sell	1.40	1.44¾	Dec. 16	Buy	1.40½		– ½
21	Dec. 16	Buy	1.40½	1.35¼	Feb. 8	Sell	1.41¼	+ ¾	

Profit (cents) per bushel	+ 44½
Losses (cents) per bushel	19¼
Gross gains (cents)	25¼
Less Commissions (17 Trades × ¼c)	4¼
NET PROFIT per bushel (cents)	21

147% ON MONEY INVESTED
On Basis of 25c per Bu. Margin

Canadian Trading Rule Checked with Chicago Wheat 1927

			Price	Stop	Date		Price	Profit	Loss
MAY WHEAT									
1	Feb. 8	Sell	1.41¼	1.46	Mar. 4	Buy	1.41½		− ¼
2	Mar. 4	Buy	1.41½	1.35¾	Mar. 9	Sell	1.40		− 1½
3	Mar. 9	Sell	1.40	1.45	Mar. 26	Buy	1.34¾	+ 5¼	
4	Mar. 26	Buy	1.34¾	1.29	April 9	Sell	1.32¾		− 2
5	April 9	Sell	1.32¾	1.38¼	May 2	Buy	1.38¼	Stopped	− 5½
SEPT. WHEAT									
6	May 2	Buy	1.34¼	1.28	May 31	Sell	1.45½	+ 11¼	
7	May 31	Sell	1.45½	1.51¾	June 28	Buy	1.41¾	+ 3¾	
8	June 28	Buy	1.41¾	1.36	July 12	Sell	1.42½	+ ¾	
9	July 12	Sell	1.42½	1.49¼	Aug. 4	Buy	1.38½	+ 4	
10	Aug. 4	Buy	1.38½	1.33½	Aug. 12	Sell	1.41¼	+ 2¾	
11	Aug. 12	Sell	1.41¼	1.48¼	Aug. 26	Buy	1.38¾	+ 2½	
12	Aug. 26	Buy	1.38¾	1.33¾	Aug. 29	Sell	1.36½		− 2¼
13	Aug. 29	Sell	1.36½	1.41¾	Sept. 24	Buy	1.28½	Est. + 8	

Profits (cents) per bushel	+ 38¼
Losses (cents) per bushel	11½
Gross gains (cents)	26¾
Less Commissions (13 Trades × ¼c)	4¼
NET PROFIT per bushel (cents)	22½

90% ON MONEY INVESTED
On Basis of 25c per Bu. Margin

Canadian Trading Rule Checked with Chicago Wheat 1928

MAY WHEAT			Price	Stop	Date		Price	Profit	Loss
1	Jan. 13	Buy	1.31¼	1.26¼	Jan. 24	Sell	1.30¾		− ½
2	Jan. 24	Sell	1.30¾	1.35	Feb. 20	Buy	1.33½		− 2¾
3	Feb. 20	Buy	1.33½	1.29¼	May 3	Sell	1.58½	+ 25	
SEPT. WHEAT									
4	May 3	Sell	1.55½	1.68	May 5	Buy	1.56½		− 1
5	May 5	Buy	1.56½	1.49	May 10	Sell	1.56¾	+ ¼	
6	May 10	Sell	1.56¾	1.63¾	May 23	Buy	1.52½	+ 4¼	
7	May 23	Buy	1.52½	1.46	May 26	Sell	1.49¾		− 2¾
8	May 26	Sell	1.49¾	1.57	June 20	Buy	1.39¼	+ 10½	
9	June 20	Buy	1.39¼	1.34	July 6	Sell	1.37½		− 1¾
10	July 6	Sell	1.37½	1.45½	Aug. 13	Buy	1.10	+ 27½	
MAY WHEAT									
11	Sept. 15	Buy	1.21½	1.16½	Sept. 25	Sell	1.24¼	+ 2¾	
12	Sept. 25	Sell	1.24¼	1.30¼	Sept. 27	Buy	1.26½		− 2¼
13	Sept. 27	Buy	1.26½	1.21¼	Oct. 9	Sell	1.24¾		− 1¾
14	Oct. 9	Sell	1.24¾	1.30	Oct. 16	Buy	1.24¼	+ ½	
15	Oct. 16	Buy	1.24¼	1.19¼	Oct. 30	Sell	1.23¼		− 1
16	Oct. 30	Sell	1.23¼	1.28¾	Nov. 14	Buy	1.24¼		− 1
17	Nov. 14	Buy	1.24¼	1.19¼	Nov. 28	Sell	1.22¾		− 1½
18	Nov. 28	Sell	1.22¾	1.27½	Jan. 10	Buy	1.19½	+ 3¼	

Profits (cents) per bushel	+ 74
Losses (cents) per bushel	16¼
Gross gains (cents)	57¾
Less Commissions (18 Trades × ¼c)	4½
NET PROFIT per bushel (cents)	53¼

213% ON MONEY INVESTED
On Basis of 25c per Bu. Margin

Canadian Trading Rule Checked with Chicago Wheat 1929

MAY WHEAT			Price	Stop	Date		Price	Profit	Loss
1	Jan. 10	Buy	1.19½	1.13¼	Jan. 29	Sell	1.26	+ 6½	
2	Jan. 29	Sell	1.26	1.33	Feb. 14	Buy	1.33	Stopped	– 7
3	Mar. 1	Buy	1.30¼	1.25¼	Mar. 4	Sell	1.28½		– 1¾
4	Mar. 4	Sell	1.28½	1.33	April 8	Buy	1.21½	+ 7	
5	April 8	Buy	1.21½	1.16	April 16	Sell	1.21½	+—0	
SEPT. WHEAT									
6	April 16	Sell	1.28½	1.32¾	May 14	Buy	1.13½	+ 15	
7	May 14	Buy	1.13½	1.08¼	May 17	Sell	1.11¾		– 1¾
8	May 17	Sell	1.11¾	1.17	June 3	Buy	1.09	+ 2¾	
9	June 3	Buy	1.09	.97¾	June 6	Sell	1.09½	+ ½	
10	June 6	Sell	1.09½	1.16½	June 19	Buy	1.12⅜		– 3⅛
11	June 19	Buy	1.12⅜	1.06½	July 8	Sell	1.25	+ 12⅝	
12	July 8	Sell	1.25	1.32	July 11	Buy	1.28¾		– 3¾
13	July 11	Buy	1.28¾	1.20½	July 19	Sell	1.44¾	+ 16	
14	July 19	Sell	1.44¾	1.53¾	Aug. 15	Buy	1.35	+ 9¾	
15	Aug. 15	Buy	1.35	1.27	Aug. 20	Sell	1.37	+ 2	
16	Aug. 20	Sell	1.37	1.44½	Aug. 30	Buy	1.33¼	+ 3¾	
17	Aug. 30	Buy	1.33¼	1.26¾	Sept. 4	Sell	1.32¾		– ½
MAY WHEAT									
18	Sept. 4	Sell	1.51⅜	1.57½	Sept. 11	Buy	1.52⅜		– 1
19	Sept. 11	Buy	1.52⅜	1.46¾	Sept. 17	Sell	1.46¾	Stopped	– 5⅝
20	Sept. 26	Buy	1.45¼	1.39⅜	Oct. 3	Sell	1.43¼		– 2
21	Oct. 3	Sell	1.43¼	1.49	Oct. 5	Buy	1.45¼		– 2
22	Oct. 5	Buy	1.45¼	1.40	Oct. 16	Sell	1.44¼		– 1
23	Oct. 16	Sell	1.44¼	1.49¾	Nov. 15	Buy	1.27¼	+ 17	
24	Nov. 15	Buy	1.27¼	1.19¼	Dec. 5	Sell	1.38⅞	+ 11⅝	
25	Dec. 5	Sell	1.38⅞	1.45¼	Dec. 17	Buy	1.32¾	+ 6⅛	
26	Dec. 17	Buy	1.32¾	1.26⅜	Dec. 19	Sell	1.31⅛		– 1⅝
27	Dec. 19	Sell	1.31⅛	1.36⅛	Dec. 24	Buy	1.36	Stopped	– 5

Profits (cents) per bushel	+110⅝
Losses (cents) per bushel	36⅛
Gross gains (cents)	74½
Less Commissions (27 Trades × ¼c)	6¾
NET PROFIT per bushel (cents)	67¾

271% ON MONEY INVESTED
On Basis of 25c per Bu. Margin

Trading Rule Number Eighteen

I will now repeat Trading Rule Number Eighteen and apply it to an actual market without using stops.

When the market has closed lower than the preceding close for two days in succession, the market indicates a *selling signal* and a sale is made at the opening on the following morning. If the market closes lower on the fifth day than on the fourth day (the day when sale was made at opening) then a second line is sold at the opening of the sixth day. If the market continued to close lower each day for many days in succession, it means that a short sale is made every other day.

When the markets close higher two days in succession, it indicates *a change in the trend,* and all short lines are covered at the opening of the third day, and the trader gets long one line at the same time and price. In no case are purchases or sales made closer than every other day.

Trades are never made on those days that show *buying* or *selling signals,* but always at the opening of the following day. No stop loss trades are ever made, since the trader will hardly over-extend himself *except* when he is carrying a large number of lines at a profit.

The following table of markets shows the actual application of this rule in the months of July, August, and September, 1928.

In order to simplify the table, I use the low of the opening, as well as the low of the close. The same results would be obtained were we to use *average* opening prices and *average* closing prices.

Daily Price Range of September and December Wheat in July, August, and September, 1928

SEPTEMBER WHEAT

	Open	High	Low	Close	
JULY					
2	142½	143	141	141¼	
3	147⅞	141⅛	140⅜	140⅝	
5	140⅝	141	138½	138¾	Selling signal
6	137⅛	138	136⅝	136⅝	Sold 1st short line at 137⅛

	Open	High	Low	Close	
7	136⅜	137⅞	136¼	136⅝	
9	136¾	137⅛	132⅝	132¾	Selling signal
10	133¼	136⅜	132⅞	134⅞	Sold 2nd short line at 133¼
11	134	135	131⅝	132¼	
12	132	134⅜	132	134	
13	134⅜	134¾	132¾	132⅞	
14	132¼	132⅞	132	132¾	Selling Signal
16	132	132¼	130½	131⅝	Sold 3rd short line at 132
17	131	132⅛	131	131½	Selling signal
18	131½	131¾	128⅞	129⅜	Sold 4th short line at 131½
19	128½	129⅜	127¼	127¾	Selling signal
20	128⅜	129¼	128⅜	129⅛	Sold 5th short line at 128⅜
21	128⅜	128½	126⅜	126½	
23	125	125¼	121⅜	121⅝	Selling signal
24	122	123½	119¾	123⅜	Sold 6th short line at 122
25	123	123⅞	122	122⅛	
26	120¼	124⅛	120¼	124	
27	123¼	124	121¾	122½	
28	122¾	123	121⅜	122⅝	
30	122⅛	122½	120⅜	121¼	
31	121¼	121½	120⅛	120½	Selling signal
AUGUST					
1	119	120	118½	119¼	Sold 7th short line at 119
2	119⅝	120¼	119¼	119⅛	Selling signal
3	119¼	119½	117⅜	117¾	
4	116⅞	117⅜	115⅝	116⅛	Sold 8th short line at 116⅛
6	115¼	115⅝	114¼	115	Selling signal
7	114⅝	115⅝	113⅛	113¼	Sold 9th short line at 114⅝
8	112	112½	109⅝	110⅞	Selling signal
9	112½	113¾	112	112¾	Sold 10th short line at 112½
10	108	109½	108	109⅛	
11	108¾	109¾	108⅛	109½	
13	109⅜	111½	108¼	111	Buying signal
14	114¼	114¼	111¼	113¾	Bought 10 short lines at 111¼, and long one line December Wheat at 116¼
15	113⅛	113½	111½	111½	Changed to December.

DECEMBER WHEAT

AUGUST					
16	115½	118	115⅜	117⅞	
17	116¾	118½	116¾	117½	
18	117⅛	117¾	116⅞	116⅞	Selling signal
20	115¾	116	114⅝	113¾	Sold one long line at 115¾ and one short line at 115¾
21	114¾	116¼	113⅛	113¼	
22	112⅝	114⅝	112½	114½	
23	115	117¾	114⅝	117	Buying signal
24	116½	117	114⅝	115	Bought one short line at 116½ and one long line at 116½
25	114¼	116	114¼	115¾	
27	115	116⅝	115	116½	Buying signal
28	115¾	118¼	115⅜	117⅞	Bought 2nd long line at 115¾

	Open	High	Low	Close	
29	117½	118⅛	116⅜	116⅜	
30	116¼	116⅝	115½	115½	Selling signal
31	115¾	116⅜	115¼	115⅞	Sold two long lines at 115¾ and one short line at 115¾
SEPTEMBER					
1	116¼	116⅝	116	116¼	
4	115¾	116	114½	115	
5	114⅞	115⅛	114¼	114¼	Selling signal
6	114¼	115¼	114	114⅞	Sold 2nd short line at 114¼
7	115	115¾	114⅝	115⅜	
8	115	115⅛	112⅝	112¾	
10	112¼	112⅞	111½	112⅜	Selling signal
11	112¾	113½	112¼	112¾	Sold 3rd short line at 112¾
12	112	113⅛	111⅝	112⅞	
13	112¼	113⅞	112¼	112¾	
14	112½	113⅝	112⅜	113½	
15	114	114¾	113⅝	114¼	Buying signal
17	114¼	114⅝	113½	113⅝	Bought two short lines at 114¼, and one long line at 114¼
18	113½	113⅝	113	113⅜	
19	113⅜	115¼	113⅜	114⅜	
20	114¾	115⅛	114⅝	114¾	Buying signal
21	114⅜	119½	114¼	119¼	Bought 2nd long line at 114⅜
22	118⅜	121⅛	118½	118¾	
24	118⅜	120⅛	118¼	118⅝	Selling signal
25	118¼	118⅝	116¾	117	Sold two long lines at 118¼, and one short line at 118¼
26	116⅞	118⅜	116⅝	118¼	
27	118¾	120⅛	118⅜	118⅜	
28	118¼	118¾	118	118¼	
29	118⅞	119	116⅞	117½	Bought in one short line to close out all trades.

In order that beginners in grain trading may easily understand the very simple operation of Trading Rule Number Eighteen, we give an illustration of an actual trader who uses this rule.

The trader with $5,000 in operating capital sells 10,000 bushels of September Wheat short at 137⅛ at the opening of July 6 (as shown in the above table) because the close at 138¾ on July 5 showed a decline at the close for two consecutive days. Again on July 9, the close was lower than the close of the 6th (July 6 and 7, close was the same). Therefore, a second line of 10,000 bushels is sold short on the opening of the 10th at 113¼. Since the close of the 12th is higher than the close of the 11th, the next buying or selling indication does not come until the 14th.

Therefore, on the 16th (Sunday intervenes) a third line of 10,000 bushels is sold short at 132. It so happens that, in this major decline, ten lines are sold short before the first buying indication comes. This indication comes on August 13, when for the first time in six weeks the market closes higher for two consecutive days. Therefore, the trader buys in all ten short lines at the opening of August 14th, at 111¼, *and gets long one line at the same price.*

The above is not theory. The trades were actually made. On August 9, the broker demanded $5,000 more margin in spite of the fact that some of the first trades showed a profit of nearly 30 cents and all trades showed a profit, except the last.

On August 14, the trader had his broker pay him back all of his original capital of $15,000, and he operated to the end of the period, September 30, 1928, only on the profits which he left with his broker.

From July 1st to August 14th, the trader's total profits were $13,837.50, although the above table shows only $13,400, less commissions of $250, or $13,150.

From August 14th to September 30th, margin requirements were very small and likewise profits were small. At no time from August 14 to September 30 was this trader long or short more than three lines. In the three-month period as a whole, nineteen trades were made and closed out, and the trader's actual average profits per bushel were 7⅜ cents.

When Trading Rule Number Eighteen Should be Applied

Trading Rule Number Eighteen works better on the short side than on the long side of the market—but more of this later. The rule should never be applied to a continuous market as shown on pages 75 to 77. This rule is the best of all rules for finding the major turns. In order to give this rule a severe test we are applying it to the short side far too soon and are being forced out more frequently than would be the case in actual trading.

Trading Rule Number Eighteen should eventually show a worthwhile profit, even if applied to the short side of a bull market before the market has gone *half way* to its top. All that is needed in the way of market action is a major decline which will take place from *some point* in two to six weeks after the first trades are attempted and furthermore that the speculator will not overstay his short position and miss his chance to take big profits. This is none too easy and it goes without saying that applying the rule on the short side before a bull market is half over is sometimes rather expensive.

I will now undertake to prove the merit of this rule by applying it to the short side of every major *bull* market we have had in the past eleven years. I will apply the rule to each bull market when it is *just half way* to what later proved to be its top. In so doing, the trader is out through "stops" from one to seven times in each market. And, to make it more difficult, we will close out our short sales when the market gets just half way to what later proved to be its bottom. In actual practice, trading rules would be reversed in finding a place to take profits unless an objective on the bottom side was determined in some other manner.

We shall begin our rigid test of this rule with the first bull market of 1921. On February 8, 1921 the trader attempts to get short with a two-cent stop at 153, according to the rule. He is forced out on February 21. He is short again on March 8 at 159 and later takes 29 cents profit, assuming that he got out when the market still had another 20 to decline before it hit bottom. In this market he was forced out through only one stop.

Try this rule on February 5, 1922, to the short side of the bull market of January and February of that year and see how far the market advanced after February 5 before a short position was possible under the rule and how successful it was after it was made to *stand up*.

Let us now take the bull market of May, 1925 and apply

the rule. Remember, we are not going to be clever; we are purposely trying to be stupid. We are looking for a chance to get short when the market is still fifteen cents from what later proved to be the top. The half way point in this bull market was reached on May 25 at 152.

The first opportunity to get short after May 25 is at 157¾ at the close of June 1. The trader is out with a two-cent stop at 159¾ on June 3. He gets short again at 159¾ on June 11 and on June 15 takes profits at 152. By waiting another day he could have had another five cents profit, and by getting out at the exact bottom on July 2 his profits would have been 21¾ cents—But, we are making this *hard;* we are not trying to be *clever.* And furthermore, we are using *every* bull market and are not looking ahead to see what bear markets if any are to follow. Any one can recognize a bull market after it is past; no trouble there.

The bull market of July and August of 1925 shows even better results, but we have not time to check every market.

Next comes the bull market that started October 3, 1925 at 133 for May Wheat and culminated on December 30 at 182. But we are purposely entering this market on the short side when it is only half way to its top. We are going to try to get short at 158 (the half way place) on November 24, when the market still has 24 cents to advance before a decline sets in. The first opportunity to get short is at 160½ on November 30. The following day the trader is out through his stop at 162½. The next opportunity to get short is December 11 at 162½. The following day the trader is out at 164½. Another short position is taken at 164 on December 18. We will assume that he passes up a chance for 5½ cents profit on December 22 and is pushed out through his stop at 167 (a high opening on December 23) with a loss of three cents.

The next opportunity to get short comes on December 31 at 177¼. He is out on January 4 with a two-cent stop. The trader (now very much discouraged with fighting the short side of a bull market) gets short on January 11 at 173¼, only to be pushed out at 175¼ on January 19 after having passed up some handsome profits in this eight-day period.

On January 21 he is short at 171 and is out at 173 on the 27th. On February 8 he is short at 167⅝. On February 23 he is out at 169⅝. On February 25 he is short at 164. It is probable that he would have got out at around 155 in March, although a transfer to the short side of September would have given a chance to ride the market down to 130¼ in May. Unless the trader was clever, he would have lost in the choppy "decline" since his short sales carried him through seven stops with total "stop" losses of 15 cents to be followed by a profit of 6 to 12 cents on his successful trade. In this case, his trade, when finally established, is entirely too far from the top.

The next major bull market got its start on February 6, 1928 at 128 for May and culminated on April 27 at 163¾. (I might mention that I got long in this market at 133⅝ for September and took profits at 161⅜ as shown on page 5. On that one trade I made a net profit of $4,122.55 on 15,000 bushels.

But this is a study of short selling under Trading Rule Number Eighteen, so we will try to get short September Wheat on April 11 at 146, when the market still has an advance ahead of 21 cents. We will try to get short under the rule in a market where I actually took tremendous profits on the long side by using plain common horse sense in a year of heavy winter wheat killing.

The first chance to take a short position under the rule is on April 21 at 150⅝. The following day the trader is pushed out through his stop. The next opportunity to get short is on May 2 at 158½ (following the peak of 167¼ reached on April 30). On May 9 he is out at 160½. On May 10 he is short at 152⅝. On May 24 he is out at 154⅝, after passing up a six-cent profit. He is again short at 150 on May 26. He later sells out at the high of July 23 at 125½. Understand, there was no reason for selling out here. We have shown it only because later it proved to be the half-way point in the decline.

The next day, if he had waited, his profits on his successful trade would have been 32 cents, and on August 10 there would have been 43 cents profit, but we are assuming that our trader, following this rule, is not clever but purely mechanical in making his trades. We are assuming that he ignored the remarkable crop improvement throughout the summer of 1928.

I need not go into detail regarding the profits I took on the long side of the bull market in October of 1931 with even larger profits on the short side of the market that followed in November.

On November 9, 1931 I stated the rule which gave me and my following an opportunity to switch from the long to the short side on November 10 at 65¾ cents. Trading Rule Number Eighteen got us out of this short market with profits of approximately ten cents a bushel.

I will now get back to my first statement where I claimed that Trading Rule Number Eighteen works better on the short side than on the long side of the market. The reason for this is interesting. Every major bull market is sooner or later followed by a major bear market; and likewise every major bear market is eventually followed by a bull market. This is an axiom. The life span from the initial start of a major bull market until the culmination of the following bear market ranges from approximately 60 days, which is a very short span, to as much as six months, which is an exceedingly long span. Frequently only half the gain in a bull market is lost and sometimes twice the gain is lost. Beyond these two extremes a new plateau of very high or very low prices is unusual.

But here is where a bull market differs from a bear market. Bull markets always gather hundreds of thousands of amateur traders on the way up and their trades are frequently followed by close-up stops or (as is more often the case) by inadequate margin. A reverse from what appears to be a bull market into a major decline causes losses to at least nine-tenths of the traders who are in the market, but a reversal from a major bear market into a major bull market usually does not cause a loss to more than one-fourth of the traders, as explained in chapter two.

The question naturally arises, "How can this be possible when for every million bushels of long grain there must be a million bushels of short grain?"

This is the answer: At least one-half of all the short trades and frequently as much as three-fourths of the short trades in a market are placed as hedges against the holding of actual grain. Therefore, a major advance does not work any hardship whatsoever on a large percentage of those who are short the futures since they are also long the actual grain.

On the other hand, a major decline frequently does not give a profit to more than one-tenth of those who are in the market, purely as a speculation. Thus a bull market is always a "hope" market if it is not a profit market, whereas a bear market is a "fear" market and in nine cases out of ten is a loss market.

It naturally follows that, after having had a major advance which has accumulated tens of thousands of amateur longs, a decline of two days in succession creates doubt and fear among that group of traders who are least able to stand punishment, either from financial or psychological reasons. A cautious opening following a decline of two days in succession that was preceded by a fifty per cent advance is a logical expectation which makes it easier for *stops* to stand up. The same can not be said for the culmination of a major bear market, which is frequently left largely in the hands of professionals.

Because of the *fear* that a sudden decline from a bull market creates, it becomes easier to forecast a major bear market following a major bull market than it does to forecast a major bull market following a major bear market. A bull market following a long sidewise market is the easiest of all markets to forecast. Such was the bull market in April 1933. It was just a simple case of getting in and taking the profits.

CHAPTER XI

Trading Rule Number Eleven

IN MAKING a study of grain speculation, it should be clearly understood that trading in grain futures would never be permitted if speculation did not, in itself, tend to steady a market. In other words, the daily, weekly, monthly, and yearly extreme price range of wheat is more narrow than would be the case if trading were confined entirely to the buying and selling of actual spot grain. Because soy beans have no futures market, the price may drop or advance 200 per cent in a twelve-month period. This actually occurred in 1931 when soy beans were 80 cents, followed by a decline to 20 cents, and, later, an advance to 40 cents.

The buying of wheat on weak spots and the selling on hard spots is the most professional of all trading practices and acts as a great price stabilizer. The most successful of all grain market scalping rules is what I choose to call *"Trading Rule Number Eleven"*. While the broad principles of this rule are used by more successful market operators than any other trading rule I think I am the first trader to state this rule and show its application to actual markets.

Successful Grain Scalping Methods

It is absolutely essential that any scalping or short swing plan, to succeed, must attempt to sell on *minor advances against the trend* and buy on *minor declines against the trend*.

Occasionally, a man will make a big profit on the purchase of bids or offers, but in the long run a loss is inevitable. Money is made by *selling* bids and offers, and not by *buying* them. Money is made by selling bids and offers because it incorporates the broad principles of Trading Rule Number Eleven. A successful scalping rule must not only attempt to buy and sell *against the trend* in the hope that the trend will shortly turn; but, it must also keep the buying and selling orders *centered with the market*. And, furthermore, trades must be kept fairly well evened up by the use of *"Differentials,"* as shown in columns 12 and 13 on pages 92 to 102.

I shall now state Trading Rule Number Eleven just as I used it in actual markets from January 18 to April 30, 1932 when my net profits over all losses and commissions were 24½ cents a bushel.

"Trading Rule Number Eleven"

Whenever possible *sell* 5,000 bushels of May Wheat at one-half cent *above* the *high* of the previous day, and whenever possible *buy* 5,000 bushels of May Wheat at one-half cent *below* the *low* of the previous day.

Each day just *one buying* and *one selling* order is placed, good only for that *one day*.

Before the opening of the market, regardless of whether you are *out* or *long* or *short*, you enter an order (good only for the day) to sell 5,000 bushels at one-half cent above the highest price reached on the previous day, and you enter an order to buy 5,000 bushels at one-half cent below the lowest price reached on the previous day.

The literal application of this rule gave me profits as stated above. In practice I consider 5,000 bushels a unit or line. Cub traders trade in "jobs" of 1,000 bushels each.

Adding the Buying and Selling Differentials to "Trading Rule Number Eleven"

Without the use of what are called "buying and selling *differentials,*" the above trading rule would, in time, cause the trader to have a net long or short position of ten, twenty, or thirty lines—which would, of course, exhaust his margin and end in failure. Therefore, when the trader is long over two lines, there must be a plan which makes it *easier* to sell and close out a unit or line than to buy more units or lines that might be burdensome to carry. When short, it must be made *easier* to buy than to sell.

Therefore, when the trader is long *two lines,* he stops trying to buy a *third line* at ½ cent below the low of the day before. He enters an order to buy the third line at ¾ of a cent below the previous day's low and, at the same time, he enters an order to sell one of his two lines at ¼ cent above the previous day's high. If you will refer to the tables on pages 94 and 95 you will see that in every case where the trader is long two lines of wheat, the buying difference as shown on the following date in the table is ¾ of a cent, and the selling difference is ¼ of a cent (See Jan. 23, March 14 and 29, April 1 and 8, 1932).

But, let us assume that the trader, in spite of his buying *differential* being farther away from the *market center* than his selling differential, gets long a *third line*. Then, he enters an order to buy a *fourth line* only if it can be had at one full cent below the low of the previous day. (On March 18, the trader was long three lines. Therefore, on March 19, he tried to buy a fourth line at 54¾ and to sell at the high of the previous day, which price was 57⅞. The sale could not be made. The purchase of the fourth line was made at 54⅜—which was the opening— on the buying order at 54¾. Thus, the order to buy at 54¾ was executed at 54⅜.)

A big decline between the 8th and the 19th of March got the trader long four lines. He was very anxious to unload some of his lines before buying more. An order to buy a fifth line at 1¼ cent under the low of March 19th and to sell one of the four lines at ¼ cent under the high of the 19th, resulted in a sale made at 54¾. Thus the trader's lines of wheat were reduced to three lines, and he was in a more comfortable position.

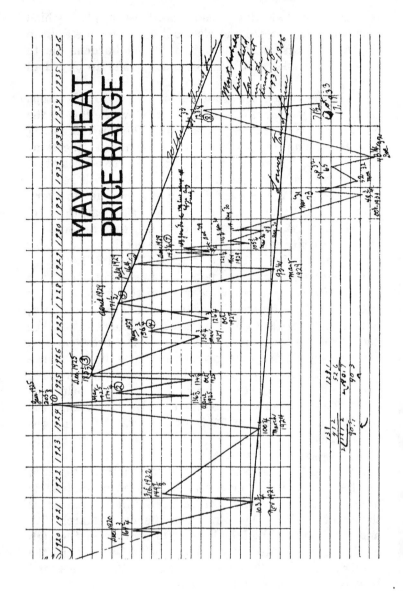

When the trader is short two or more lines, his *buying differentials* are always smaller than the *selling differentials*. Thus, on the day *following* a position of two short lines, the *buying differential* is ¼ cent, and the *selling differential* is ¾ cent. When short three lines, the order on the *following day* is to buy at the *low* of the previous day and sell a fourth line short at *one cent* over the *high* of the previous day.

Remember, each morning before the market opens, all orders of the previous day are cancelled, and a new order is placed to buy just one unit or line, and also to sell just one line. Occasionally, both buying and selling orders are filled in one day, as occurred on February 16, 1932.

When wheat is selling at $1.00 a bushel, then all buying and selling differentials should be multiplied by two; and when wheat is selling at $1.50 per bushel, all buying and selling differentials are multiplied by three.

The ideal situation is for trades to run one, two and three lines long, and then one, two, and three lines short. Four or more lines long or short are always hard on the margin, and five lines are difficult if not impossible for the average trader to carry.

Study the Table Carefully

Readers who desire to trade according to *Trading Rule Number Eleven* should not only study the table carefully, but they should keep a table of their own.

Ordinarily, I like to have all trades paired up just as soon as they are closed out, regardless of whether they show a profit or a loss. I made one exception and paired up the purchase of February 29 with the sale of February 13. In all other cases, the profits as shown in column eight were taken up just as soon as sales could be paired up with purchases. The same applies to the losses shown in column nine.

You will also note that while I confined my trades to the more active futures in all cases I switched my trading to the more distant futures at times when I was *out of the market* and all trades had been closed out.

In giving the opening price, I have simplified the table by always giving the *low* of the opening. If I had given the *high* of the opening the results would have been practically the same.

An order to buy at a higher figure than the opening naturally becomes a *market* order if the opening range is *lower* than the buying order; and an order to sell at a lower figure than the opening is also filled at the opening. The abbreviation "Mkt. Ord." in column one of the table means *"Market Order."*

Also keep in mind that up to *one* or *two lines* long or short the *buying* or *selling* difference is always ½ cent below the low of the day before or ½ cent above the *high* of the day before, as the case may be. In order to make myself perfectly clear, I shall now repeat what I have already said.

After the trader is long two lines, he will try to buy a *third line* or *unit* at ¾ of a cent below the *low of the previous day* and he will try to sell one of his two lines at ¼ of a cent above the *high of the previous day.* Don't be confused because you see ½ cent *buying difference* after *two lines long* and in other cases when you see ¾ cent or 1 cent. Just keep in mind that when you are long *two lines* you don't know until the day is over whether you will be long *three lines* or *one line,* or if no trades are made you will still be long *two lines.* In keeping a table the columns of *"buying difference"* and *"selling difference"* are always kept *one line ahead* of all other figures. (See Oct. 1.) In other words, the column following *two lines long* always shows an order to buy at ¾ of a cent below the low of the day before. But the figure in the same column as *two lines long* may be ½ *cent* or ¼ *cent, if no trade has been made;* or, it may be 1 cent if the trader had been long three lines on the day before.

It is just possible we may have overlooked some trades

or got a quotation wrong. If so, don't feel that the long or short position of September 30 would have been materially different. In all probability a different set of differentials would have shown the trader long or short on September 30, just as we have indicated in the table. Please keep in mind that the ever-changing *buying differences* and *selling differences* tend to keep the trader 5,000, 10,000, or 15,000 bushels *short* or *long* or *out of the market and ready for a new start.*

Trading Rule Number Eleven is just as hazardous as it is sporting. I repeat that big profits and safe profits are dependent on a successful forecast of a side-wise market. This rule has been checked with more markets than any other one trading rule. While the trader is seldom long or short more than four lines there was one market found in Winnipeg May wheat in the summer of 1929 when the trader would have been long eight lines.

Over 91,000 market quotations were used in checking the rules offered in this book. About one third of the checking was done in Canada.

Wheat Trading Rule Number Eleven Applied to the Market of 1932

MAY FUTURE

Date		Open	High	Low	Sold	Bought	Gains	Losses	Lines Short	Lines Long	Buying Difference	Selling Difference
JANUARY												
14	......	57⅛	57⅜	56¼	......	......	......	......	......	......	½ cent	½ cent
15	......	56	56¾	55¾	......	55¾	......	......	......	1 line	½ cent	½ cent
16	......	56⅜	59⅜	56¼	57¼	......	1½	......	out	out	½ cent	½ cent
18	Mkt ord	60	61¾	59⅞	60	......	......	......	1 line	......	½ cent	½ cent
19	......	60⅛	60¾	59⅜	......	59⅜	⅝	......	out	out	½ cent	½ cent
20	......	59¼	60⅛	58¾	......	58⅞	......	......	......	1 line	½ cent	½ cent
21	......	60¼	60⅞	59¾	60⅝	......	1¾	......	out	out	½ cent	½ cent
22	......	59¾	60	59⅛	......	59¼	......	......	......	1 line	½ cent	½ cent
23	......	58⅞	59	57¾	......	58⅝	......	......	......	2 lines	½ cent	½ cent
25	No trade	57¾	58½	57¾	......	......	......	......	......	2 lines	¾ cent	¼ cent
26	No trade	57¾	58	57¼	......	......	......	......	......	2 lines	¾ cent	¼ cent
27	No trade	57	58	56¾	......	......	......	......	......	2 lines	¾ cent	¼ cent
28	......	57⅞	58⅜	57⅜	58¼	......	......	1	......	1 line	¾ cent	¼ cent
29	......	58⅛	60⅛	57⅞	58⅞	......	¼	......	out	out	½ cent	½ cent
30	......	61	61⅛	58¾	60⅝	......	......	......	1 line	......	½ cent	½ cent
FEBRUARY												
1	No trade	59⅛	61⅜	59⅛	......	......	......	......	1 line	......	½ cent	½ cent
2	No trade	60	60¼	59⅛	......	......	......	......	1 line	......	½ cent	½ cent
3	No trade	59¾	60⅜	59⅛	......	......	......	......	1 line	......	½ cent	½ cent
4	No trade	60	60⅛	58¾	......	......	......	......	1 line	......	½ cent	½ cent
5	......	58⅝	59	58	......	58¼	2⅜	......	out	out	½ cent	½ cent
6	No trade	58	58⅝	57¾	......	......	......	......	out	out	½ cent	½ cent
8	No trade	58⅜	58⅝	57⅝	......	......	......	......	out	out	½ cent	½ cent
9	......	57¾	58	57	......	57⅛	......	......	......	1 line	½ cent	½ cent

Wheat Trading Rule Number Eleven Applied to the Market of 1932—*Continued*

Date		Open	High	Low	Sold	Bought	Gains	Losses	Lines Short	Lines Long	Buying Difference	Selling Difference
					MAY FUTURE—*Continued*							
FEBRUARY—*Continued*												
10	No trade	56⅝	57⅞	56⅝						1 line	½ cent	½ cent
11	Mkt ord	58⅝	59⅜	58⅝	58⅝		1½		out	out	½ cent	½ cent
13	Mkt ord	60⅛	61½	59⅞	60⅛				1 line		½ cent	½ cent
15	No trade	60⅝	61	59⅞					1 line			
16	Bot & sold	59⅜	62½	59⅜	61½	59⅜	2⅛		1 line		½ cent	½ cent
17	No trade	61¾	62⅝	60½					1 line		½ cent	½ cent
18	No trade	60⅝	61⅞	60⅝					1 line		½ cent	½ cent
19		62⅜	63	61⅞	62⅜				2 lines		½ cent	½ cent
20		61¼	61¾	61		61⅛	1¼		1 line		¼ cent	¾ cent
23		60⅝	62⅜	60⅜	62¼	60½	1¾		1 line		½ cent	½ cent
24	No trade	61⅛	62¼	60⅞					1 line		½ cent	½ cent
25		61⅜	62⅞	61⅜	62¾				2 lines		½ cent	½ cent
26	No trade	61⅞	62¾	61⅞					2 lines		¼ cent	¾ cent
27		61¾	62¼	61⅜		61⅜	1⅜		1 line		¼ cent	¾ cent
29		61¾	61⅞	60⅞		60⅞		¾	out	out	½ cent	½ cent
MARCH		(Purchase of February 29 paired up with sale of February 13)										
1		60¾	61	60⅛		60⅜				1 line	½ cent	½ cent
2		60⅝	61⅝	60⅝	61½		1⅛		out	out	½ cent	½ cent
3		61⅞	62	61⅛					out	out	½ cent	½ cent
4	No trade	60⅞	61½	60¾					out	out	½ cent	½ cent
5	No trade	61	61⅞	61					out	out	½ cent	½ cent
7	No trade	61⅞	62⅛	60¾					out	out	½ cent	½ cent
8		60⅞	61⅝	60¼		60¼				1 line	½ cent	½ cent
9	No trade	61¼	61⅝	60¾						1 line	½ cent	½ cent
10	No trade	60⅝	61⅛	60⅝						1 line	½ cent	½ cent

Wheat Trading Rule Number Eleven Applied to the Market of 1932—*Continued*

Date	Open	High	Low	Sold	Bought	Gains	Losses	Lines Short	Lines Long	Buying Difference	Selling Difference
MARCH—*Continued*											
MAY FUTURE—*Continued*											
11	No trade 605/8	603/4	603/8						1 line	1/2 cent	1/2 cent
12	No trade 603/8	603/4	603/8						1 line	1/2 cent	1/2 cent
14	603/8	607/8	577/8		597/8				2 lines	1/2 cent	1/2 cent
15	No trade 581/4	583/4	571/4						2 lines	3/4 cent	1/4 cent
16	No trade 581/4	583/8	571/4						2 lines	3/4 cent	1/4 cent
17	No trade 571/2	577/8	567/8		561/8				3 lines	3/4 cent	1/4 cent
18	No trade 575/8	577/8	553/4		541/2				3 lines	3/4 cent	1/4 cent
19	Mkt ord 543/8	55	535/8	543/4					4 lines	1 cent	high
21	541/4	555/8	541/4				1/2		3 lines	11/4 cent	1/4 under
22	547/8	551/8	527/8		531/4				4 lines	1 cent	high
23	No trade 523/8	543/8	521/4						4 lines	11/4 cent	1/4 under
24	No trade 541/2	543/4	533/8						3 lines	11/4 cent	1/4 under
26	No trade 531/4	531/2	521/4						4 lines	1 cent	high
28	521/4	535/8	52	531/4			25/8		3 lines	11/4 cent	1/4 under
29	533/8	541/4	525/8	535/8			21/2		2 lines	1 cent	high
30	541/8	551/4	531/2	541/2					1 line	3/4 cent	1/4 cent
30	No trade 543/4	551/8	54						1 line	1/2 cent	1/2 cent
APRIL											
1	537/8	541/2	531/8	543/4	531/2	11/2			2 lines	1/2 cent	1/2 cent
2	531/2	561/4	531/8	57		31/2			1 line	3/4 cent	1/4 cent
4	56	577/8	553/4					out	out	1/2 cent	1/2 cent
5	No trade 563/8	567/8	56					out	out	1/2 cent	1/2 cent
6	533/8	571/8	553/8		551/2				1 line	1/2 cent	1/2 cent
7	No trade 563/8	567/8	555/8		551/8				1 line	1/2 cent	1/2 cent
8	563/8	565/8	537/8						2 lines	1/2 cent	1/2 cent

Wheat Trading Rule Number Eleven Applied to the Market of 1932—*Continued*

MAY FUTURE—*Continued*

APRIL—*Continued*

Date		Open	High	Low	Sold	Bought	Gains	Losses	Lines Short	Lines Long	Buying Difference	Selling Difference
9		56	57⅜	55⅞	56⅞		1⅜			1 line	¾ cent	¼ cent
11		56¾	59¾	56¾	57⅞		2¾		out	out	½ cent	½ cent
12		59½	61⅛	58⅝	60¼				1 line		½ cent	½ cent
13	No trade	60½	60⅝	59⅜					1 line		½ cent	½ cent
14		59⅜	62	59⅜	61⅛				2 lines		½ cent	½ cent
15	No trade	60	61¼	59⅝					2 lines		¼ cent	¾ cent
16		60	60¼	58¾		59⅜	⅞		1 line		¼ cent	¾ cent
18		58⅞	59¾	58¼		58¼	2⅞		out	out		

JULY FUTURE

Date		Open	High	Low	Sold	Bought	Gains	Losses	Lines Short	Lines Long	Buying Difference	Selling Difference
18		62	62½	60¾								
19		60¼	61⅜	59⅞		60¼				1 line	½ cent	½ cent
20	No trade	61	61⅛	59¾						1 line	½ cent	½ cent
21	No trade	60	60¾	59½						1 line	½ cent	½ cent
22		60	60⅛	58⅞		59				2 lines	½ cent	½ cent
23		58	59	58	59	58⅛				3 lines	¾ cent	¼ cent
25		58⅝	59¾	58⅜	60			1¼		2 lines	1 cent	high
26		59⅝	60½	59⅜			1			1 line	¾ cent	¼ cent
27	No trade	60⅛	60¼	59¼						1 line	½ cent	½ cent
28		59⅛	59¼	56¾		58¾				2 lines	½ cent	½ cent
29		56¾	56¾	54½	56¾	56				3 lines	¾ cent	¼ cent
30		56⅝	57¾	56⅜				1⅜		2 lines	1 cent	high

Wheat Trading Rule Number Eleven Applied to the Market of 1932—*Continued*

JULY FUTURE—*Continued*

Date		Open	High	Low	Sold	Bought	Gains	Losses	Lines Short	Lines Long	Buying Difference	Selling Difference
MAY												
2	....	57⅛	58	56¾	58	....	¾	....	....	1 line	¾ cent	¼ cent
3	....	57	57¾	55⅜	....	56¼	....	....	....	2 lines	½ cent	½ cent
4	No trade	55¾	56⅜	55	....	....	....	....	....	2 lines	¾ cent	¼ cent
5	No trade	55⅞	56⅜	54⅝	....	....	....	....	....	2 lines	¾ cent	¼ cent
6	....	55¾	57½	55¾	56⅝	....	⅝	....	....	1 line	¾ cent	¼ cent
7	No trade	57	57½	56⅜	....	....	....	....	....	1 line	½ cent	½ cent
9	No trade	57¼	57½	56¾	....	....	....	....	....	1 line	½ cent	½ cent
10	No trade	57⅛	57⅜	56⅞	....	....	....	....	....	1 line	½ cent	½ cent
11	Mkt ord	58⅛	58¾	57⅝	58⅛	....	1⅞	....	....	out	½ cent	½ cent
12	Mkt ord	57	57⅜	55⅞	....	57	....	....	....	1 line	½ cent	½ cent
13	....	56	56⅝	55⅞	....	....	....	....	....	1 line	½ cent	½ cent
14	....	55⅝	55⅞	55⅛	....	55⅜	....	....	....	2 lines	½ cent	½ cent
16	....	55¼	57⅛	55¼	56⅛	....	....	⅞	....	1 line	¾ cent	¼ cent
17	....	56¾	58⅜	56¾	57⅝	....	2¼	....	out	out	½ cent	½ cent
18	No trade	57⅜	58⅜	56⅞	....	....	....	....	out	out	½ cent	½ cent
19	No trade	57¼	57¾	56⅞	....	....	....	....	out	out	½ cent	½ cent
20	....	57⅝	59	57⅝	58¼	....	....	....	1 line	....	½ cent	½ cent
21	....	58½	59¾	58¼	59½	....	....	....	2 lines	....	½ cent	½ cent
23	....	59¾	61½	59¾	61½	....	....	....	3 lines	....	¼ cent	¾ cent
24	....	60½	60¾	59⅜	....	59¾	....	1½	2 lines	....	low	1 cent
25	No trade	59½	60¾	59¼	....	....	....	....	2 lines	....	¼ cent	¾ cent
26	....	60⅛	60¼	58¾	....	59	½	....	1 line	....	¼ cent	¾ cent
27	No trade	59⅝	60½	59⅜	....	....	....	....	1 line	....	½ cent	½ cent
28	No trade	58⅝	59⅜	59⅝	....	....	....	....	1 line	....	½ cent	½ cent
31	Mkt ord	58	58¼	57⅛	....	58	3½	....	out	out	½ cent	½ cent

Wheat Trading Rule Number Eleven Applied to the Market of 1932—*Continued*

Date		Open	High	Low	Sold	Bought	Gains	Losses	Lines Short	Lines Long	Buying Difference	Selling Difference
JUNE					JULY FUTURE—*Continued*							
1		57⅝	58	55⅜		56⅝				1 line	½ cent	½ cent
2	No trade	55¼	56⅜	55⅛						1 line	½ cent	½ cent
3	No trade	56	56⅞	54¾						1 line	½ cent	½ cent
4		55⅛	55⅝	54		54¼				2 lines	½ cent	½ cent
6		53⅝	53⅞	51⅝		53¼				3 lines	¾ cent	¼ cent
7	No trade	52⅛	52¾	51¼						3 lines	1 cent	high
8		50⅝	51	49⅝		50¼				4 lines	1 cent	high
9	No trade	49½	50¾	49⅜						4 lines	1¼ cent	¼ under
10		50⅜	51¼	50	50½			6⅛		3 lines	1¼ cent	¼ under
11	Mkt ord	51½	52¼	50⅞	51½			2¾		2 lines	1 cent	high
13		50⅞	51	49¾		50⅛				3 lines	¾ cent	¼ cent
14		49¼	49½	48¾		48¾				4 lines	1 cent	high
15		48¾	50¾	48¾	49¼			4		3 lines	1¼ cent	¼ under
16		50¼	51¼	50	50¾		½			2 lines	1 cent	high
17		50⅜	51	48⅛		48¼				3 lines	¾ cent	¼ cent
18	No trade	47¾	48¾	47⅝						3 lines	1 cent	high
20		48¾	49⅝	48¾	48¾			1⅜		2 lines	1 cent	high
21		48⅞	49¼	47⅞		48				3 lines	¾ cent	¼ cent
22		47¼	48¼	46⅞		46⅞				4 lines	1 cent	high
23	Mkt ord	48¼	48⅝	47⅞	48¼			½		3 lines	1¼ cent	¼ under
24		47⅞	48¼	47⅜	48¼					2 lines	1 cent	high
25		46⅞	48⅞	46⅞	48½		½			1 line	¾ cent	¼ cent
27		48¾	49⅝	47¾	49⅜		2½		out	out	½ cent	½ cent
					DECEMBER FUTURE							
28	No trade	53¾	54⅜	53					out	out	½ cent	½ cent
29	No trade	54¼	54½	53½					out	out	½ cent	½ cent
30	No trade	54⅜	54⅞	53⅝					out	out	½ cent	½ cent

Wheat Trading Rule Number Eleven Applied to the Market of 1932—*Continued*

DECEMBER FUTURE—*Continued*

Date		Open	High	Low	Sold	Bought	Gains	Losses	Lines Short	Lines Long	Buying Difference	Selling Difference
JULY												
1	No trade	53½	53⅝	53¼	......	......	......	......	out	out	½ cent	½ cent
5	No trade	53½	53⅝	53	......	......	......	......	out	out	½ cent	½ cent
6	......	53⅛	54⅞	53⅛	54⅛	......	......	......	1 line	......	½ cent	½ cent
7	......	54½	55½	54⅛	55⅜	......	......	......	2 lines	......	½ cent	½ cent
8	No trade	54⅜	54¾	54	......	......	......	......	2 lines	......	¼ cent	¾ cent
9	......	53⅞	54⅛	53½	......	53¾	⅜	......	1 line	......	¼ cent	¾ cent
11	......	53⅛	53½	53	......	53	2⅜	......	out	out	½ cent	½ cent
12	Mkt ord	52⅛	52½	52	......	52⅛	......	1⅜	......	1 line	½ cent	½ cent
13	No trade	52⅜	52¾	52¼	......	......	......	......	......	1 line	½ cent	½ cent
14	......	52¾	53⅛	50¾	......	51½	......	......	......	2 lines	½ cent	½ cent
15	No trade	51⅜	51⅝	50½	......	......	......	......	......	2 lines	¾ cent	¼ cent
16	No trade	51⅜	51½	49⅞	......	......	......	......	......	2 lines	¾ cent	¼ cent
18	No trade	50¼	50½	49⅞	......	......	......	......	......	2 lines	¾ cent	¼ cent
19	......	50⅛	51⅛	50¼	50¾	......	......	......	......	1 line	¾ cent	¼ cent
20	......	51¼	51¾	50¼	51¾	......	¼	......	out	out	½ cent	½ cent
21	No trade	50⅜	51	50¼	......	......	......	......	out	out	½ cent	½ cent
22	......	50⅜	51⅝	50⅜	51½	......	......	......	1 line	......	½ cent	½ cent
23	No trade	51⅜	51¾	51¼	......	......	......	......	1 line	......	½ cent	½ cent
25	......	51¾	51⅞	50½	......	50¾	¾	......	out	out	½ cent	½ cent
26	......	51⅛	52¾	51⅛	52⅜	......	......	1⅞	1 line	......	½ cent	½ cent
27	......	52¾	55⅛	52⅛	53¼	......	......	......	2 lines	......	½ cent	½ cent
28	......	54¾	56½	54¾	55⅞	......	......	......	3 lines	......	¼ cent	¾ cent
29	......	54⅝	56	54¼	......	54¼	......	......	2 lines	......	low	1 cent
30	No trade	54⅝	55⅜	54½	......	......	......	......	2 lines	......	¼ cent	¾ cent

Wheat Trading Rule Number Eleven Applied to the Market of 1932—*Continued*

Date		Open	High	Low	Sold	Bought	Gains	Losses	Lines Short	Lines Long	Buying Difference	Selling Difference
AUGUST					DECEMBER FUTURE—*Continued*							
1		54½	54⅞	53⅞		54¼		1	1 line		½ cent	½ cent
2		53¾	54	52¼		53⅜	2½		out	out	½ cent	½ cent
3		51¾	54¼	51½		51¾				1 line	½ cent	½ cent
4		54¾	55⅞	53¾	54¾		3		out	out	½ cent	½ cent
5	No trade	55½	56	54⅞					out	out	½ cent	½ cent
6		56	57⅞	56	56½				1 line		½ cent	½ cent
8		57½	59½	57	58⅜				2 lines		½ cent	½ cent
9	No trade	57¾	58⅝	57¼					2 lines		¼ cent	¾ cent
10		58¼	60⅛	57¾	59⅜				3 lines		¼ cent	¾ cent
11		59	59⅜	57⅜		57¾		1¼	2 lines		low	1 cent
12		57¾	58	56		57⅛	1¼		1 line		¼ cent	¾ cent
13		55½	56¼	54¾		55½	3⅞		out	out	½ cent	½ cent
15	No trade	55⅛	56⅛	54⅞					out	out	½ cent	½ cent
16	Mkt ord	56¾	57⅜	54⅝	56¾				1 line		½ cent	½ cent
17		55¼	55⅝	53¾		54⅛	2⅝		out	out	½ cent	½ cent
18	No trade	54⅛	55⅞	53¾					out	out	½ cent	½ cent
19	No trade	55¼	55¾	54⅛					out	out	½ cent	½ cent
20		53⅝	54	53⅛		53⅝	1⅛			1 line	½ cent	½ cent
22	No trade	53⅝	54¼	53¼						1 line	½ cent	½ cent
23		54⅝	55⅜	54¼	54¾				out	out	½ cent	½ cent
24		54½	54⅝	53⅝		53¾	1⅜			1 line	½ cent	½ cent
25		54⅞	56¾	54⅞	55⅛				out	out	½ cent	½ cent
26	No trade	55⅞	56¼	55					out	out	½ cent	½ cent
27	Mkt ord	57¼	58	57¼	57¼				1 line		½ cent	½ cent
29		57¾	58⅞	57	58½				2 lines		½ cent	½ cent
30	No trade	57¾	58¾	57½					2 lines		¼ cent	¾ cent
31		57¼	57⅝	55¾		57¼			1 line		¼ cent	¾ cent

Wheat Trading Rule Number Eleven Applied to the Market of 1932—*Continued*

Date		Open	High	Low	Sold	Bought	Gains	Losses	Lines Short	Lines Long	Buying Differences	Selling Difference
SEPTEMBER					DECEMBER FUTURE—*Continued*							
1	No trade	56⅜	57	55⅞	....	....	....	....	1 line	....	½ cent	½ cent
2	....	56⅞	57½	56	57½	....	....	....	2 lines	....	½ cent	½ cent
3	....	58⅛	58½	58	58¼	....	....	....	3 lines	....	¼ cent	¾ cent
6	....	59½	60	58¼	59½	....	....	....	4 lines	....	low	1 cent
7	Mkt ord	58¼	58½	57½	....	58¼	¼	....	3 lines	....	¼ over	1¼ cent
8	....	57⅞	58⅜	56¾	....	57½	....	....	2 lines	....	low	1 cent
9	....	56⅝	57¼	56½	....	56½	1¾	....	1 line	....	¼ cent	¾ cent
10	....	56⅜	56¾	55⅞	....	56	3½	....	out	out	½ cent	½ cent
					MAY FUTURE							
10	....	61⅝	61⅞	61	....	....	....	....	....	....	....	....
12	....	61	61⅛	59½	....	60½	....	....	....	1 line	½ cent	½ cent
13	Mkt ord	58¼	59¾	58¼	....	58¼	....	....	....	2 lines	½ cent	½ cent
14	....	59⅞	60¼	57½	....	57½	....	....	....	3 lines	¾ cent	¼ cent
15	No trade	58	58⅝	56⅞	....	....	....	....	....	3 lines	1 cent	high
16	....	58	59⅛	57⅞	58⅞	....	....	1⅞	....	2 lines	¾ cent	¼ cent
17	No trade	57⅞	58½	57¾	....	....	....	....	....	2 lines	¾ cent	¼ cent
19	....	58¼	59⅛	57¼	58¾	....	½	....	....	1 line	¾ cent	¼ cent
20	No trade	57½	58¼	57½	....	....	....	....	....	1 line	½ cent	½ cent
21	....	58⅝	60⅝	58⅝	58¾	....	1¼	....	out	out	½ cent	½ cent
22	Mkt ord	61¼	61½	59⅛	61¼	....	....	....	1 line	....	½ cent	½ cent
23	No trade	59⅜	60	59	....	....	....	....	1 line	....	½ cent	½ cent
24	....	59⅜	60⅞	59⅜	60½	....	....	....	2 lines	....	½ cent	½ cent
26	No trade	60⅜	60½	59⅜	....	....	....	....	2 lines	....	¼ cent	¾ cent
27	....	59⅝	59¾	59	....	59⅛	2⅛	....	1 line	....	¼ cent	¾ cent

Wheat Trading Rule Number Eleven Applied to the Market of 1932—*Continued*

MAY FUTURE—*Continued*

SEPTEMBER—*Continued*

Date		Open	High	Low	Sold	Bought	Gains	Losses	Lines Short	Lines Long	Buying Difference	Selling Difference
28	....	59⅜	60⅜	58⅝	60¼	....	....	....	2 lines	....	½ cent	½ cent
29	No trade	59½	59⅞	58¾	....	....	....	....	2 lines	....	¼ cent	¾ cent
30	....	58½	58¾	58	....	58½	2	....	1 line	....	¼ cent	¾ cent

	Buying Difference	Selling Difference
Buying and Selling Differences for October 3, 1932	½ cent	½ cent

30 Bought one line at today's close to even up trades 58½ 1¾

Gross Gains on 46 profit trades .... 75⅛ cents

Gross Losses on 19 loss trades .... 34½ cents

Gross Gains over Losses .... 40⅝ cents

Commission on 65 trades .... 16¼ cents

NET PROFIT per bushel on 65 trades .... 24⅜ cents

Conclusion

If the market in the first nine months of 1932 had had the normal wide daily swings instead of very narrow daily price swings, the profits from the use of *"Trading Rule Number Eleven"* would have been two to three times what we have shown.

Because I deviated slightly from the rule, I obtained profits far in excess of those shown for the same period.

Under no circumstances would I ever buy or sell more than one line a day.

When Margin Requirements Were Greatest

On June 9, 1932, the margin requirements for the trader who followed *"Trading Rule Number Eleven"* reached their peak, at which time he was long four lines with an average loss of 3 cents a bushel. Allowing ten cents a bushel for normal margin meant thirteen cents a bushel to carry through the loss. If the speculator traded in units of 5,000 bushels, he was long 20,000 bushels, which required $2,600 for margin. But, because his profits since January 14 were far in excess of $2,600, the trade was carried through this anxious period on past profits that were left with the broker.

The "cub" trader operating only in jobs required $600 in margin at the time when margin requirements were heaviest.

Successful Scalping

Anyone can take worthwhile profits in scalping a market, providing the market has a sidewise movement with occasional wide daily fluctuations and does not run into a major bull or bear market.

The statement I have just made is an axiom among professional traders. To scalp a market successfully a trader must have a proper technique and he must be correct in his forecast of a sidewise market. Nothing else is needed.

CHAPTER XII

The Short Side of the Market

IT IS claimed the man who is long grain futures pays the storage charges in the premiums of the futures over the cash, while on the other hand the man who is short gets these carrying charges as a "present". This, of course, is not literally true, but it does tend to work out that way. In the following table I show the profits from a *continued* short position in May Wheat from the first trading day in the May future to May 1 of each year since July 3, 1929. We then assume a switch is made to September until May Wheat again comes on the board, thereby showing a short position in either May or September Wheat throughout the whole period.

Decline in Futures from July 3, 1939 to May 1, 1933 Compared to Cash

July 3, 1929	Sold May Short 137	
May 1, 1930	Closed trade @ 102⅞	Gain 34⅛
May 1, 1930	Sold Sept short 109⅜	
Aug. 1, 1930	Closed trade @ 87⅝	Gain 21¾
Aug. 1, 1930	Sold May short 99⅝	
May 1, 1931	Closed trade @ 57⅛	Gain 42½
May 1, 1931	Sold Sept short 62¾	
July 30, 1931	Closed trade @ 51⅜	Gain 11⅜
July 30, 1931	Sold May short 60	
May 2, 1932	Closed trade @ 55⅝	Gain 4⅜
May 2, 1932	Sold Sept short 55⅜	
Aug. 2, 1932	Closed trade @ 50¾	Gain 4⅝
Aug. 2, 1932	Sold May short 58	
May 1, 1933	Closed trade @ 72¼	Loss 14½

Net gain over losses in a continual short position from July 3, 1929 to May 1, 1933 as shown in the above table would be 104¼ cents a bushel. Cash wheat sold at $1.21¾ cents on July 3, 1929. The price of cash wheat on May 1, 1933 was 74 cents, which shows a decline of only 47¾ cents in cash wheat compared to 104¼ for the futures.

The trader who was long May Wheat throughout this period, switching at the market to September in the interval when May was not quoted, lost in the three-year period 104¼. The man who held cash wheat lost on the cash wheat decline only 47¾ cents. Of course the holder of cash wheat had three years storage interest and insurance to pay.

Conclusion

When the more distant futures continually sell at a premium over the near-by futures the *technical advantage* lies with the short seller, as shown in the above example. This is a necessary market situation; otherwise, no one would care to own and store cash grain for delivery on short sales to those who are long grain futures.

When the near futures, due to a tight situation, advance rapidly to a big premium over the more distant futures, the *technical advantage* lies with a long position. This situation seldom happens when there is a large visible and carryover.

CHAPTER XIII

Scale Buying

THOMAS GIBSON says scale buying has a place in speculation. My answer is no; emphatically no. I mention Thomas Gibson, because Gibson, so far as I know, is the only financial writer of note who has ever advised the use of the scale, either up or down.

Right at the start I wish to say that adding to a line of grain or stocks, as the market advances, is commonly practiced by successful traders, as shown in "Speculative Transactions of Eight Leading Traders in the May Future" by G. Wright Hoffman (Department of Agriculture Bulletin No. 1479). In spite of this endorsement by leading traders, I do not believe in scale trading with the trend. However, it is not our purpose in this article to discuss *scale trading as the trade goes in the trader's favor* except in exceptional cases when following "Trading Rule Number Eighteen." This point is covered in "Trading Rule Number Eighteen" on Page 75.

This article is concerned only with scale buying for the purpose of *averaging down,* and with the scale selling for the purpose of *averaging up* and also to prove that the placing of scale buying or selling orders, for the purpose of lowering the buying level or raising the selling level is the exact opposite procedure to that of using "stops". You can't use both methods at the same time. Try it and find out.

I shall illustrate: I advised the purchase of September wheat in 1930 at $1.09. Trader A buys 10,000 bushels and places an order to add to the line 10,000 bushels on each two cent decline. Trader B also buys 10,000 bushels but places a two cent stop loss order behind his trade. Therefore, when the market reaches $1.07 A has bought

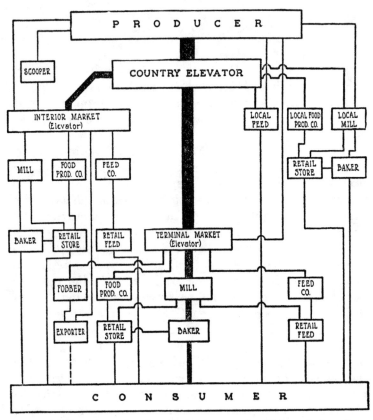

The principal channels of trade in the merchandising of the wheat crop. This chart was obtained from "Futures Trading" by G. Wright Hoffman. Mr. Hoffman is undoubtedly the best authority on this subject.

an additional 10,000 bushels of wheat at exactly the same price at which B has sold 10,000 bushels of wheat. A now has 20,000 bushels of wheat and B is out of the market with a 2¼ cent loss, after adding commission. In speculation the buyer and seller can never both be right at a given price, although both may make a profit eventually.

On page 121 I stated that the use of "stops" is illogical and poor trading practice except when taking on additional "lines" after the trend has become established. Now I am going to prove that while "scale trading against the trend" is the exact opposite to "stops" it is also a very bad trading practice.

Before taking up the use of scale trading, I wish to make a passing comment on "stops".

My condemnation of "stops" in a previous book touched a tender spot with a number of traders. One man wrote, "I quite agree with you that the use of 'stops' is decidedly wrong if it means to get out and stay out for an indefinite period. With this assumption you are right in your conclusions; and your examples of your own trading are very convincing. But, as used in my own trading, I have found the stop loss device a life saver on more than one occasion." What was being done by this trader who claimed to use "stops" with success? He was scalping the market, which, in his particular case has meant little or no profits over a long period of time.

On the subject of many small and frequently made trades (scalping) I wish to quote from a member of one of the leading brokerage houses in Chicago. "Our grain market sheet is edited by the best grain trader we have ever found. He has made and retained a comfortable fortune in grain trading. Of course, his trades are mostly held open for big profits and for a considerable period of time, which accounts for his success. He has on one occasion kept a wheat trade open for seven months and secured a profit of 92 cents a bushel, which is a record for our house on a single trade. It naturally follows that our house did not wax fat on commissions from a trade held open for seven months. We would have much preferred having a writer of a trading market or scalping type if such methods could be made profitable, but, unfortunately, such methods have never been made to work except in quiet markets. Our house stands ready to pay $25,000.00 a year to any man who can give scalping advice at three o'clock P. M. good for the next day and can show net profits of three times the amount of the commission."

While the "stop" is the exact opposite of the scale order to lower the buying average there is also this marked distinction. The stop loss device is economically absurd, while the scale buying order to lower the buying average is economically very sound. Certainly, if wheat is a good purchase at $1.09, it is a better purchase at $1.07. The trader who uses the scale to lower his average is simply backing up his judgment when he buys more grain on each two cent decline. Now, if the scale order is economically sound, what is wrong? Here is the answer: The scale order to lower the buying average or raise the selling average is financially impracticable. The trader is placed in deep water by every series of scale trades which run into big paper losses.

I shall now assume that each of twenty-two successful traders is able to margin his initial trades to the extent of *five times the initial quantity traded in.* We shall now see what happens if we make these traders use scale trading. Bear in mind I am taking actual trades from invoices of twenty-two traders, every one of whom has made money in the past five year period.

The outstanding trader of this successful group has frequently added just one more line when he was 10 or 15 cents wrong and was generally rewarded for his faith and courage, but he did not in any case use the scale device.

Here is what might have happened to each of these traders if we assume that they scaled on a two cent scale on their first trade, which ran into a fourteen cent loss before it was closed out. Allowing ten cents for margin, only five sales are possible.

We start with 1925. "A" actually bought 10,000 bushels of May Wheat at $1.90 on Feb. 6th, 1925, which he sold on March 3rd at $2.00. Scale buying on each two cent decline would have forced him out on February 11th.

"B" actually bought 50,000 bushels of wheat at $1.82 on Feb. 13th, 1925, on which he took a ten cent loss on March 13th. While the two cent scale would have permitted only a purchase at $1.80 and $1.78 in February, he would have failed financially on March 13th, just the same as though he had made the five scale purchases.

"C" is so successful in picking highs for selling short and lows for getting long that his two cent scale trading would have carried him to May, 1927, without financial failure, at which time he sold short 15,000 bushels of September Wheat at $1.31 on May 6th, getting out on September 10th without a loss. Had he sold short 15,000 bushels on each two cent advance, he would have been closed out on May 26th if not sooner. (September Wheat sold as high as $1.48 on the last day of May, 1927.)

"D" has an enviable record. While he did not make the money made by C, in proportion to his trading capital, his ratio of gains to losses was almost $11.00 to $1.00, a record which is seldom equaled. D's failure to make a financial showing equal to that of C is due to the fact that he remained out of the market for long periods.

D's most unfortunate trade was made on November 26, 1925. D had just taken tremendous profits in May Wheat. He was long 175,000 bushels bought from $1.35 to $1.45, adding to his line as the market advanced. On November 26th he closed out his long trades as $1.61 and got short 50,000 bushels at the same price. On December 28th this short sale showed a paper loss of 20 cents. The trade was closed out March 22, 1926 at $1.54 with a profit of 7 cents. Had D sold 50,000 bushels short on each two cent advance, he would have failed financially on December 3rd or 4th, when his average paper loss would have exceeded ten cents.

Without going into detail we will see when the other traders would have failed had they resorted to scale trading to lower buying levels and raise selling levels.

E would have failed in 1925; F in 1925; G in 1926; H in 1926; I in 1925; J in 1926; K in 1926; L in 1927; M in 1925; N in 1925; O in 1925; P in 1927; Q in 1924; R in 1926; S in 1925; T in 1930.

T's case deserves some comment. I am giving T's experience with his permission. Since 1931 he has been one of my closest friends. His record of grain trading accomplishment surpassed anything I had ever known up to April of 1933. For the past six years T has followed the advice of a member of the Chicago Board of Trade who lives in Monticello, with this exception: He has added a line on each three cent advance or decline, as the trade went against him, and since the lines were rather small in proportion to his very ample capital, he succeeded in spite of the very great risk he was taking. On October 17, 1933 he met his Waterloo and is now bankrupt.

Scale Trading in Very Small Quantities

I have now shown that twenty-two successful traders would have failed financially at some time in the past eight years had they resorted to scale trading for the purpose of averaging down in buying or averaging up in selling, *assuming that each additional scale order was for a quantity of grain equal to the first order.*

It is only fair to make some comment as to what might happen if all scale trades were made in very small quantities.

For example, let us assume that the trader who is in the habit of trading in 30,000 bushel lots, desires to buy only 5,000 bushels of September Wheat at $1.09 and 5,000 bushels on each two cent decline, rather than to take on a full line of 30,000 bushels at $1.09. Certainly this is conservative trading practice, which no one can deny. However, it is not very profitable for the simple reason that a good market accomplishment is made possible only when the trader is very much wrong, at the start, as we shall see from the following illustration.

A buys 5,000 bushels of September Wheat at $1.09 and places an order to buy 5,000 bushels at each of the following prices of $1.07, $1.05, $1.03, $1.01 and 99 cents. If he is right marketwise at the start, he has only 5,000 bushels although his capital justifies trading in 30,000 bushels. To enable A to make a worthwhile showing for a man of his means, the market must decline to 99 cents and then make a good advance. Any market technique that calls for being wrong first in order later to be right, is absurd and ridiculous.

Successful Speculation Calls for Being Right

The successful speculator must be right more often than he is wrong. He must buy on major declines and sell on major advances. There is no technique that can possibly take the place of thinking. Trading rules are good; in fact they are necessary in making careful forecasts. Note what rules were used and what rules were not used in making the forecast of a 30 cent decline in May wheat. This forecast was made and published on July 18th and August 14th, 1933 and was fulfilled in less than ninety days.

A study of supply and demand in commodities and of current and prospective earnings in common stocks is made for the purpose of arriving at a *fair and reasonable price*. After determining this, the trader tries to buy on major declines of five to ten per cent below this fair price and to sell at ten to twenty per cent above this price. This is real speculation and is the foundation on which all successful traders operate.

CHAPTER XIV

Statistical Charts

I AM offering the following charts as an example of the splendid work the United States Department of Agriculture and Agricultural Economics is doing in presenting graphically to the grain trade comparative figures on supply and demand, carry-over, world supply and all other factors which affect wheat prices.

The chart below shows world wheat stocks as of July 1, 1925 to 1933. The continually mounting stocks are due to three prime factors, which in order of their importance are: 1. World wide depression. 2. The expansion of wheat acreage. 3. The exceedingly high tariff walls by importing countries.

Wheat: World Stocks as of July 1, 1925-1933

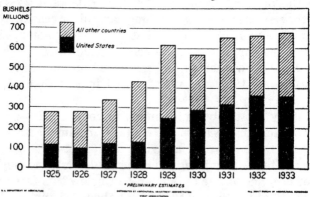

The next chart shows the United States carry-over of wheat on July 1, from 1920 to 1933. According to the Uhlmann Grain Co. the stocks of all wheat in the United States in all positions, were 383,000,000 bushels on July

112

1, 1933, which was an all time record for carry-over. The reason for the large world wheat stocks and United States wheat stocks from 1925 to 1933 inclusive, was due largely to activities of the Canadian Wheat Pool and the American Farm board in holding wheat back from consumptive channels and consequently causing wheat prices in Canada and the United States to remain far above a world parity. Looking at these abortive activities in the light of present knowledge the whole program has been a panorama picture of a great market mistake. As this book goes to press, there is no longer a Canadian wheat pool nor a United States Farm Board, with the result that private interests which now control the wheat trade will in their own selfish efforts, undertake to dispose of the short wheat crop grown in the United States in 1933, for the best price that can be obtained.

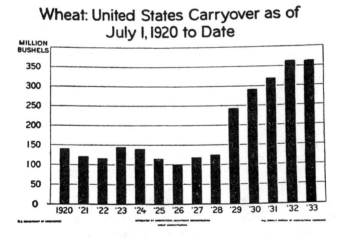

Wheat: United States Carryover as of July 1, 1920 to Date

Next, we have a chart which shows United States exports from 1921–1933 and the production in Europe including Russian shipments. United States exports have shown an alarming decline since 1927, which is due primarily to the fact that our wheat has not sold on a parity with other countries as well as the fact that high tariff walls have made it difficult to place the wheat of the United States and other exporting countries into those countries which are normally the heaviest importers. As the price of wheat has advanced in Europe due to import duty protection, the production has constantly mounted, reaching its peak in the fall of 1933.

A recent French law which places a tax on farmers who produce too much wheat, will probably be a factor in reducing the wheat production in France. This measure is a part of the French program to lift grain prices to the levels of 1913–1917, inclusive.

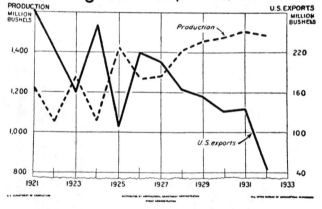

The chart that is illustrated below is extremely interesting from an economic standpoint in that it tends to show what might be considered a fair price for wheat in relationship to what the farmer is required to buy. Where the two lines frequently recross each other, the price relationship between wheat and what the farmer must buy should, in my opinion, be considered as normal and therefore, equitable. Such a price relationship ex-

isted from 1911 to 1916. Then for four years bonanza
conditions prevailed for the wheat farmer in the United
States and Canada. The result was a tremendous amount
of new wheat land put into production, high prices encouraged, use of tractors, combines and other modern
farming machinery, thus making it possible for the
farmer to tend a larger acreage and at the same time increase his yield per acre. This introduction of modern
wheat growing and harvesting machinery has undoubtedly
been a major factor in bringing about the low price that
farmers have had to contend with since 1929.

It may be said to the credit of the Department of Agriculture that they have been exceedingly painstaking and
accurate in compiling their figures for the charts. The
result is that the grain speculator who comes into the
market at times, knows exactly what he is dealing with as
far as supply and demand and farm purchasing power
are concerned.

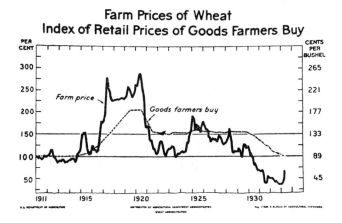

The chart that follows has not been brought entirely
down to date. In fact, few of these charts are down to date
and are offered only as an example of the good material
which the wheat forecaster, trader and farmer have at

their command. Those who are interested in these charts should write to the United States Department of Agriculture and ask for the more recent additions.

This chart shows the scale of import duties as imposed by Germany, France, and Italy from 1921 down to date. These import duties, by making the price of domestic wheat very high in importing countries, have so encouraged German, French and Italian farmers to expand their acreage and increase their yields as to keep out from 100 to 300 million bushels of imported wheat that probably would have been utilized by these countries had the duties never been imposed.

The German duty of slightly over $1.60 a bushel practically excludes all foreign wheat except Russian wheat, which is accepted under certain reciprocity agreements.

Foreign Import Duties on Wheat, and United States Stocks of Wheat, July 1, 1920-1932

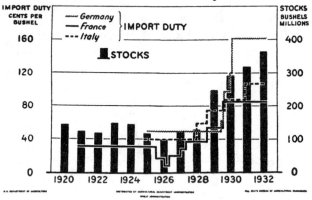

The next chart tells its own story of wheat, which since 1930 has been one of over supply and low world price. This low price is due partly to over supply but in the main it is due to impoverished world conditions. Europe is determined to raise her own wheat until her buying power improves.

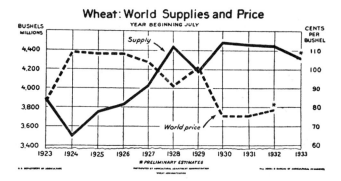

The chart below is a more recent chart than that shown on page 115.

When agricultural commodity prices are above non-agricultural commodity prices, the farmer's buying power is above normal and those who produce non-agricultural commodities or finished products are required to pay a price for food and clothing that is too high compared to their income.

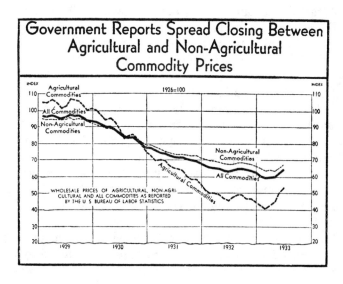

CHAPTER XV

Applying the Popular Two Cent Stop

IT HAS been said by at least one of the world's greatest commodity traders that "if traders would attempt to trade on values, buying on major breaks and selling on major advances, exercise more patience, trade in amounts that can be easily financed when the trader is temporarily wrong, and not place 'stop' orders behind trades, practically every trader would make money in each five year period".

I do not believe there is a grain trader in the United States who, having made money in grain trading in the past five years without resorting to the use of "stops" could have added one nickel to his income by using a one, two or five cent "stop" behind every trade he entered into. We don't buy farm land or city property that way.

After all, an ounce of evidence is worth all the theory in the world. I have just gone to a tremendous amount of work to examine the five year trading records of twenty-two traders whose operations were profitable over a five year period.

The average of all results shows that a one cent "stop" would have cut net profits 72 per cent, a two cent "stop" would have cut profits 54 per cent and a five cent "stop" would have cut net profits 47 per cent. On the other hand, all but six of the twenty-two traders would have benefited in the summer of 1933 had they used "stops" and not re-entered the market, which proves that 1933 was one of those exceptions to a good trading rule, which is, "Use no stops".

It appears that only those traders who lost consistently over a period of years have their net losses reduced by the use of "stops". In my own case the use of "stops" would have helped only in the years 1915, 1921, 1923, 1926, 1930, and 1931, which were mostly years of big losses.

The test of any mechanical device is to apply it to actual trades. So let us apply a two cent stop loss to every trade I made in nearly nineteen years of trading, in which $1,000.00 grew to over $100,000.00 in eighteen years. Please note that while losses were not limited, in no case after the first four years, was as much as half of the profits ever required for margin, but you may be assured my capital was where it could be quickly obtained when and if needed.

In 1912 I made $1,025.00 net profit, but with a two cent stop loss the May trade would have been caught and the net profit for the year would have been $374.00 on July Corn, minus $100.00 lost in May Corn stop trade, or $275.00 net.

Beginning with the year 1913, the first figure shows profits just as they were made without the use of stop losses, and in which judgment was not allowed to be interfered with by a stop loss order. The *second figure* under each year shows what the result would have been had I limited all my trades to a two cent stop loss.

1913

Trades made without stops—year's profits..		$ 560.25
Stops would have caught May Corn trade— profits		325.00

1914

Trades as made without stops—year's profits.		200.00
Stops caught all trades, loss..............	$200.00	

1915

Trades as made without stops—year's profits.		1,552.50
Stops caught September Wheat trade and saved $253.75—year's profits............		1,806.25

1916

Trades as made without stops—year's profits.		6,987.55
Stops caught all trades but May Wheat— year's profits		1,350.00

1917

Trades as made without stops—year's profits.		5,891.00
Stops caught all trades—year's losses......	675.00	

1918

Trades as made without stops—year's profits.		8,790.00
Stops would have caught July Corn—year's profits		2,465.00

1919

Trades as made without stops—year's profits.		32,025.00
No two cent stops would have been reached——profits		32,025.00

1920

Trades as made without stops—year's profits. (May Corn was actually carried through a 17 cent loss)		16,181.25
Stops would have caught all trades—loss....	2,000.00	

1921

Trades as made without stops—year's losses.	11,650.85	
Stops would have caught all trades and limited losses to.........................	2,250.00	

1922

Trades as made without stops—year's profits.		12,968.50
Stops would have caught May Wheat and May Corn—profit.....................		2,505.00

1923

Trades as made without stops—year's profits.		6,193.25
Stops would have caught September Wheat and saved a loss of $2,070.00—year's profits with stops		8,263.25

1924

Trades as made without stops—year's profits.		10,726.52
Stops would have caught all trades except July Corn—net gains for year with stops..		725.83

1925

Trades as made without stops—year's profits.		1,756.54
Stops would have caught all trades—year's losses	2,700.00	

1926

Trades as made without stops—year's losses.	4,062.03	
Stops would have caught all trades—year's losses	2,500.00	

1927

Trades as advised without stops—year's gain.		7,437.50
Stops would have caught all trades except Sept. Wheat—year's losses..............	750.00	

1928

Trades as advised without stops—year's gain.	20,625.00
Stops would have caught most of the trades and profits would have been.............	3,827.41

1929

Trades as advised without stops—year's gain.		6,639.65
Stops would have caught most of the trades and losses would have been.............	2,761.21	

Without resorting to any mechanical method of stopping losses, my grain trades from 1913 down to 1929 showed a net profit of $108,488.10. Had I used a 2 cent "stop" my net profits would have been only $36,779.01.

The Use of Stops

When I feel that the market has developed momentum in a certain direction and is going to continue to move in that direction to the extent of five to twenty cents, I advise the use of stops—*but only when I feel somewhat insecure in my position.*

The first two weeks in May, 1933, is a typical case of when I like to use "stops". In the first half of May I felt that the market was destined to sell much higher, due to currency inflation and the price-raising campaign at Washington. Under these circumstances it would have been foolish to advise a short position *for a turn*, without the use of stops. But in July, 1933, when I advised a short position I felt certain that the administration would not care to push grain prices any higher than the July first price. Why should President Roosevelt and Secretary Wallace desire higher prices when the farm price of corn had increased four times in less than six months? Short sales made in July was no place to use stops.

A Stop Loss Fable

Once upon a time ten wheat dealers, courageous and true, entered the wheat market after a 20 cent decline. The first trader bought at 120 and placed his stop at 118. The second trader bought at 118 and placed his stop at 116.

The third trader bought at 116 and placed his stop at 114 and so on until after another 20 cent decline all ten traders had taken each his two cent loss plus his commission of $\frac{1}{4}$ cent. Since each trader got out of the market just where another trader got in, $2\frac{1}{2}$ cents commission could have been saved had all the traders agreed to assume the others obligation.

The Fable of the Broker Who Gave Buying and Selling Advice at the Same Price

Once upon a time a poor man bought his job of wheat at 120 and the broker advised a stop at 118. At the same time a rich man bought a large line of wheat at 120 and the broker advised him, because he was rich, to buy an equal line on each two cent decline. Thus the broker advises the poor man to sell at 118 and the rich man to buy at 118. The poor man disregarded the broker's advice since he considered wheat really worth 120. The market broke 20 cents and later advanced 40 cents. Now the poor man is still poor but he is $200.00 richer than he was before he made the trade, while on the other hand the rich man failed financially when he tried to margin his tenth line on his broker's advice to buy an equal amount on each two cent decline. The poor man was able to carry his 1,000 bushel job through a 20 cent decline and later sell at a 20 cent profit.

CHAPTER XVI

Short Swing Trading

THE idea of making frequent small profit trades (so called scalping trades) is very tempting to say the least. If a correct forecast can be made of a sidewise market running two to four weeks then short swing trades may be profitable in what is called a scalping market.

The theory is so attractive that more money is undoubtedly lost in this form of trading than is lost by traders who actually take big occasional losses.

In a short chapter I am going to show that the big traders are almost never short swing traders; that those who attempt frequent small profit trades are not using supply and demand factors, but are really depending on mechanical methods.

The Technique of Famous Traders of the Past

If the trader will get "Speculative Transactions of Eight Leading Traders on the Chicago Board of Trade" he will see that the methods of all but two are very much the same. First, a position is taken in a market and then purchases or sales are made and trades are *held open* for weeks and months at a time, or long enough to allow supply and demand factors to bring about the anticipated change in price. Big traders frequently do *add to their line* as the market goes in their favor.

After reading Bulletin No. 1479, which may be obtained from the Government Printing Office, Washington, D. C. for 15 cents, I suggest that traders read "In the Wheat Pit" by James A. Patten; and "The Plunger" by E. J. Dies. These books tell of most of the big successful deals of the past and refer to the thousands of losing "in

and out traders" as small fish nibbling at the tails of the
larger fish.

Short Swing Versus Long Pull Trading

I shall now try to show without the use of algebraic
equations that the long pull trader always has an advantage over the short swing trader. (The fallacy of all short
swing small profit trading is definitely and conclusively
proven by higher mathematics and can be found in
"Chance and Error" by Hopkins, "Forecasting the Yield
and Price of Cotton" by Moore, and "Risk and Risk Bearing" by Hardy.

Since I am not going to use higher mathematics, I will
start with the *axiom* that the market must either go up
or down. But from a purely technical standpoint the market has *ten chances* to decline *one point* to *one chance* of
advancing *ten points* and vice versa. I challenge anyone
to disprove the above theory, either by mathematics or by
actual market citation.

Three Hypothetical Traders

We are going to leave market judgment entirely out in
a test we shall make between one long pull trader and two
scalping traders.

Three traders enter the market on the flip of a coin in
order to determine their market position for each trade,
and all get an *average expectancy* as they say in life insurance actuary tables.

The long pull trader makes four trades and will take
10 cents profit or 10 cents loss on each trade, or, which-
ever limit is first reached.

In a year this trader makes four trades in which he
hopes to make 10 cents on each trade or 40 cents on the
four trades. If he gets an even expectancy (even market
break) he gains on two trades and makes 19½ cents (commissions paid) and on two trades he loses 20½ cents
(commissions paid). His net loss on the total of four

trades is exactly 1 cent in commissions, plus banking interest on his capital used as margin.

The first market scalper is satisfied with 1 cent gross
profit or 1 cent gross loss. Therefore, he makes forty
trades as equivalent to the four trades of the long pull
trader. He gets an even market break and has gross gains
of 20 cents and gross losses of 20 cents. Now we add
twenty commissions of ¼ cent each to the loss trades
and we have 25 cents net loss on the loss trades. We now
subtract ¼ cent each for twenty commissions on the gain
trades, which gives us 15 cents net gain on twenty gain
trades. Thus, with an even market break, the trader has
a net gain of 15 cents on all trades showing a profit and
a loss of 25 cents on all trades showing a loss.

Our second scalper, in addition to taking only one cent
profit per trade, limits his losses to just ¼ of a cent per
trade. As stated in our axiom, *loss* trades will be exactly
four times as frequent as *gain* trades (on a four to one
ratio or ten to one ratio) and the stop loss scalper will
therefore make exactly four times as many trades as the
first scalper, or one hundred and sixty trades in all.

Assuming *average expectancy,* our second scalper
using the ¼ cent stop loss, loses on one hundred and
twenty trades exactly 30 cents. Now we add 30 cents for
commissions and we have 60 cents net loss for the scalper
who goes out for one cent profits and ¼ cent losses. He
makes 40 cents on forty gain trades from which we must
subtract 10 cents for commissions, which gives the trader
30 cents net gain on his gain trades. *This last trader is
really in bad.* He gets an even break in the market, but
his net losses are *double* his net gains, due to an overhead
of 40 cents in commissions.

Application of Skill

We Shall Now Apply Skill. All three traders suddenly
become so skillful that they can add 50 per cent to their
gain trades and can cut their losses in half.

The long pull trader who got 20 cents gross on all gain trades now makes 30 cents, less ¾ cent commissions, or 29¼ cents on all gain trades. He cuts his losses in half and loses only 10 cents plus ¼ cent commission or 10¼ cents on his one and only trade showing a loss.

The first scalper now makes 30 cents gross less 7½ cents in commission, or 22½ cents net on all gain trades. He cuts his losses to 10 cents and loses only 12½ cents after adding his commissions of 2½ cents.

The "stop loss" scalper who was so clever as to make four times as many gain trades as he had loss trades, now makes not 40 cents gross, but 60 cents. We subtract a commission of 10 cents for forty trades, which gives 50 cents net gain on all trades showing a profit. The market loss on all trades showing a loss is cut from 30 cents to 15 cents, but we must add 30 cents for commission on one hundred and twenty unprofitable trades, which gives us 45 cents net loss on all loss trades.

Thus we see that after allowing for very unusual skill on the part of all three traders the long pull trader's gain trades are 29¼ cents to 10¼ cents loss on loss trades, or nearly three times the losses.

The penny scalper who is willing to have equal losses per trade to gains has only 22½ cents in gains to 12½ cents in losses, while the close up stop loss scalper with better judgment than the world has yet discovered, has only 50 cents in gains to 45 cents in losses.

Conclusion

Thus we see that the long pull trader having unusual skill can make profits of nearly three times his losses, while the stop loss scalper of equal skill has only 50 cents in gains to 45 cents in losses.

At one time I asked a member of one of Chicago's largest brokerage firms if he had any customers not members of the exchange who made a living by scalping the grain or stock market. This was his answer: "There sit two of the only four outside scalpers I have ever known who really make a living at scalping. But the living is not so good. Their net profits run from $3,000.00 to $5,000,00 a year on a working capital of $10,000.00 to $15,000.00." He then added, "A Monticello, Illinois trader who places most of his trades through our house has made more money in commodity trading in the last five years than all the scalpers who live in Chicago and scalp the Chicago grain market. In the fall of 1924 this Monticello trader bought May wheat and then went to Europe. He returned in December and closed out his trades, which netted him over a million dollars in profits."

When Short Swing Advice Is Opportune

There are times when an advance or decline already overdue, synchronizes so nicely with a *current* market factor that a short swing forecast can be expected to be fairly accurate. On April 8th, 1929, with a minor advance in corn already overdue and *farm marketing* in Illinois and Iowa suddenly stopped on account of field work, it was quite easy to say, "It is only natural to expect a small advance this week of one to three cents." I therefore took advantage of both the long and short side of a very small two weeks advance and decline.

CHAPTER XVII

The Economics of Price

I HAVE just received a letter from a client who has this comment to make:—

"Sept. 28, 1933

"I value your letters especially because they give reasons for expecting an advance or a decline of, let us say, ten or twenty cents a bushel and for the most part, you are right. In your bulletins of July 17th and August 14th, you convinced me that wheat would decline forty cents a bushel, but I am not convinced to my entire satisfaction that ninety cents is a cheap price for wheat for the next six months; $1.05 a logical price, and $1.24 a high price.

"It is rather hard for me to make myself clear in the criticism I am about to make, but what I am perplexed about is this:—If wheat had been selling at $2.00 a bushel on July 17th, would you have still forecast a decline of only forty cents, in which case would you have considered $1.60 rather than 90 cents a cheap price? Am I right or not in this conclusion? In other words, does a grain market forecaster attempt only to interpret market forces and add to or take from the current price an amount that compensates for his forecast of changing conditions, or does he go deeper than this and determine a *reasonable price for wheat, independent of what the market may be at the time?* If there is some basic law that helps a student of market conditions to arrive at a logical price for wheat without adding to or subtracting from the current price I would like to know what that is."

I consider the above letter one of the most logical inquiries regarding price analysis that I have ever received and for that reason I am pleased to approach the present price of wheat from the angle of economics. In so doing

I wish to express appreciation and give credit to such economists as Fairchild, Taussig, Seager and John Stuart Mill. While the forecaster frequently makes his forecast by adding to or subtracting from the current market price, *price is based on something deeper and more profound than the simple statement that the market price is too high or too low when judged by current price making factors.*

The Economic or Natural Price Level For Wheat

Throughout the ages the price of wheat has moved up and down through a figure that is called the *cost of production.* Over a period of one hundred years wheat has sold below the cost of production as often as it has sold above the cost of production, and this is the economics of price. What is the cost of production? It is the cost of producing wheat in terms of the cost of producing gold.

Some economists claim that wheat averages selling at the cost of production plus a nominal profit of ten to twenty cents, in which case the cost of management and supervision is not figured as a part of the cost of production. However, the United States Department of Agriculture chooses to allow the producer of wheat a wage for his supervision in addition to his labor and this is included as a part of the cost of production. This is the logical course and eliminates the necessity of setting aside a certain amount for profit. It eliminates confusion.

The United States Department of Agriculture claims that in the winter wheat belt of the United States it cost approximately ninety cents a bushel in 1931 to produce (and deliver to market) a crop of wheat in which the yield ran from thirteen to eighteen bushels per acre.

The ninety cents is, of course, figured in gold dollars and not in terms of present inflated currency. In estimating these costs the United States Department of Agriculture does not place any definite value on land, since to do so would be very confusing. After all is said and done the

market value of an acre of land is only a matter of opinion.
Since some land is worth more than others the rent on
some land is higher than it is on other lands. Therefore
the indeterminable item of land value is taken care of in
the item of rent. The United States Department of Agriculture is very specific in determining the cost of producing wheat that yields from thirteen to eighteen bushels
per acre and they have set down the acre cost as follows:

Cost of preparing and planting	$ 3.20
Harvesting and threshing	4.70
Fertilizer and manure	.80
Delivering to the market	.83
Seed	1.34
Average land rental	6.31
Miscellaneous, which includes sacks, twine, crop insurance, investment and depreciation of implements, use of storage, etc	2.36
Making a total acre cost of	$19.64

This total cost includes all hired labor as well as the
farmer's own labor and the reward for supervision which
after all is a part of cost. The wheat grower's profit is
what he makes from his own labor as well as his job of
supervision (or reward for supervision if you prefer that
word).

Without stating it in further detail these itemized costs
when expressed in terms of gold dollars are dependent on
the cost of producing gold as much as they are on the cost
of growing wheat. Beginning with about 1884 when modern wheat harvesting machinery was perfected and when
modern gold mining machinery was perfected, it has taken
approximately the same amount of labor and capital to
produce twenty-one bushels of wheat under average conditions as it has cost to produce one ounce of gold under
average conditions. Obviously, the cost of production and
likewise the economics of production must be based on
average conditions. If the cost of producing gold could
suddenly be cut in half then wheat would double in price,
contrariwise without adding to marketing and other costs
if some variety of wheat could be found that would double

the yield per acre, then the price of wheat in gold dollars would drop to half the average for the past forty-five years.

It naturally follows that the poor devil who stakes out his gold claim in the sand beds of Cherry Creek, Colorado, spends more energy in producing one ounce of gold than the most favorably situated wheat farmer would consume in producing 100 bushels of wheat, which would buy nearly five ounces of gold. On the other hand in the very productive Rand Mines of South Africa, an ounce of gold can be produced with less effort than it would take to produce even five bushels of wheat on certain thin marginal lands of North Dakota or Southern Michigan; but economics must deal with *average cases* and average cases are what we are considering.

All the farm legislation in the world cannot make it permanently more profitable to produce wheat than to produce gold, although this is exactly what is being attempted at the present time by every major wheat exporting country.

When, for a short period, it becomes more profitable to produce wheat than to produce gold, tens of thousands of laborers leave the gold mines for the wheat fields and settle on marginal wheat farms. In few cases does an actual gold miner become a wheat grower but for purposes of illustration it amounts to the same thing.

For several months in 1932, the production of gold was far more profitable than the production of wheat on marginal lands. The result was that nearly 90,000 people in the United States alone settled along the banks of the streams of our West that had gold bearing sands, and attempted the production of gold. Hard workers who were willing to learn and who found good locations could pan $5.00 in gold a day. Out of this number, 11,000 were farmers who had failed to make a profit in the production of wheat and other grains.

The profit in producing gold and the profit in producing

wheat, regardless of legislation, will always be kept in close balance and over a long period of years the profit from neither industry will be large. Wheat and gold are both commodities and must therefore conform to the old economic law of relative costs. Notwithstanding the above statement, we know that the price of wheat in the past twenty years has moved over a very wide range in terms of gold money. When wheat was high in price and more profitable to produce than gold, the high price for wheat always occurred in and just following a major war period when the demand for wheat was almost equal to the supply. For a few years following the world war America forgot all about the high cost of producing gold and rushed pellmell into the production of wheat which yielded a profit of several times the profit made in the mining of gold. But these 1914–21 prices were scarcity prices and could only be temporary when studied in the light of economics.

Economics prove there can be no such thing as permanent over-production of any commodity and neither can there be such a thing as a permanent scarcity. As water seeks its physical level, a commodity is always attempting to return to its economic price level as determined by supply, demand, and cost of production. When the price of wheat is high, millions of workers in other industries become producers of wheat and compete with those who have always been in the wheat-growing business. When wheat is high in price less is eaten and less is wasted. Thus, an acute scarcity becomes gradually transformed into a burdensome, albeit temporary, over-production.

A high price greatly increases the supply and likewise greatly decreases the demand for wheat and to a like extent a low price decreases the supply and increases the demand. Fairchild covers this point when he says: "the supply of producible goods is governed by the expected future cost of production".

Monopolistic and Mandatory Prices

In times like these, when our government is making strenuous efforts to improve the condition of the farmer, it is worthwhile to devote a little time to *monopolistic price* and *mandatory price* which are too often futile attempts to advance the price of certain commodities at *the expense of other commodities*. Such a course is economically unfair and unsound and for this reason such efforts are doomed to failure, although for a year or two they may succeed in temporarily advancing the price.

In the past five hundred years the price of wheat has been high only in times of major wars, with the result that wheat growing was rapidly expanded following each of these major wars; and in time the expansion in acreage pushed the price as far *below* the cost of production as it had previously been *above* the cost of production.

A monopolistic wheat price undertakes to ignore the relative cost of producing wheat and gold and undertakes to place the production of wheat in a more favorable position than the production of gold, but such efforts always have had an ugly fly-back. For example, our government has undertaken to cut the acreage of wheat 15 per cent by paying the farmers a bonus for reducing their acreage. This effort will be temporarily beneficial to wheat prices but in the end it will increase that group of farmers who have quit growing wheat only to become once again wheat growing farmers. In the long run the wheat acreage of the United States, whether it be fifty million, sixty million or seventy million acres, will depend on how profitable it is to produce wheat and nothing else.

The government plan to reduce the wheat acreage is an attempt to establish a monopolistic price by creating a scarcity value as the result of controlled acreage.

A mandatory price contemplates even more radical measures than a monopolistic price. When it comes to wheat, milk or any other standard commodity, a mandatory price results in a certain definite price as determined by law for a portion of the out-put that will be consumed at that price but with no price whatsoever for the over-supply. If the mandatory price is far above its economic price as determined by relative costs, the portion of the output which cannot be sold *at any price,* increases rapidly with each succeeding year of artificially high levels.

Milk is the best illustration of how a mandatory price fails to function. On more than one occasion the officials of large milk consuming centers have said to dairy men: "If you will quit striking among yourselves and stop destroying milk that is on its way to market, we will pay you the price you are asking, but we will only agree to take a certain definite output, and the portion you have left we will not use at any price. Therefore, for that part we cannot consume you will have to seek another market," which in most cases is a cheese or butter factory in some other dairy section. In every case where high mandatory prices have been placed on milk, there has been a drastic curtailment in the demand, which has been so great as to bring about a pronounced undernourishment in the children of the poor with no offsetting benefit to the producer.

Economic law fairly shrieks a word of warning and admonition which is this: "Over a long period of years the production of any staple commodity barely pays the cost of production and if for a short period the production of a commodity becomes exceedingly profitable as occurred in wheat growing from 1914 to 1920, there must naturally follow a long period of exceedingly low prices and over production. Low prices—and low prices alone—will, in a period of years, (usually from ten to fifteen) so discourage production and so increase demand as to change the situation from *temporary over-production* and *low prices to temporary scarcity* and *high prices.*

Currency Inflation

Currency inflation does not in any way disturb the relative cost of producing wheat and producing gold. The

average price over a long period of years is about equal
to the cost of production; nothing more, nothing less. If
money is inflated until the gold content in the dollar is half
of the old gold standard measurement, then wheat should
double in price (in terms of paper dollars but not in terms
of gold dollars) and it will double in price without any
change in supply and demand factors.

All economists agree on one point and that is that when
the *general price level of all commodities rises,* we may
assume that the cause is the cheapening in value of money
whether it be cheaper gold production costs or currency
inflation. In other words, high prices and cheap money
mean the same whereas low prices and dear money are
likewise synonomous. To inflate currency makes it easier
for the borrower to pay off old gold dollar debts and likewise it makes it harder for the lender of money to live,
which includes the holder of government bonds, postal
savings certificates and other high price bonds.

Price is the one dominating factor which controls production and when expressed in terms of gold it has nothing
to do with currency inflation or the price of wheat as expressed in currency inflation. Currency has no value
whatsoever except for the gold or silver that is pledged to
make it good. When all gold support was removed from
the old German mark the mark declined to nothing. I
know of a man who has a trunk full of German marks
that are without any value whatsoever.

All economic life centers around the exchange of goods
and services through the medium of money. Even the
choice between substitutes is determined by their relative
prices. From the viewpoint of consumption, price is like
the governor on a steam engine; the higher the price, the
smaller the consumption, until finally over-supply de-
velops and prices must collapse in order that consumption
may increase.

More tons of water are consumed by a civilized people
in a year than the total consumption in tons of all other

commodities including food, steel, concrete, etc. This is due to cheapness. In fact, water is so cheap in price that many people consider it free; yet it does cost something as I realize when I pay the $50 a year for the 170,000 gallons I use on my garden and lawn.

Price behavior is complex and sometimes it appears without rhyme or reason. A famous painting costs $100,-000 because it cannot be duplicated or if it can be duplicated the job would cost approximately $100,000. In this case $100,000 in the price of production, the same as 10 cents is the price of an article in a ten cent store. Remember normal profit or effort of supervision is considered as a part of cost. It is the reward that causes industry to continue to produce. So, in the final analysis, whether we like it or not, we must assume that the price of wheat and all commodities gyrates through, above and below the cost of production.

For the past twenty years the wheat market forecaster has looked upon 98 cents as a fundamentally sound economic price for a bushel of contract wheat delivered in the Chicago market. He realizes that this is a distress price for the debt-ridden farmer, but he accepts it as a fact that cannot be side-stepped. He knows that lower operating costs can make this price lower than 98 cents and he knows that higher operating costs can put the price well above $1.25. He also knows that a crop shortage can temporarily create a scarcity value that would make dollar wheat far too cheap and he also knows that currency inflation must add to the paper dollar price of wheat for the estimated loss in the gold content of the dollar. Either consciously or unconsciously, all wheat price forecasts are built around that item of 98 cents a bushel. A forecaster knows that sixty cents is so low that it can only be temporary and likewise, two dollars is so high it must necessarily be short lived.

In giving this analysis of why 98 cents is a sound basic price for wheat, I do not believe I have varied one iota from the principles which are laid down by such econo-mists as Fairchild, Taussig, Seager or Mills.

Keep in mind that 21 bushels of wheat, produced under average conditions of climate and soil fertility, cost one ounce of gold; and, adversely, one ounce of gold costs approximately 21 bushels of wheat. Also, remember that adverse weather conditions which lower the yield, tend to increase the price of wheat and likewise, currency infla-tion also tends to increase the cost of wheat because it increases the cost of labor and living conditions.

In arriving at 98 cents as the average cost of producing wheat for a period of 45 years, we started with 1884, when modern wheat harvesting machinery tended to cheapen the cost of wheat and we end with 1932. We have elimi-nated the years of 1917 to 1920, inclusive, since the high prices in this period were based on an unsound credit ex-pansion, for which the world has been paying a dear price for the past several years. In the 45 years we have used in making this check, the average annual price of wheat has exceeded $1.50 in only two years. We must, therefore, assume that $1.50 a bushel for wheat when expressed in terms of gold dollars, is an exceedingly *high price*. In this 45-year period, wheat has sold below 75 cents in only ten years. Therefore, a price of 75 cents must be considered exceedingly low.

The current price of 95 cents for Chicago May Wheat is quoted in inflated United States currency and is equiv-alent to only 66 cents when based on gold dollars, such as prevailed in February of this year. Since the yearly aver-age price of wheat has been below 66 cents only three times in the past 45 years, the present inflated dollar price of 95 cents, must be considered *very low*. Therefore, the next broad move in the economic price cycle must be up-ward. In the next ten years it seems logical to expect the average price of wheat to be at least 98 cents in terms of gold. In terms of inflated currencies, the price could easily range from $1.25 to $1.75 per bushel.

The Secular Trend of Grain Prices

(A Ten Year Forecast)

The secular trend of grain prices in the next ten years will be toward distinctly higher levels. Many devices have been tried to give the farmer a reasonable return for his capital and toil expended in growing a crop but mostly they have ended in failure because economic laws have been ignored. At last the wheat, corn and cotton producing nations of the world have come to the realization that high prices can come only when the consumer is gripped by the fear of a shortage. Therefore surplus grain producing countries are working on plans that will so reduce the acreage in a few years as to create an actual shortage.

The United States can boast of having led the way in a price lifting program that is as sound as the everlasting laws of economics. Unfortunately the program because of its very soundness and far-reaching force cannot immediately advance the products of the farm to a price level that will give the farmer a decent living.

As this book goes to press in November of 1933, we hear the threat of uprisings in farm communities in the middle-west. The National Farm Holiday Association is telling the farmer that anything is better than the condition under which he existed from 1929 to 1933. Demands are being made for a mandatory price of $1.00 for wheat and 60 cents for corn. This rapid spreading of discontent among that group which has always constituted our most solid and conservative class of citizens is stirring Washington on to action as never before. Something must be done. Something is being done. In the short space of eight months processing taxes have been levied that will yield over a billion dollars a year. This revenue will be paid back to farmers who agree to cut their acreage in crops and numbers of livestock. It is the administration's program for a gigantic retreat in farm production. At last the cry of the farmer is being taken seriously.

My people have been big scale farmers for three generations and many of my relatives are farmers at the present time. No one who is not in close touch with the farmer can know what he has been made to suffer in loss of income, pride and self-respect in the last five years. Farmers' wives who were raised in thrifty farm homes and who graduated from our great state universities have, in many cases, been forced to leave their household duties, and do the heavy work of men in the fields. Thus their health and spirit have been broken. When farmers' wives and daughters are forced to do the work of men, millions of farm laborers in tens of thousands of small towns in the farming sections of the middle-west are forced into idleness.

What caused all this misery? The answer can be found in two words and these words are "low prices". What caused the low prices? The answer to this can also be found in two words which are "over production". Each year for the past five years farmers have produced just a little more than was needed and each year the annual surplus was added to the accumulated surplus of preceding years. Many traders who bought cash grain and futures in the past five years have failed in business. Grain elevators became useless because money could not be found to make repairs. The grain trade did not dare to pay an honest price for unwanted and unneeded grain and store it at a charge of two cents a month for years until it might possibly be needed. The Farm Board made a try at government buying and lost a half billion dollars of tax payers' money in trying to force a "scarcity price" on a "surplus product". It all ended in failure as the surplus continued to grow.

At last a planned agriculture is in the making. It is working slowly—too slowly—for millions of farmers who are about to lose all; but it is working along sound lines. Scarcity will advance grain prices in a free and natural market in which a short crop will sell at a much higher price than a bumper crop—which is as it should be.

A planned reduction in agricultural crops is the only way out and, best of all, it is a sure way out.

Because I have faith in a planned decrease in farm production that will meet the demand, I am claiming that by 1936 grain, fruit, vegetables and livestock will be selling at the 1912–16 level of prices, and people will look back on the 30 cent wheat and 12 cent corn of February, 1933 and say: "If we had known then what we know now about how to cut production, we would have saved ourselves all the misery of those terrible years of 1930 to 1933."

Thanks to planned curtailment of farm output the secular trend of grain prices is toward much higher levels. Not a guaranteed price—no, that would ruin the whole plan. It will be a scarcity price—a free price and one that moves down in seasons of bountiful crops and then moves very high when only a few bushels per acre are produced.

As acres are taken out of production, farm lands will advance to double the prices seen in the fall of 1933.

Yes, the secular, or long pull, trend of grain prices is toward higher levels.

Chapter XVIII

A Study of Spreads

THIS comparison between the prices of two futures was inspired by the March issue of "Wheat Studies" of the Food Research Institute of Stanford University, California. This is a very technical analysis of the price relationship of two wheat futures and requires fifty pages to make the presentation. I am here attempting to reduce this treatise to the simplest and most academic form possible. Where *"Wheat Studies"* has been very scientific and technically cautious in its analysis, I have taken the liberty to state arbitrarily a definite figure which was not in all cases obtained from the above-mentioned book.

Traders who are long wheat in the spring months are interested primarily in two situations:

1. Should their long commitments in wheat be made in the July or the September futures?

2. Is wheat due for a major advance from current levels?

September Wheat Is a Better Speculation Than July

This article was written in April of 1933 when I was long three lines of wheat as a long pull investment. Many of my friends were holding July at the time. Conditions were such as to warrant a switch from July into September. Those who read this analysis of the relative merits of July and September were given an opportunity to switch into September. The later future gained nearly two cents over the July in May and June of 1933. The purpose of this analysis is to show the conditions that make for a wider or narrower spread in the months of May and June.

After making a very careful study of the March issue of *"Wheat Studies"*, I have come to the conclusion that

September Wheat has one chance in two of selling at a premium of 2¾ cents over July in the last ten days in June. Furthermore, September Wheat has one chance in two of selling 2 cents over July Wheat in the last week in May. September Wheat also has as good a chance of selling as high as 3¼ cents over July Wheat in the last week in June as it has of selling as low as 2¼ cents over July in the last week in June.

Assuming that September Wheat should sell at a premium of 2¾ cents over July Wheat in the last week in June, then the trader who switches from July Wheat to September Wheat at the present time would be 2 cents better off by his switch; or, a spread can be made at the present time by buying September Wheat and selling July Wheat, which would give the trader a gross profit of 2 cents. After paying commissions and tax he will have almost 1½ cents a bushel for profit.

Total stocks, July 1st	September over July	September under July
Above normal by 100 million bushels or more	2¾	—
Above normal by 50 million bushels	1⅝	—
Above normal by 20 million bushels	⅛	—
Normal	—	1
Below normal by 20 million bushels	—	2⅝
Below normal by 40 million bushels	—	4⅜
Below normal by 60 million bushels	—	6¼

"*Wheat Studies*" arbitrarily defines normal carryover as "the level of July first stocks which tends to be accompanied by a price of Chicago September one cent per bushel under the price of July." But, in order to simplify matters, I prefer to make the arbitrary statement that *120 million bushels of wheat in the July first* carryover is normal. A lower figure is below normal, and a higher figure is above normal. The table shown above was obtained from "*Wheat Studies*" and shows the most logical price difference between the two futures on July 1st with the different carryovers.

Assuming that 120 million bushels is *normal,* a study of the above table would indicate that a carryover of 220 million bushels or more should show a logical premium of September over July of 2¾ cents. A carryover of only 60 million bushels would be 60 million bushels below normal and would indicate an acute if not an alarming shortage, in which the September should sell under the July by approximately 6¼ cents, as shown in the above table.

Comparing this with the present market, no one knows just what the carryover will be on July 1, of 1933, but it will probably be around 370 million bushels. But it is a foregone conclusion that the carryover on July 1 will be at least 220 million bushels, making it more than 100 million bushels above a normal carryover of 120 million bushels. Thus we have a right to expect that during the first three weeks of June the price of Chicago September Wheat will average about 2¾ cents over the price of July Wheat and that by the end of June the premium of September over July should be in the neighborhood of 3 or 3¼ cents over July. If there ever was a year in which the September future in June should sell at a full carrying charge over July, it is this year when we are confronted by a burdensome supply of old wheat as opposed to a supply of new wheat which will probably fall short of domestic requirements.

As speculators, we wish to take full advantage of any increase in the spread. Therefore, when we dispose of our present holdings of May and July Wheat, it is only logical that we will reinstate in the September if, at that time, we are bullish. And if we are bearish it is logical to assume that our short sales will be made in the July. I have now answered question (1) showing that this year (1933) the September Wheat future is better for a long position than July.

Forecasting the Price

We will now make a study of the probable trend of wheat prices between April 10th and June 1st, 1933, by an analysis of the *positive* and *negative* spreads between July and September Wheat.

In years when there is a burdensome supply of old wheat, as exists at the present time, it is natural to assume that wheat should sell at a relatively low price level and also that the September future should sell at a premium over the July. When a composite price curve is made of all years that fit into this *"low-price high-carryover"* situation, we have a pronounced price advance for both the July and September futures throughout the month of April and a somewhat smaller price advance throughout the month of May with the high point reached in the latter part of May, followed by a gradual decline in June. In years when the price of wheat is very high and the carryover on July 1 appears to be exceedingly small, it then follows that there should be a major price advance in April followed by a major decline in May; then a reversal of the trend, to be followed by a secondary major advance in June.

I would not want to be long wheat solely because this happens to be a year of relatively low prices, an indicated huge carryover on July 1, and the prospect of a short crop. Yet, it is comforting for the man who is long wheat to know that the present July and September futures fit into a situation which calls for a major advance in April to be followed by a somewhat less pronounced advance in May.

Those who want to make a careful study of the positive and negative spreads between July and September wheat by years and their relationship to carryover should study the table below and particularly the next to the last column (June column). Except for 1931, when the two futures sold at practically the same price, September Wheat sold at a premium over July in each of the last five years of heavy carryovers. In 1917 the premium of 22.17 of July over September was due to a "squeeze" as well as to a shortage of cash grain. In 1918 to 1920 there was no trading in wheat futures.

If the 1933 July-September Wheat future is to have a normal performance the man who switches from the July to the September at the present time will be about 1½ cents better off than would be the case if he were to hold on to his July Wheat, assuming of course that he retained his July Wheat until the first of July.

This forecast worked out within one-fourth of a cent of what I claimed in the above article.

United States Wheat Stocks, July 1, and March 1, and Average July-September Price Spread by Months, 1896–1932

(Million bushels; cents per bushel)

Year	July 1 Stocks			March 1 Stocks	July-September Spreads				
	Visible	All Commercial	Commercial and Farm	Commercial and Farm	March	April	May	June	July
1896	47.3	118.1	175.2	335.2	. . . .	+ 0.33	+ 0.83	+ 0.77	+ 1.04
1897	17.3	67.5	100.4	258.9	− 2.12	− 2.21	− 4.42	− 4.77	− 4.62
1898	14.6	36.1	58.7	246.1	− 7.38	− 7.21	− 19.04	− 8.47	− 7.92
1899	31.4	118.2	195.8	383.7	+ 0.42	+ 0.75	+ 0.21	+ 1.30	+ 1.33
1900	44.6	125.6	188.2	385.5	. . . .	+ 0.83	+ 1.12	+ 1.40	+ 1.17
1901	29.3	96.8	134.2	357.7	. . . .	. . . .	− 1.75	− 2.17	− 1.21
1902	18.3	72.9	130.4	332.0	− 0.04	− 0.50	− 1.29	− 1.40	− 3.75
1903	14.9	63.6	109.7	307.1	− 1.29	− 2.92	− 2.58	− 2.33	+ 0.67
1904	11.1	68.0	106.3	271.7	− 5.58	− 4.25	− 5.29	− 4.80	− 6.58
1905	10.8	53.3	78.1	240.7	− 6.08	− 4.62	− 6.67	− 4.73	− 2.12
1906	23.0	92.2	139.7	314.3	− 0.12	− 1.04	− 1.96	− 0.27	+ 0.71
1907	37.8	136.7	192.4	375.6	+ 0.50	+ 1.04	+ 1.46	− 2.57	− 2.58
1908	10.9	62.3	95.5	281.6	− 2.83	− 2.46	− 3.92	− 2.47	+ 0.29
1909	9.8	45.4	59.8	227.4	− 6.38	− 8.50	− 7.75	− 6.73	− 7.21
1910	12.0	72.7	110.1	280.9	− 2.33	− 2.33	− 2.12	− 2.13	− 1.96
1911	23.9	91.9	126.0	301.1	− 0.25	− 0.54	− 1.08	− 0.67	+ 2.04
1912	23.3	80.7	104.6	277.3	− 2.17	− 3.17	− 5.00	− 3.07	− 3.25
1913	29.9	95.0	130.5	327.4	− 0.33	− 0.67	− 0.46	− 0.23	+ 1.00
1914	15.0	77.3	109.5	304.2	− 0.50	− 0.33	− 1.17	− 1.53	+ 0.50
1915	7.9	40.7	69.7	321.0	− 11.92	− 13.50	− 6.12	− 2.03	− 6.08
1916	41.1	151.6	226.3	465.4	− 1.25	− 1.79	+ 0.33	+ 2.07	+ 1.42
1917	14.1	37.2	52.8	268.7	− 12.08	− 24.33	− 28.42	− 26.23	− 22.17
1918	0.8	12.8	20.9	207.9	. . . .	. . . .	. . . .	. . . .	. . . .
1919	8.5	41.6	60.9	302.1	. . . .	. . . .	. . . .	. . . .	. . . .

United States Wheat Stocks, July 1, and March 1, and Average July-September Price Spread by Months, 1896–1932

(Million bushels; cents per bushel)

| Year | July 1 Stocks | | | March 1 Stocks | July-September Spreads | | | | |
	Visible	All Commercial	Commercial and Farm	Commercial and Farm	March	April	May	June	July
1920	19.5	115.2	164.8	387.5	....	....	....	−10.20	+ 0.58
1921	7.8	72.7	129.4	380.1	− 6.67	− 7.00	− 5.29	+ 0.40	− 2.38
1922	17.8	84.1	116.6	321.7	− 1.79	− 2.12	+ 1.50	+ 0.93	− 1.00
1923	26.3	110.5	145.7	345.4	+ 0.88	+ 1.00	+ 0.96	+ 1.60	− 1.08
1924	34.9	113.2	142.5	328.8	− 9.67	− 8.25	− 8.21	− 2.83	− 3.42
1925	29.1	85.2	113.8	325.0	− 5.79	− 5.96	− 4.08	− 4.17	− 0.17
1926	12.3	77.9	98.5	298.4	− 2.29	− 1.42	− 2.79	− 1.97	− 2.33
1927	22.1	91.2	117.9	333.0	− 1.67	− 3.12	0.00	+ 1.84	+ 2.92
1928	38.9	100.7	124.1	318.8	+ 1.67	+ 3.00	+ 3.75	+ 4.42	+ 4.29
1929	92.7	196.4	242.2	450.1	+ 1.96	+ 2.96	+ 2.71	+ 2.92	+ 2.96
1930	107.5	243.4	290.8	497.6	− 0.04	− 0.75	− 0.21	+ 0.01	+ 0.54
1931	187.3	286.7	318.6	511.2	+ 2.04	+ 2.21	+ 1.92	+ 2.49	+ 2.38
1932	163.2	290.7	362.6	560.4					

The spreads are for averages for the second, third, and fourth Fridays of each month, except for June which are the daily averages for the first three full weeks of June.

CHAPTER XIX

A Study of Major Declines

BECAUSE the institution of futures trading is designed to give a constant market for grain, regardless of how great the current receipts may be or how small the current demand, the short interest is largely a hedging interest in which those who are short are not concerned about whether or not the market goes up or down since each day their grain is sold in the futures as fast as it is bought on the cash grain tables. What the cash buyer wants in August is a *wide premium* in May over September, and the wider the premium the greater are his merchandising profits.

When a major bear market gets under way there is *never* a large speculative short interest that rushes in to *buy—take profits—*and incidentally *support* the market. The speculative short interest just isn't there and never was there. The short interest which, of course, is always exactly equal to the long interest is mostly a merchandising short interest. It is a hedged interest and is *closed* and *completed* when the cash grain is delivered on the short sale in the delivery month.

Under such conditions, what is the result in the beginning of a major bear market? First, there is a group of thinly margined accounts which must be closed out, and this causes the first drastic break such as occurred on July 19 of 1933. Since the speculative short interest is always very small, the buying after the first collapse must be done by a second group of would-be longs or by those who are long and willing to increase their holdings as the market declines. After a month or two of declines, tired longs whose accounts were better margined begin to unload their grain—not to shorts who are taking profits—

148

but to a third group of investment buyers who are willing to take the long side as a long pull investment. All this time the merchandising short side (or cash grain trade if you prefer) sees its profits in its millions of bushels of cash grain vanish and, to offset this, it sees the profits accrue from the short sale of the futures.

Regardless of how much profit or loss is shown in the merchandising short sales of the grain trade, these short sales remain undisturbed until the actual grain is sold to some consumer, which may be a miller, a wet process grinder, a farmer feeder, or an exporter.

I have now given the most logical reason why major bear markets (which follow major bull markets) are of long duration and average 86 days in length. Just remember that in a major bear market a new class of traders who are willing to take the long side must be found before the market can find its bottom and later its "balance".

A major bear market has a set of rules that are all its own. It ignores the "head" and "shoulders" that the graph seeks to find. The only charts that work following a major bull market are charts of major bear markets.

Right now, as I write this article, there are ten tired longs who *know* that some time in the next six weeks they will close out their trades and take their losses and possibly profits to where there is one man who is out of the market and *knows* he will buy grain in the next six weeks and hold for the long pull. When these two groups are equal in number the market will be in balance and ready to be influenced equally by bullish or bearish news.

The above article was published on Sept. 25, 1933.

The End of a Bull Market

The experienced forecaster and trader has little trouble in determining the end of a major advance in grain although the same cannot be said regarding the stock market. The stock market frequently has a bad "shake out" only to recover on constructive news and move on to higher levels. Not so with grain. Bull markets in grain are often weather affairs; they must necessarily be seasonal and they must be followed by a major decline which is often a bear market of long duration.

A major bull market in grain usually lasts from three to six weeks in which most of the advance occurs in the last two or three weeks of the period. It is recognized by head-liners in daily papers; general comment is heard forecasting much higher prices than ever occur.

The experienced trader will try to be long grain at the start of a bull market and will sell at the first sign of extreme weakness, which means he never sells out his line at the top. He waits for the decline to get under way.

The charts on the two following pages show arrows where a short sale should have been made in the summer of 1933, which by the way, was where I took a short position in both Chicago and Winnipeg wheat. The invoice on page 7 shows where I sold Chicago May wheat short on the first sign of pronounced weakness.

Many traders mistook June 29th for the beginning of a major decline and transferred from the long side to the short side of the market on that date. Although June 29th proved later to be too soon to reverse one's position, the patient trader who reversed his position then and there took large profits on both the up and down side of this historic advance and decline.

Just remember that after a major advance (which is always a period of great public participation in the market) a 10 cent decline in one day or a 15 cent decline in two or three days is always a true indication that the major advance is over and that a major decline will shortly start that is due to last from two to five months. The decline may be slow or it may be precipitous but it is sure to come. The first sharp decline may be more than regained in the following two weeks as occurred between July 18th and 26th of 1929, but just the same the bull market is over with the first sharp break.

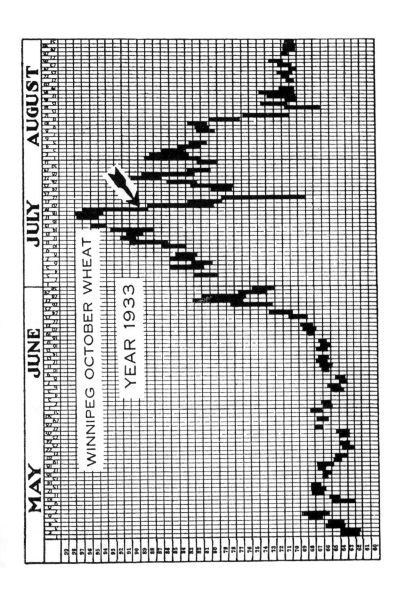

WINNIPEG OCTOBER WHEAT

YEAR 1933

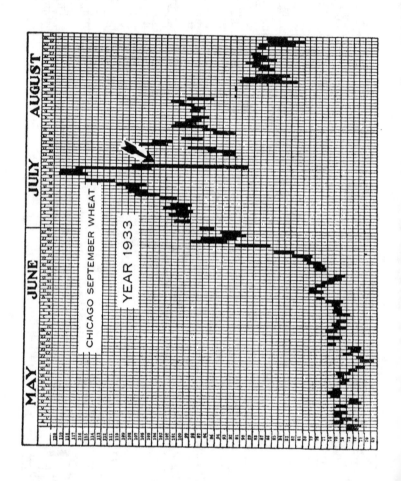

There has not been a single bull grain market in the past 12 years that has shown an exception to this rule. The reason for this is simple.

The first shakeout shatters confidence as calls for additional margin are telephoned to traders. While most traders refuse to believe that the top has been reached hundreds of thousands of traders resolve to sell out at the top figure that has just been passed, when and if, the opportunity is again offered. With thousands of would-be sellers wanting to take profits at the peak that has just been passed, a second higher peak is seldom made. When made, it is of very short duration.

The above rule which never fails, applies only to the major bull markets that occur about twice in three years. It does not apply so well to the many small advances of ten to twenty cents a bushel.

Price Range of Past Bull Markets

The best way to study the extent of bull markets in past years is to give typical cases. After I give these cases I will offer my conclusions. My comments will be confined only to wheat advances that started from a more or less quiet market. (When I use the term "congested market" I refer to a market that has remained within a narrow price range for one or more weeks and making no headway in either direction.)

On July 12 of 1921, a bull market got under way after wheat had sold at an average price of $1.20 in a widely congested market that lasted about three weeks. In four days 15 cents was added to the price of wheat. The top was made at $1.35 on July 15.

April of 1922 saw wheat in congestion for a period of four weeks. The average price in this period of congestion was $1.33. The advance lasted nine days and reached $1.49¼ on April 22.

In 1924, wheat had been in a congestion for a period of three weeks. The average price in this period of congestion was $1.17. The bull market started on July 12 and culminated on July 29 when the price was $1.36.

Wheat had been in a congestion for three weeks in November and the first part of December in 1924. The average price during this period was $1.61. The bull market extended from the first day of December until the 27th day of December when the price was $1.85.

During October and the first week in November of 1925, wheat was in a broad congestion with an average price of $1.41. The bull market started on the 9th of November and culminated on December 6 when the price was $1.74½.

September Wheat was in a broad congestion all through May and June of 1926. The average price in this congestion was $1.35. A bull market started on July 7 and culminated on July 19 when the price was $1.47⅜.

In the first three weeks in June of 1929, September Wheat was in a broad congestion at an average price of $1.11. A bull market started on June 16 and culminated on July 18 when the price was $1.51.

On October 8, 1931, December Wheat had been in a narrow congestion at an average price of 48 cents. The bull market got under way on October 8 and culminated on November 9 when the price was 67¼ cents.

I shall now show the above periods of time and price changes in tabulated form:—

Bull Market No.	No. of Days in congestion before advance	Length of Bull Mkt.	Extent of Advance	Per cent of Advance
1	21 days	4 days	15c	12%
2	28 days	9 days	16c	12%
3	21 days	17 days	19c	16%
4	28 days	27 days	24c	15%
5	30 days	27 days	33c	23%
6	60 days	12 days	12c	9%
7	21 days	32 days	40c	36%
8	21 days	30 days	19c	40%
Average ..	30 days	19 days	22c	20%

Let me make it perfectly plain that the above table does not mean a great deal. Certainly it does not actually prove anything. However, it is interesting in that it shows that the length of the *average* bull market is nineteen days; that the shortest bull market following a congested market was four days in duration, and that the longest was thirty-two days in duration. It is also interesting to note that the average extent of the advance was 22 cents; or, when expressed in terms of percentage, 20 per cent. It is worth noting that the nineteen-cent advance of October 1931 was one of the greatest bull markets in the last twenty years when judged by the percentage of advance, although in cents it was not as large as the July, 1933 advance.

CHAPTER XX

Trading in Cotton

THERE are certain well defined technical factors which form the background for successful long pull cotton traders. All who intend to trade in cotton should learn the following rules so well that they become the foundation of their trading knowledge. We are publishing a table below, which is of great value to the student of cotton price fluctuations. This table requires some explanation.

First, no allowance is made for carryover in the following table. (In order to simplify matters it is assumed that each crop is consumed in the twelve months following harvest.)

Second, it is not customary for spot people to carry cotton *open*.

Third, there is always some carryover from the previous crop, and it is reasonable to suppose that the visible supply is *hedged* and perhaps some of the cotton in mill stocks for which the mills have no orders, is also hedged.

Fourth, as a rule mills *fix* the price on their cotton only as they book orders for goods to be made from that cotton.

In your study of the chart below you will notice that at the beginning of the season the *into sight* is not as great as the Mill Consumption, consequently we have to borrow some from the carryover until such times as the new crop movement is large enough to take care of the mill demand, usually about the middle of September.

Up to that time there has been no pressure from the new crop but from the middle of September until about February the "*into sight*" is so large that it is a constant weight upon the market. The cotton which cannot be sold to the mills is bought by the Spot firms and *hedged* in the market, which makes the Trade a constant Seller of Hedges for months. After the heavy movement is over and the Trade begins to take its cotton out of the warehouses and sell it to the mills, the Trade is a constant buyer of hedges until the new crop moves.

Thus it would appear that the Trade is "against the market" during the heavy movement and "for the market" after the movement is over, whereas the Trade is not interested in *price* at all but in the difference between the price at which they can buy spot cotton and at which they can Hedge. The same applies to grain as brought out in Chapter II.

Most persons do not stop to think about it but handling a cotton crop is a big financial problem. When you consider that the average value of the cotton crop for a normal five year period like 1924–29 is about $1,400,000,000 and the seed $200,000,000 to $250,000,000 more and that 67% of the cotton and perhaps nearly all the seed that is going to be marketed is thrown on the market from Sept. to Dec. inclusive, it is no wonder that this weight of actual cotton has a depressing effect on prices. The Supply is twice the needs of the mills until the first of the year. Now look at the other side of the picture. In the four months of May, June, July and August immediately preceding this period an amount equivalent to only 11% of the crop comes on the market. The Supply during that period is only one-third of the mills' needs and the balance must be taken out of storage and the Hedges bought off. Add to this, the fact that this is the crop scare period and you can easily see why most of the Annual Highs are made during that period except that we allow for a month's *lag* which makes it necessary to include the month of September.

From the column of Annual Highs you will notice that there are usually three times in the year when trades can be made profitably.

Purchase on declines in February with a view to get

ting out in April or May on some bulge made by Price Fixing and talk of delay or damage to the new crop.

Purchase on declines in June with a view of getting out on some crop scare later in the season, more often around the first of September, than any other time. In June we always get the big acreage and fine condition gossip, when the crop looks like a bale to the acre. Later when we have high temperatures, drought and perhaps hot winds, or rumors of them, the crop begins to look like a bale to ten acres; at least that is the way the gossip goes.

Sell on bulges when the crop begins to move, usually in early September, with a view to covering when the weight of the movement is at its height.

Every cotton trader should have two U. S. Government publications on cotton which I consider well worth reading: "Report of Lloyd S. Tenny, before Senate Committee Investigating Cotton Price Decline." Bureau of Agricultural Economics. *Free.* "Technical Bulletin No. 50. Factors Affecting the Price of Cotton." Government Printing Office. Price 15 cents.

The Cotton Traders Table

Month of Season	Percentage of crop INTO SIGHT Each Month	Percentage of crop CONSUMED Each Month	Percentage of crop HEDGED in Future Market	No. of Annual HIGHS during Each Month 58 year period	Avg. Monthly Fluctuations (3 years) (1924–26 inc.)
August	4%	8%	4%	10	295 points
September	14%	9%	1%	15	371 points
October	20%	9%	12%	4	360 points
November	18%	9%	21%	1	178 points
December	15%	9%	27%	3	151 points
January	8%	8%	27%	3	122 points
February	5%	8%	24%	2	150 points
March	5%	8%	21%	2	134 points
April	4%	8%	17%	4	98 points
May	3%	8%	12%	4	160 points
June	2%	8%	6%	2	124 points
July	2%	8%	0%	8	216 points
Totals	100%	100%		58 yrs	

Month of annual highs and *lows* and number of points decline for four typical years:

1924	1925	1926	1927
High—Aug.	High—Sept.	High—Sept.	High—Sept.
Low—Sept.	Low—Oct.	Low—Dec.	Low—Dec.

Average Annual Decline (under weight of movement, liquidation, etc.) 668 points.

Notations

Practically all big movements (both ways) come in July, August, September and October. Widest monthly fluctuations come in months when *least* and *most* actual *cotton* is handled.

Most *annual highs* are made when very little *cotton* is coming on the market and when practically none is left in *hedge account* from the previous crop.

Fewest *annual highs* are made when greatest weight of the crop is left and liquidation of speculative holdings in advance of the December delivery.

Usual Time for Planting and Picking Cotton

North Ala. plants April 26. First picking Sept. 7.
South Ala. plants April 12. First picking Aug. 18.
North La. plants April 17. First picking Sept. 1.
South La. plants April 8. First picking Aug. 20.
North Okla. plants May 10. First picking Sept. 15.
South Okla. plants April 25. First picking Aug. 25.
Northern Tex. plants Apr. 27. First picking Aug. 25.
Central Texas plants Apr. 17. First picking Aug. 20.
Southern Texas plants Mar. 7. First picking Aug. 7.

CHAPTER XXI

Forecasting Past Markets

I SHALL now discuss in a general way many of the more important methods and material used in making a grain forecast. I have no secrets whatsoever and feel honored if I can be of help in training those who are not professionals to do a large part of their own forecasting thereby helping them to accept or reject some of my own methods.

Mechanical or Technical Methods

Mechanical or technical methods naturally play a more important part in forecasting the trend of grain prices than they do in forecasting the trend of the stock market. Each individual corporation may be considered animate —or perhaps I should say human. The course of each company depends upon its ability to meet competition as well as honest and efficient management that is careful not to pay out too large a portion of the earnings in salaries to executives or in fine office buildings that are not needed to manufacture the product or merchandise it as the case may be.

On the other hand, grain is a commodity, and while produced by human effort it does not depend so much on honesty of management as does the stock of a corporation. A part of its cost, of course, is the labor involved, which means that, unlike common stocks, commodities can never sell down to nothing. Neither can commodities sell at several times the cost of production, since too high a price would result in a great overproduction which would, in itself, bring about a decline in price.

The most time-honored of all mechanical grain trading methods is the "Head and Shoulder Method" of determining the turning points in a bull or bear market. This is explained very nicely by Mr. George Cole, on page 62.

Traders may be interested to know that I paid less attention to the "Head and Shoulder Method" in reversing my position in the bull market of July 1933.

The extent of an advance or decline and the length of time spent in a bull or bear market is an important factor for the trader to consider. Off hand, I should say that it is very professional for the man who is long grain to wait until the top is made and then close out on the decline. When short, he should wait until the bottom is made and then close out on the advance. To follow such a plan, the trader never has the happy and lucky experience of getting out of his trades at the exact top or bottom, but year in and year out he will average bigger profits than if he tries to call the top and bottom.

Anticipating the Probable Effect of Coming Events or Conditions

I can best illustrate this by examples. Ample subsoil moisture which delays the planting of corn and cotton is invariably construed as bullish when the planting or cultivation of the crop is being delayed. But the forecaster knows that subsoil moisture will probably be needed in July and August; so, while others look upon a wet spring as a bullish factor, his experience teaches him that it should be considered bearish later on in the season when the stored-up moisture may be needed. Unseasonably hot weather that causes the corn crop to curl in the afternoons but rushes it on to maturity ahead of frost is usually considered bullish at the very time when it should be considered as a favorable crop factor and therefore bearish.

Political events, like the processing tax, which was considered by most of the trade as bearish on the week ending June 19, 1933 proved, in the following month a major bullish factor just as I claimed it would. The price-advancing force of this contemplated processing tax had un-

doubtedly been fully discounted in the rush of wheat
buying by millers, to be followed later in July by an offsetting decline in buying.

Currency inflation, increase in business activity—are
all factors which the forecaster must take into consideration. Since the price force of coming events can never be
reduced to a formula the forecasting of the price effect of
these events becomes the most interesting and skillful of
all forms of forecasting.

Supply and Demand and Its Effect on Price

This is mostly a rule-and-thumb method. Seasoned
speculators claim that the percentage of price change
should be three to four times the percentage of bushel
change as the crop is favored or injured by weather conditions.

Study Past Markets When Similar Conditions Prevailed

Some forecasters prefer to call this a study of the *history of markets*. This study offers some of the most valuable data for the forecaster and helps him materially in
determining his position in the market. I am somewhat
surprised that this method is not used by more forecasters.
Personally, I consider it one of my most valuable and de-
pendable methods. Under this might be included *calendar trading*, also the statement: "Never bull the tail end
of a short crop."

Let us take, for example, the corn crop of 1930, which
was only 2,060,000,000 bushels. In August of 1930, when
the short crop became an assured fact, due to serious damage in July and August, May Corn advanced to $1.03 a
bushel with the result that farmers sold their short corn
crop in place of feeding it. As a result of a too generous
marketing of the crop, the May future declined from the
August high of $1.03 to 54 cents in May of 1931.

A study of exceedingly large corn visibles in July at
a season of the year when the actual use of corn reaches

the lowest ebb oftentimes correctly forecasts a major decline in August and September.

Psychological Factors

Public participation in the market, volume of trading, and the breaking through of resistance points as weak holders are pushed out through stops may be considered as psychological factors. Attempting to forecast prices by weighing public enthusiasm undoubtedly causes more mistakes to be made by forecasters than any other single method. I do not attempt to let public psychology play a very important part in my forecasting but I do not ignore it.

Now let us take the market of July 1933 and see what course I followed. (This article was published by Ainsworth in Financial Service in July 1933 and at the peak of a wild bull market.)

If I were to depend entirely upon the *length of time* spent in the bull market, I would have to delay my short sale about seven days; but if I had depended only on the *extent of the advance* I would have sold my wheat about ten cents cheaper than the price I obtained.

I have given the bearish effect of the processing tax after it goes into operation an important part in taking my short position, and feel that it will be a major price-depressing factor in the last half of July. All political factors are now bearish since the Roosevelt administration will not want to see a "Roosevelt Grain Market" like the "Hoover Stock Market" to be followed later by a major collapse at the end of four years in office.

If we claim that the *percentage of price advance* should be three or four times the percentage of bushel losses under a normal crop, we would need to assume that wheat is only slightly too high in price. The short position I have just taken in corn was largely influenced by the impressive declines that followed adverse weather conditions in past corn markets.

In stating the material used by grain market forecasters, I hope I have enabled traders to see the manner in which I arrive at my conclusions. I want it distinctly understood that no forecaster would think of using these methods in the same manner twice in succession. Some price-making forces will impress him as being very important under certain conditions while under other conditions they would be given only passing notice.

Forecasting the October 1933 Low for Chicago May Wheat From Five Lines of Approach

This forecast was made on July 17th and August 14th, 1933 when May wheat was selling at $1.10 to $1.28.

There is no study as interesting and as profitable as the long pull forecasting of commodity prices. It carries with it so much more logic than the hit-and-miss forecasting that is based on *resistance points, top* and *bottom formations* and charts as shown on page 88.

Now I do not want to belittle the splendid arguments for resistance points. They are very important. In fact, they are so important that the Chicago Board of Trade got permission from Washington to place a minimum on the bottom side of wheat prices in July of 1933 because they knew full well that longs who had put wheat up to unreasonably high levels were so pressed for additional margin on the decline that no bottom was in sight. Without this minimum our objective of 93 cents on the bottom side of May Wheat would have been reached on two different occasions; but that is beside the point.

We are now looking for the October *low* or the November *low* of Chicago May Wheat by five different lines of approach, and remember we are not looking for average prices; we are looking for the probable lows of the crop which are frequently made in October or November for many reasons which will be discussed in later bulletins. These five different lines of approach show a probable low in the fall months of *93 cents, 96 cents, 93 cents, 86⅝ cents, and 86 cents.*

After the excitement of a great bull market which resulted from crop damage, it is well to forecast the October low by examining the history of the great crop scare in 1893.

In 1893 crop damage to wheat was the greatest ever experienced in the United States. That year the majority of brokers predicted famine prices before another crop was produced. Yet no famine ever occurred. I commented on this market in detail on July 31 under the heading, "Wheat Supply and Market Action Following Short Crops."

The 1893 crop of 396,000,000 bushels (for all wheat) was the shortest crop grown in the United States since records have been kept. In "theory" it fell short of domestic requirements for food, seed, and feed by 108,000,000 bushels. Now, pay careful attention to this analysis which is typical of crop scare psychology.

In July and August of that greatest of all crop damage years, public excitement was at fever heat. Then in September, after the crop was raised, there was nothing to worry about. The damage was accepted and the fire of enthusiasm burned itself out just as it is doing this year. Wheat prices weakened each month until May. The September *low* was 75⅛ cents, October *low* 70 cents, November *low* 66½ cents, and on down with each succeeding month. But the point we want to bring out right here is that the October low was 4¾ cents lower than the lowest price reached in August and 5⅛ cents lower than the lowest point reached in September. This represented a decline of 7 per cent from the average of the August and September lows.

Conclusion: If the market in this 1933 crop damage year is going to perform like it did in 1893, May Wheat should make a low in October of 7 per cent below the low in July or August. One dollar was the *low* in July and, assuming one dollar as the *low* in August for May Wheat, a 7 per cent decline would mean *93 cents for May Wheat* in order to duplicate the 1933 wheat market action.

We shall now take a second line of approach, which is that of seasonal decline. We shall use the last ten-year average of 1923 to 1932, inclusive. The ten-year average *high* reached in August for Chicago May Wheat was $1.26 and the ten-year average *low* reached in October was $1.13, showing an average decline of 13 cents a bushel from the July *high* to the October *low*. Assuming that the *high* in August of this year was made on August 10 at $1.09⅛, then the low in October should be *96 cents for May Wheat* in order to duplicate the seasonal decline in the fall months. In the above ten-year check it is interesting to note that in no year of the ten-year period was any bull market made after August except in 1932 and in every year in the ten-year period (including 1932) the low in October was lower than the best prices made in August.

For our third line of approach we will include world figures. Under the title, "The World Wheat Situation," we show that Winnipeg Wheat should decline 15 cents. Assuming an equal decline of 15 cents from Friday's average of $1.08 gives a price of *93 cents for Chicago May Wheat*. It is necessary to read carefully the above mentioned article on page 169 of this book in order to understand just why Winnipeg Wheat is due for a 15 cent decline.

For the fourth line of approach we shall apply the rule that the *price increase of wheat should be four times the per cent of bushel decrease in wheat supply* which of course includes *crop plus old carryover*.

	Carryover Millions	Crop Millions	Total Supply Millions
July 1, 1932.............350		727	1,070
July 1, 1933.............369		500	869

1933 shortage compared to 1932 (mil. bu.)................201

From the above table we find that the 1933 crop of 500,000,000 bushels (August 10 government estimate) plus the July 1, 1933 carryover is 18 per cent short of the 1932 crop plus the 1932 carryover. Four times 18 per cent is 72 per cent. The October *low* for May Wheat of last year was 48⅝ cents. 72 per cent of 48⅝ gives 38 cents as the proper increase under the above rule. Therefore the low of May Wheat in October should be 48⅝ cents plus 38 cents increase, or *86⅝ cents,* to be in line with the relative crop difference. Therefore we have *86⅝ for the May Wheat low* in October under our fourth line of reasoning.

We shall now use a fifth method of determining a reasonable price for Chicago May Wheat. In my opinion, this is the most interesting as well as the most inaccurate means of determining a fair price for wheat. It is political, theoretical, and obscure; but nevertheless it is alluring under present political conditions.

We shall start by quoting George N. Peek, administrator of Agricultural Adjustment, in an article that appeared in the Chicago Tribune August 10. Mr. Peek said, "We have one responsibility under the law, and that is to get farmers' prices up to parity."

Probably Mr. Peek was thinking of low-priced hogs and not $1.00 wheat, which was considered a very high price for wheat as late as 1915. Be that as it may, what is *parity,* anyway? What is the fairest price for all concerned? What price should the farmer have for his wheat this summer to compensate for the short crop and get him right in line with other workers? As a land owner, I like to feel sorry for myself at times. I like to think of myself as the forgotten man. But figures do not warrant the assumption that farmers are any more forgotten than others. Surely we have had our full share of favorable legislation.

Except for the bonanza farming period of 1914 to 1920, gross farm income and factory wage pay rolls have gone hand in hand for the past forty years. In the last three years ten homes were lost by factory workers as a result of low income where one farm was lost through fore-closure. Here is the table which shows that farm income and factory wages in America go hand in hand and prob-ably will *always* go hand in hand. If the farmer has been in the cellar of despair for the past three years, then all others have also been in the cellar. When we who own and farm land move out of the cellar of low prices, we shall all move out together.

Here is the table of income by groups as presented by the Department of Agriculture and the Department of Labor:

	Gross Farm Income	Factory Wage Pay Roll
1923	$11,041,000,000	$11,009,000,000
1924	11,337,000,000	10,172,000,000
1925	11,968,000,000	10,730,000,000
1926	11,480,000,000	11,095,000,000
1927	11,616,000,000	10,849,000,000
1928	11,741,000,000	10,902,000,000
1929	11,918,000,000	11,621,000,000
1930	9,414,000,000	9,518,000,000
1931	6,911,000,000	7,256,000,000
1932	5,143,000,000	5,022,000,000

Let us assume that the factory wage pay roll for 1933 will increase $1,500,000,000 over the five billion dollars plus shown in 1932. That would mean $6,522,000,000. No statistician expects a factory wage of over 6½ billion dollars this year.

Just what price would the wheat farmer need to get for his half billion bushels of wheat grown in 1933 to ad-vance the same distance out of this depression as the laborer hopes to advance? That is the question we are putting and the answer is easy. It is just plain arith-metic.

Assuming that factory labor gets 1½ billion dollars more than in 1932, that would be an increase of 33⅓ per cent. The average price of Chicago May Wheat last year (using December future for June and July) was 56 cents a bushel for 727,000,000 bushels grown, or $407,120,000. Now we will add 33⅓ per cent to this, which gives $542,820,000 as the proper *"parity"* or *equitable recovery price*. But the farmer had only one-half billion bushels of wheat to sell this year; so, in order to realize a return on his wheat of 33⅓ per cent over last year, the Chicago price would need to be $1.08 a bushel for the crop season of 1933–34 as compared to 56 cents for last year.

The yearly price range for the past five years has averaged 44 cents. By taking half of this range or 22 cents from $1.08, we have *86 for the bottom side of May Wheat* and $1.30 for the top side between July 15, 1933 and May 1, 1933.

In using this fifth method of forecasting I have purposely used Chicago prices in both cases. The same results would have been obtained had I used farm prices. Furthermore, I have not complicated this last price analysis by dividing farm income into its respective groups. I simply take the stand that, if factory wage is to increase a third, the farmer should get a third more for his wheat than he did a year ago; and he should also have a third more for his corn, hogs, cotton, milk, etc.

Relationship of Price to Crop

This is a bearish forecast made on August 14th, 1933.

Several years ago a Canadian brokerage house compiled a table showing that the *percentage of wheat price advance should be about four times the percentage of world crop decrease and vice versa*. This table when checked over a number of years, seemed to be fairly reliable.

Let us now take the price of wheat in Liverpool on August 9 of last year as a basis of comparison. The price of Liverpool December was then 58 cents. While I have just shown that the world wheat crop of this year might equal that of last year, I shall be conservative and assume that it will fall 200 million bushels short, according to estimates of the U. S. Department of Agriculture. This amount is approximately four per cent of a normal world wheat crop of 4,800,000,000 bushels. Multiplying this by four, we have sixteen per cent. We shall now add 16 per cent to the Liverpool price of 58 cents on August 9, 1932, which gives a logical price increase due to crop shortage of 9.3 cents. Although England was off the gold standard a year ago I am willing to add another 10 per cent to allow for the "spirit" of currency inflation rather than the actuality. This would call for an addition of 5.8 cents to the basic price.

In order to reconcile the price of wheat in Liverpool a year ago with present conditions, we shall now take 58 cents as the basic price and add 9.3 cents for crop shortage and 5.8 cents for currency inflation. This gives a price for Liverpool wheat of 73.1 cents as compared with the price on August 9, 1933 of 76 cents, when expressed in terms of inflated U. S. currency.

While it is apparent that I have added inflation in twice in performing this "operation," I am willing to do so in an effort to be conservative. This would look as though Liverpool wheat (which reflects the world market) is still four or five cents too high; but we must further assume that Liverpool wheat is now coming into the season of the year when it frequently has a major decline and seldom has a sustained advance.

Let us now look at Liverpool competitive prices, using those of July 31 which I have received direct from Liverpool. On that date No. 2 Northern Manitoba sold in Liverpool at 92¼ cents a bushel, and on that same date Argentine Baril wheat (weighing 63½ pounds per bushel) and Argentine Rosafe (weighing 64½ pounds per bushel) sold at 76 cents freight paid in Liverpool. This heavy Argentine wheat is equal in grade to No. 2 Canadian Northern, being fully as sound and heavy, although of course it does not have the strength or the bread-making qualities of Canadian spring wheat. Yet this price difference was 16 cents and, after quality is taken into consideration, indicates that Canadian wheat is fully ten cents too high to justify even one-fourth of what might be considered a normal Canadian export business. In other words Canadian wheat must quickly get in line with Russia, Argentina and other exporters or she will be left with her short crop on her hands for another year.

Therefore, after making all adjustments for theoretical rather than actual world shortage under last year, and completely ignoring the fact that world stocks are now the greatest they have ever been as of July 1 in any year, we find that Winnipeg wheat is ten cents too high compared to Liverpool and Liverpool is four or five cents too high compared to its own market in previous years. Such a course of reasoning would indicate that Winnipeg wheat is approximately 15 cents too high and that a world price-correcting decline should depress Winnipeg December Wheat to not far from the 70-cent level, which would still leave the price 9 cents higher than that of August 9, 1932.

After the story of the summer bull market in wheat is completed sometime in November by that very excellent wheat statistical service, Wheat Studies of Stanford University, California, it will probably say that—Serious crop damage in Canada and the United States so excited the speculative public in both countries that wheat prices were advanced to a level that was entirely out of keeping with supply, demand, and competitive world prices.

Regardless of what the administration may desire to accomplish for the American wheat farmer, it does not seem reasonable that Chicago December Wheat should be selling at about 15 cents over Winnipeg and 25 cents over Liverpool. This last statement applies particularly if we assume a U. S. surplus for export of 174 million bushels after allowing 125 million bushels for a normal carryover.

Those in Canada who frequently take a very discerning view of American wheat prices are very dubious about our wheat price-advancing campaign. That very excellent paper published in Winnipeg called the "Weekly Market News," which covers only grain and grain products, has this to say in its issue of August 2 :—

"If Secretary Wallace is correctly quoted, it might appear that dumping of wheat (in foreign markets) can hardly be classified as stimulating exports. Nor is it likely that domestic plans will proceed as smoothly as now anticipated. In any event, another big experiment is under way in a country that has a very large domestic consumption to fall back upon. It will be interesting to watch its progress from a detached point of view."

As far as the program at Washington is concerned, it may appear that the present administration would like for wheat prices to be maintained until farmers in the spring wheat country have had an opportunity to sell their wheat after it has been harvested. In not longer than two weeks from today this opportunity will have been offered to all farmers in the spring wheat country. After that it would seem logical that our government might be rather indifferent as to current wheat prices and devote its energies to a permanent price-lifting campaign that might extend over a four-year period rather than to exhaust most of its force in attempting to maintain current levels for the next three months.

Regardless of how you feel as to the ability or the desire of Washington to advance grain prices to higher levels, it seems that the administration should start with hogs or meat products rather than grain. Using corn as an illustration, it must be admitted by all that there is something basically unsound and economically wrong with corn selling in the market at a high price level when hogs are selling at very close to an all-time record low.

What I have just given is a forecast of a market that is now history.

CHAPTER XXII

Market Action Following Short Crops

I HAVE frequently said that the culmination of a bull market comes at a time when the crop shortage receives front page comment in our daily papers. This was true when Canada produced only half a wheat crop in 1929. The high was reached on July 29, 1929 when Chicago December sold at $1.58, and the low was made on November 13 at $1.10 which represented a decline of 47 cents a bushel. Winnipeg declined even more than Chicago in this same period.

Now let us see how the market performed following the shortest wheat crop grown in the United States since records have been kept. This was the crop of 1893 when the total wheat production in the United States was only 396 million bushels as compared with 612 million bushels produced in 1891 and 516 million bushels produced in 1892. This short crop of 1893 was considered a calamity in July and August and many market writers claimed that the people of the United States would face starvation before the season was over. It was suggested that a ban be placed on exports, which of course was not done. Dollar wheat was freely predicted.

I will now show you just what happened forty years ago to a wheat market following a period of public excitement and how speculative enthusiasm dampened as the season progressed. In July and August of 1893 May Wheat sold as high as 76⅜ cents because of repeated government statements that the supply could not measure up to the demand. Nevertheless, each month following August of 1893 May Wheat sold progressively lower until the future expired. The low in May was 52⅞ and the high was 60¼. But there is more to the story.

The visible supply on March first of 1894 following the all-time record short crop of 1893 was 75,564,000 bushels, an amount that was extremely burdensome forty years ago. It was only slightly below the then all-time record visible of 79 million bushels on March first of the year before and was more than *double* the ten-year average visible on March first. Furthermore, this major decline in wheat prices in the fall and winter of 1893 and the spring of 1894 came in the face of prospects for a rather short crop in 1894 which turned out to be only 460 million bushels. Millions were lost by speculators who had taken their first try at grain speculation.

It is also interesting to note that in 1894 we were coming out of a depression which started in 1891, the same as we are coming out of the depression now. Of course, the short crop of 1893 didn't depress wheat prices. It came as a natural aftermath to a too-great and too-rapid price advance.

Those who would like to make a further study of this short crop of 1893 which immediately preceded a major price decline in wheat should refer to page 35 of Howard Bartel's Red Book published in 1894. This can be found in many brokers' offices.

The market suggestion from this 1893 market decline is: "Don't buy wheat on crop damage after it gets in the headlines of our daily papers."

This message was also repeated in July of 1929 and again in July of 1933.

Who Gets What the Speculator Loses?

I like occasionally to write on this subject because it has a direct bearing on the length of bear markets as I shall show in an article which was written in August, 1933.

I will now make the dogmatic statement that generally speaking the farmer profits by what the speculator loses over a term of years. This applies particularly to a major bear market that takes place immediately after crops are harvested. For example, from July 7th to July 27th September Wheat sold at an average price of $1.08 and in this period the farmers of the wheat belt sold approximately 150,000,000 bushels of wheat at an average price of 97 cents at the country station. After the farmers had sold their wheat, the market declined approximately 30 cents a bushel, which means that farmers received about $45,000,000, which loss had to be stood by some other group. Probably not over one-tenth of this 150,000,000 bushels of wheat sold at the high prices of July was bought by millers or other actual users of wheat. This loss was sustained almost entirely by speculators who bought wheat so close to the July top that as a group they lost approximately 27 cents a bushel. The loss by the speculators may all have been taken on one single trade or it may have averaged through a dozen trades, but that is beside the point.

Now let us assume a hypothetical case that has never happened, which is that wheat and other grains advance from a low price level to a high price level and *remain permanently at that high price level.* In such a case speculators who bought as the market advanced, took an additional profit that the grower of grain failed to obtain. But in such a case the farmers did not lose what speculators made; they just failed to obtain the top price; in fact, speculation made and supported the market.

We will now examine the mechanics of a major bear market and see just where the profits and losses are allotted. For the past three months the speculative long interest has been about five times the amount of the speculative short interest. Approximately 80 per cent of the short interest was not speculative at all but represented short sales of the futures against actual cash holdings of grain in mills and terminal warehouses.

The cash grain trade prefers to make many *small merchandising profits that are certain regardless of the course of the market* rather than to work for a larger speculative profit that might be entirely lost. Therefore, they continue to sell the futures at a higher price than they pay for the cash grain. The grain that is purchased is warehoused and later delivered on a short sale of September or December Wheat and thus the trade is completed.

Now let me make myself clear. I do not claim that all the money lost by grain speculators *who are wrong* goes into the pockets of the producer. It is only the *difference* between what is *lost* and what is *made* in speculative grain trading that finds its way into the pockets of the farmer.

Let us assume that a billion dollars is lost in five years by grain traders who are poor traders and that three quarters of a billion dollars is made by grain traders who are clever or perhaps just fortunate. The difference of a quarter billion dollars over that five-year period must go to the farmer since it did not go to the cash grain trade, which operates on the smallest margin of profit of any group of buyers dealing in any class of commodities or merchandise. Neither does it go to the broker whose fee of $12.50 for 5,000 bushels of grain bought and sold is a small charge for the grain merchandising service he renders. This net loss of $250,000,000 just had to go to the farmer because there was no other group in a position to take it.

Selling Cash Grain at Harvest Time

Early in July when bullish enthusiasm was advancing the futures, and receipts of both corn and wheat were running ten to twenty times the sales to mills, feeders and other actual consumers, some of my trader friends in the markets who are not familiar with the mechanics of marketing wondered who bought the wheat, corn and oats that arrived in such vast quantities.

The man who is long the futures buys the actual grain, as I shall show. He buys it without knowing he has done so.

Let us assume that John Smith and Company are track

buyers of corn in Chicago and know corn grades from A to Z. They bought Number Two Mixed Corn on Tuesday, July 18 for 62¾ cents, which they probably delivered on a September contract for 70¾ cents. They did this by selling September Corn short the minute the purchase was made. Nothing else was necessary to complete the trade. The grain was then stored for seven weeks at a cost of three cents and delivered on September 1. The grain that cost 62¾ cents is sold for 70¾ cents the moment it is purchased, and the net profit after paying the storage is 5 cents a bushel regardless of how the market acts. Such wide premiums in the futures over the cash occur only in wild bull markets and are real danger signals.

In a declining market a dozen speculators may take their turn at owning the September Corn and each may take a loss or some may lose and some may gain; but the *final holder* sometime after September first will *own the actual corn at some price.*

Then John Smith and Company may choose to buy back the actual corn delivered in September and sell the December at a wide premium over September and store the corn and deliver it again on a December contract. Obviously the man who is short grain futures without owning the actual grain for delivery must buy in his short future sale at *some price* and take his profit or loss, but the cash grain handler need only deliver the actual grain that he bought at a lower price than he sold the future. Smith's trade is completed when he sells short what he has in storage; he has nothing to buy back since he has filled his contract.

The fact that cash grain houses were buying cash grain on July 17, 18, and 19 at the biggest discount below the futures that has been seen in years was a strong argument in favor of a decline in grain futures, since the cash and the futures could not continue to remain so far apart.

CHAPTER XXIII

The Safety of Funds with the Broker

FOR more than ten years I have claimed that margin money left with a broker who is a member of the New York Stock Exchange is more secure and easier to obtain on demand than when deposited with the average bank. This also applies to funds of five thousand dollars or more that are left in a customer's stock account to draw the prevailing call-money interest rate. Past events have more than verified the correctness of my statement.

Except for the period from March 4 to March 14, any and all funds left with brokers who are members of the New York Stock Exchange have been paid to customers on demand, except of course that part which was required to margin open trades. In the above-mentioned ten-day period, a New York Stock Exchange ruling was made prohibiting brokers who were members of this exchange to pay balances to customers until the leading banks of the country opened. This ruling has now been lifted and customers have access to all funds left with their brokers that are not needed for margin purposes.

Brokerage houses that are members of the New York Stock Exchange are more conservative financial institutions than even the best of banks because the rules that govern their actions are more severe and more exacting than are the rules of the Federal Reserve banks which govern the action of member banks. For example, no broker is permitted to lend the funds of customers unless these funds can be loaned on listed stocks and bonds. In the event these securities used as collateral depreciate in value to the extent that the loan is endangered, the broker is required to sell the securities in order to protect the loans he has made.

Banks are not held to such rigid requirements. Under no circumstance is a broker who is a member of the New York Stock Exchange permitted to speculate with the funds of his customers. This has not always been the case with banks. If a member desires to make speculative commitments in the market, he is required to use his own funds, the same as you or I.

In the past, many of our largest banks, (particularly those in New York City) have seen fit to speculate with millions of dollars that belong to depositors. Furthermore, many banks have seen fit to reap large profits by urging depositors to buy South American bonds and other bonds that have since gone bad. As far as I know, no member of the New York Stock Exchange has ever been guilty of asking a customer to buy unlisted securities and most brokerage houses hesitate to make any specific recommendations whatsoever regarding individual stocks. A brokerage house can collect all money due it on demand, which is not true of banks. Because of the jealous guardianship and supervision of the New York Stock Exchange over its members, it naturally follows that the houses of broker members are the most liquid of all financial institutions. When rated on the basis of safety, they stand far ahead of banks and life insurance companies when considered as a whole.

From 1931 to 1933 there have been only six failures of New York Stock Exchange members and with but two exceptions, these failures have not been important houses. In this same period of time, over half the banks in the United States have gone into permanent receivership. It naturally follows as a logical conclusion that funds left with a New York Stock Exchange brokerage house are safeguarded to an unusual degree.

Just What Is Speculation

Every wage earner, every producer of capital, is a speculator whether he would be or not. We must speculate on how we are to make our income, and after we have made it, we must speculate on how we are to keep it where it will be safe until it is needed. Speculation is just another name for intelligent assumption of risks.

Now, most of my friends who are out and out speculators frankly admit the fact, as opposed to that so-called investment class who would like to think that they take no speculative risks. By all the time-honored yardsticks of financial measurement these out and out speculators should have failed in the last two years of declining stocks and grain futures, and those who invest only for a six per cent return should have their capital intact. But such has not been the case. As a matter of fact, very few of my old speculator friends have lost *all* they had, yet every speculator I know of has less in 1933 than he had in 1929. On the other hand, millions of people who never meant to risk a dime have lost their lifetime savings in the four years following 1929.

Many of my very close friends who look with horror on so-called speculation have lost all they had through the failure of banks, building and loan associations, and defaulted bonds, where they had their savings invested; or else they have failed through the decline in farm lands and city real estate. This doesn't seem quite fair since those who never asked more than a six per cent return certainly had a moral claim to safety of principal.

The question arises, "Is speculation as hazardous as some forms of so-called investment?"

The investing and saving class have lost heavily through a "speculation" and too great a trust in time-honored financial institutions in which capital appreciation of property was not even a part of their financial program. W. G. Sibley, in the March 24th, 1933 issue of the Chicago Journal of Commerce, admits that "where to put savings" is a delicate subject.

I have this much to say. When I want to save a little

money and know I can get it when I need it, I prefer an old brokerage house that has weathered many a financial storm, to the average bank; and right now I should prefer it to any building and loan association, no matter how honest and capable has been the management. I should prefer having money permanently invested in American Tobacco or Coca Cola stock (and I have some in each) rather than having it invested in ten of the best first mortgage real estate bonds in the United States. Postal Saving certificates are good investments for $2,500.00 (or less) that may be needed on demand.

When I invest for safe-keeping, I want to know that I am not speculating. Seven per cent return with some risk to my capital never looked good to me. I prefer to speculate on "doubles or quits" rather than to risk capital to obtain seven per cent when by no risk whatsoever I can get two to three per cent. But, I haven't told you what speculation really is. Here is the classic definition—

Any contract to purchase or sell goods or shares by which either or both parties may gain or lose is speculation. So, I shall now select an ideal speculation that is not permanently disturbed by bank failures, insurrections, or government politics, and to which cannot be attached the stigma of hoarding.

I might buy ten bars of silver at 29 cents an ounce and bury it on a farm, leaving a note to my estate in a safe deposit box stating where the silver is buried. In case of insurrection, I would destroy the note before my lock box was discovered. No matter what happens, I still have that silver at a price that will undoubtedly stand up, and in five years it may double or treble in market value. The silver will not corrode; and closed banks, burglars, insurrections, high taxes, or what not will not disturb my secret. Of course I would be speculating, because I hoped and expected my metal to advance in price. But I would be taking little risk because I bought far below the cost of production.

Now, as a matter of course, I have never bought an ounce of metal as a speculation in my lifetime. I prefer to take a greater risk for a greater and quicker profit in wheat futures. But the silver illustration shows us a safe and sound *speculation*. If such a deal shows a profit, no other person takes an offsetting loss because of my purchase, since I buy when the world has more silver than it knows what to do with, and so little gold that it is hard to keep on a gold standard. When I buy silver I am exchanging much-needed gold (or its equivalent in currency) for silver that is not needed, and we might also add—not wanted.

Now, strange as it may seem, this imaginary purchase of silver which would be an out and out speculation is far safer for a ten-year long pull trade than 99 per cent of investments that cannot at best yield more than a low rate of interest. In any case, I still have my silver, but in buying *debt* obligations like bank savings certificates, bonds, and building and loan shares, I stand a chance of eventually owning only pieces of paper that have no value.

The above article appeared in Ainsworth's Financial Service in March of 1932. Since then silver has advanced and thousands of financial institutions closed their doors. Under present conditions I consider a savings account in a good bank as an ideal investment.

(The Above Article Was Published in 1932)

CHAPTER XXIV

Qualifications for Successful Trading

FIRST AND FOREMOST, the Trader must have money, but a "Cub Trader" with a capital of $1000 is just as well protected as the Trader with a capital of $30,000, if he trades within his modest means. Don't forget all Traders were first small Traders before they became big Traders. Don't venture beyond your depth. Remember no chain is stronger than its weakest link. Don't overtrade. Sometimes you will have a big paper loss when your profits are just around the corner. If you have overtraded you cannot ride out the loss. Do not force your broker to call on you for margin. Send it to him before he asks you for it, or better still keep it with him all the time.

Remember the small Trader is not a piker; he is a business man who is trying to conserve his capital, while on the other hand, the plunger is a gambler. Your broker wants you to make money and for that reason he will also advise you not to overtrade.

Second, the Trader must have an abundance of patience. He should realize that half of the time grain is neither a purchase nor a sale, as far as he is concerned. He is either waiting for an opportune time to buy, or he is waiting for an opportune time to sell. Only a few have the necessary patience to wait out their market. To trade all the time or to make a trade every week is a gamble in which the Trader cannot expect as much as an even break. There are some pit Traders (who pay no commission) who can take advantage of situations which arise on the floor of the Exchange itself. But "eighth chasing" is not for you or for me.

At times I have spent as much as three months trying to buy our line of May Wheat at a price I considered profitable and then occasionally I have had to do without it. That calls for patience.

It is my earnest desire that all new Traders start in as "Cub Traders" and gradually grow into bigger Traders as their capital increases. In this way there is little to lose and everything to gain. It will take a few years longer to reach a given goal but what of it? It will be worth just that much more when once it is attained. If some unexpected chain of events should cause you to lose, there is some satisfaction in being able to say "I have lost only what I had made."

The element of time and successful trading go hand in hand the same as in other business. They cannot be divorced. So do not let paper profits or paper losses keep you awake nights.

Successful grain trading is hard work and it is not a get-rich-quick business. You *must* go slow and that takes time. I spent twenty years getting what I have and I don't intend losing it, if hard work, patience and conservative trading can prevent it.

If you expect to get rich quick at grain trading, you are going to be disappointed. I have met most of the big grain Traders and they are men of middle age or past, and what is more, they are business men who never expected to get rich in one year. Don't expect to get something for nothing.

James J. Hill, the empire builder, said, "A new force is born into the world when a man has saved his first thousand dollars for investment."

This brings us up to the point of thrift, because only the thrifty can keep money and money is a necessary part of successful trading. If you spend your profits you will never be a big Trader. The same factors, which make for success in farming or merchandising, are required in the field of investment and speculation. Success in any field of endeavor, calls for work, thought, self-denial and sacrifice.

Chapter XXV

Mistakes Made in Grain Trading

THERE are but few who are willing to submit to the discipline or to undergo the toil essential to success in speculation.

Some of the most common mistakes made may be summarized briefly as follows:

Buying when the price level is too high. Eleventh hour bulls.

Overtrading—Trading on insufficient capital, and forgetting that the successful trader must be a financier, and help to finance the movement of the crop.

Depending on market telegrams—The grain market is not so fast that successful traders require a daily telegram.

Trading on weather reports.

Trading on crop prospects and ignoring other factors.

Taking profits when the prospects are still bullish.

Taking small profits.

Making too many trades.

Trading in one grain only, or in one future only, **and** trading in but one market.

Over-enthusiasm—Remember every market has two sides. You are not always right.

Refusing to take delivery under any circumstances, **by** always selling out before the first of the delivery **month.** Buying in the more distant futures when the discount **for** the nearby future is unreasonably wide.

Constant Shifting from one future to another.

Reversing the Position, which usually means getting "whip-sawed" in the market.

CHAPTER XXVI

Market Factors

REDUCED to its lowest terms, the action of any organized commodity market includes only three basic factors, which are:

    (1)   Price Level
    (2)   Element of Time
    (3)   Volume of Trading

The above is technically correct. It is the way the subject is presented in Economics. However, the grain trader will get a clearer picture of the factors which make up a grain futures market if he will think of the market in terms of

(1) PRICE LEVEL
{ Supply and Demand
Cost of Production
Acreage

(2) SEASONAL TRENDS
{ Accelerated, offset and sometimes reversed by weather and Crop News

(3) VOLUME
{ And the effect it has in Producing wide or narrow price fluctuations

These factors of price level, seasonal trends and volume of trading, have an important bearing on the future action of the market, but there is not room in this book to analyze this correlation.

I refer the reader to Brookmire's Chart *"Wheat Production to Price"* which illustrates this correlation; also to *"Risk and Risk Bearing"* by Hardy, pages 157 to 236; *"Principles of Economics"* by Seager, pages 263 to 300; *"Principles of Economics"* by Taussig, pages 109 to 195 and pages 285 to 303; *"Speculation—Its Sound Principles and Rules for Its Practice"* by Thomas Temple Hoyne, (read the whole book); *"The Art of Speculation"* by

Philip L. Carret; *"The Value of Organized Speculation"*
by Brace, pages 50 to 96; *"Myself and Fellow Asses"* by
Hoyne, pages 217, 218, 219. For a very simple well-
written chapter on the *"Forces and Conditions Which Determine Grain Prices"* read Chapter VIII of *"Agricultural
Economics"* by Taylor. *"Marketing Agricultural Products"* by B. H. Hibbard, pages 171 to 180. Every grain
trader should read *"The Pit"* and *"The Octopus"* by Frank
Norris. The Norris books are just interesting novels
which feature the trader, the producer and the consumer.
They are not Economics, but they are good reading.

All the above books, and hundreds like them may be
obtained from The Dixie Business Book Shop, 140 Green-
wich Street, New York, N. Y.

Individual Factors Affecting Price

World Crop. World Demand. U. S. Crop. U. S. Demand. Canadian Crop. Farm Reserves. Visible Supply.
Hog Population. Volume of Futures Trading. Wide or
narrow price range in determining probable price field.
Seasonal trends. Condition of national prosperity. Rela-
tion of cash prices to futures. Comparison of prices in
different markets. Quality of U. S. crop compared with
average world quality. Note: In spite of many opinions
to the contrary good quality is bullish and poor quality is
bearish.

Chapter XXVII

Increasing the Risk

IF THE Cub Trader will trade in quantities not to exceed four times as many bushels as he has dollars, and if the margin of from twenty-five cents to fifty cents per bushel is never used up (and the consecutiveness broken off—see note), and if I can make an average yearly profit of twelve and a half cents a bushel for my efforts in each of four futures, the goal should be realized. Yet there is not one chance in a million that this goal would be reached. There are too many "ifs" in the road. This table reminds me of a certain book issued by a bond house which said, "Retire in 15 years on your present living budget." It didn't "pan" out.

Except for 1930 to 1932, my average net gains have been over twelve and a half cents a bushel per year in each future. In fact they have been nearly twelve and a half cents per trade and many trades are often made in one grain future in a year.

In order to reach the above goal, it would be necessary for many factors to work out right, and most important, it would be necessary at all times for the trader to have practically all of his profits in the enterprise.

I also warn the trader that by following a progressive plan of speculation, his capital will be well eaten into on more than one occasion. (Look at my profits by years as shown on page 23—you will see that I did not increase my quantities after I got into the thirty thousand bushel class in each of three or four futures. Now, I am risking in the market only a small part of what I made there.

The above plan if it succeeded, would require an average return of fifty per cent each year on an ever-increasing capital.

The Table below shows how your capital would increase on a fifty per cent return, beginning with a capital of $1,000. (Of course, in speculation the percent of return would be very uneven by years, but if the average was fifty percent over a number of years the result, in the end, would be the same as shown in the following table:

End of first year...$	1,500.00	End of tenth year...$57,664.99	
End of second year..	2,250.00	End of eleventh year 86,497.48	
End of third year..	3,375.00	End of twelfth year. 129,746.22	
End of fourth year.	5,062.50	End of thirteenth	
End of fifth year...	7,593.75	year 194,619.33	
End of sixth year..	11,390.62	End of fourteenth	
End of seventh year.	17,085.93	year 291,928.99	
End of eighth year.	25,628.89	End of fifteenth year 437,893.48	
End of ninth year..	38,443.33		

The success of nearly all great business organizations has been the result of a steady policy of progressive expansion. Also a large number of big failures since 1929 have been due to this same policy.

The trader should not forget that to increase quantities means to incur additional risks. However, the Cub Trader, which is my name for the man with only $1000.00 he can risk, should increase his quantities slightly each year as his capital increases. Do not mistake me to mean pyramiding grain trades with paper profits. Both are ambitious policies, but the former has real merit and the latter absolutely none.

NOTE: In my last seventeen years of trading, there were two occasions when I required over twenty-five cents per bushel to margin any trades. These years were most of 1921 and July of 1933. I took the short of the market too soon in July, 1933.

Chapter XXVIII

Conservative Trading

I LIKE to trade in conservative quantities and by so doing I never have any big worries when I go to bed at night. I like to be on one side of the market and not be short one future and long another. I am determined to carry on year in and year out and be able to survive three bad trades in a row if called upon to do so. In fact, I have had that unpleasant experience on two occasions in twenty-five years when it was necessary for me to carry through three loss trades in succession before I came into a trade showing a profit.

I have met most of the big successful grain traders in my time. As a whole they impress me as being a bit old-fashioned, which is a valuable trading quality. These veteran traders all know something of the principles of banking and a lot about the merchandising of cash grain. At least half of them own from one to a dozen farms and many of the older traders are top-notch farmers. While no two traders use precisely the same methods, they do seem to have many of the same traits in common. One impressive quality is that after accumulating grain at low prices, they do not set a definite price at which to close out their trades, but stand aside and watch the public buy until the market looks top heavy. Then after the first big collapse, which marks the beginning of most bear markets, these experienced traders sell out and stand aside, allowing several weeks or months for the market to regain its equilibrium before again taking the long side. Another trait of most successful traders is that they will carry their trades into a tremendous loss if they are convinced all the time that they are right in their position. I think this applied particularly to James A. Patten whom I wish were living today to have a hand in this market. Another trait which most of the successful traders show to a more or less degree is the patience to hang on to a trade month after month through all the minor ups and downs. Possibly they will pass up a profit of 30 cents a bushel and end up by taking 15 or 20 cents, and be happy in the fact that the trade at least yielded a worthwhile profit. Since successful speculation can never be a game of doubles or quits, the veteran trader who has made and retained his fortune in the commodity market is always a man who is careful not to be long or short more bushels than he can comfortably margin.

CHAPTER XXIX

My Trades for 1933

THE trades as shown below and on the following page were, with only two exceptions, made without the use of stops. The purpose and need for the grain speculator is to come into the market on the buying side and halt a decline. If he uses stops that are quickly caught, he has rendered little service except excitement and enthusiasm which some writers claim helps to make a market. A study of the trades below should convince any man who remembers the market of 1933 that trades such as these tend to narrow the range by supporting the market on the bottom side and checking it on the top side. One hundred cub traders with one thousand dollars each and trading in job lots will help to finance a crop just as effectively as the trader with one hundred thousand dollars who trades in one thousand bushel lots.

The following is the complete list of my own trades for a twelve month period, except for four efforts to take a short position at times when I was afraid to make short sales without the use of "stops". The "stops" were placed one cent away from the short sales with the result that four cents was lost, that is not included in the list as itemized below.

A Complete List of All Trades Made in the Past Year

Oct. 6, 1932 Bought May Wheat at............$ .55
April 10, 1933 Sold May Wheat at............. .57⅝
    (A long position) Profit.................   .02⅝
April 10, 1933 Bought Sept. Wheat............ .59⅝
April 19, 1933 Sold Sept. Wheat.............. .70
    (A long position) Profit.................   .10⅜
March 16, 1933 Bought July Wheat........... .53⅞
April 19, 1933 Sold July Wheat............... .68¼
    (A long position) Profit.................   .14⅜
May 13, 1933 Bought Dec. Wheat............. .78
June 30, 1933 Sold Dec. Wheat............... .93½
    (A long position) Profit.................   .15½

May 13, 1933 Bought Sept. Oats	$ .27⅛		
June 30, 1933 Sold Sept. Oats	.42⅝		
(A long position) Profit			.15½
May 13, 1933 Bought Dec. Corn	.51¼		
June 30, 1933 Sold Dec. Corn	.58⅜		
(A long position) Profit			.07⅛
June 30, 1933 Sold Dec. Wheat	.93½		
August 17, 1933 Bought in at	.85¾		
(A short sale) Profit			.07¾
July 19, 1933 Sold Dec. Wheat at	1.13½		
August 17, 1933 Bought in at	.89⅞		
(A short sale) Profit			.23⅝
July 24, 1933 Sold Dec. Wheat at	1.02		
August 17, 1933 Bought in at	.89⅞		
(A short sale) Profit			.12⅛
July 10, 1933 Sold May Corn at	.73¼		
August 21, 1933 Bought in at	.63⅜		
(A short sale) Profit			.09⅞
June 30, 1933 Sold Dec. Corn at	.58⅜		
August 21, 1933 Bought in at	.56		
(A short sale) Profit			.02⅜
August 17, 1933 Bought May Wheat at	.89⅞		
Sept. 25, 1933 Sold May Wheat at	.96		
(A long position) Profit			.06⅛
Oct. 6, 1933 Bought May Wheat at	.90		
Oct. 19, 1933 Sold May Wheat at	.79⅝		
(A long position) Loss		.10⅜	
Oct. 4, 1933 Bought May Corn at	.53		
Oct. 30, 1933 Sold May Corn at	.53½		
(A long position) Profit			.00½
Oct. 16, 1933 Bought July Wheat at	.76⅝		
Oct. 30, 1933 Sold July Wheat at	.90		
(A long position) Profit			.13⅜
Oct. 16, 1933 Bought July Corn at	.48¼		
Oct. 30, 1933 Sold July Corn at	.55¼		
(A long position) Profit			.07
Oct. 18, 1933 Bought May Wheat at	.81⅝		
Oct. 30, 1933 Sold May Wheat at	.92¾		
(A long position) Profit			.11⅛
Oct. 21, 1933 Bought May Wheat at	.85		
Oct. 30, 1933 Sold May Wheat at	.92¾		
(A long position) Profit			.07¾
Oct. 30, 1933 Sold May Wheat at	.92¾		
Nov. 1, 1933 Bought in at	.85⅛		
(A short sale) Profit			.07⅝
Gains per bushel on Profit Trades for Year			$1.74¾
Losses on all Loss Trades			.14⅜
Net Gains per bushel over Losses			$1.60⅜

Chapter XXX

Some Interesting Wheat Figures

	Low price in March	Range for three months	High price in May
1933	$ .46½	$ .46½ @ .73¼	$ .73¼
1932	.52	.52 @ .62⅛	.60⅜
1931	.81¼	.81¼ @ .86¼	.86¼
1930	1.05¾	1.00 @ 1.16¾	1.08½
1929	1.18	.93¼ @ 1.31⅞	1.14½
1928	1.33⅞	1.33⅞ @ 1.71½	1.70
1927	1.31½	1.30¾ @ 1.56¾	1.56¾
1926	1.58⅜	1.50 @ 1.71½	1.71½
1925	1.40½	1.36½ @ 1.74¼	1.74¼
1924	1.00¼	1.00¼ @ 1.06¾	1.06¾
1923	1.16¼	1.11½ @ 1.27¼	1.23⅞
1922	1.28½	1.16 @ 1.49⅛	1.47½
1921	1.37½	1.19½ @ 1.87	1.87
1920	Only trading was in Dec., $1.50½ @ $1.64½		
1918–19	Trading Suspended		
1917	1.75¾	1.75¾ @ 3.25	3.25
1916	1.05⅞	1.04 @ 1.21½	1.18
1915	1.35¾	1.35¾ @ 1.65½	1.64
1914	.90⅝	.90⅛ @ 1.00	1.00
1913	.88⅛	.88⅛ @ .93⅜	.92¾
1912	1.00⅝	1.00⅝ @ 1.19	1.19
1911	.85¾	.84⅜ @ 1.04¾	1.04¾
1910	1.10⅛	.93½ @ 1.16¼	1.16¼
1909	1.12⅜	1.12⅜ @ 1.35¼	1.35¼
1908	.92	.89 @ 1.11	1.11
1907	.74⅝	.74⅝ @ 1.00¼	1.00¼
1906	.76¼	.76¼ @ .86¾	.86¾
1905	1.09	.86½ @ 1.18¾	1.07
1904	.90¾	.85½ @ 1.01½	1.01½
1903	.71½	.71½ @ .80⅝	.80⅝
1902	.70½	.70½ @ .78¼	.78¼
1901	.74⅝	.69⅝ @ .77⅝	.75⅛
1900	.64⅝	.63½ @ .68¼	.66⅝
1899	.66⅜	.66⅜ @ .78	.78
1898	1.01½	1.01½ @ 1.85	1.85
1897	.70⅛	.64½ @ .78	.76

The table on the preceding page exhibits the lowest prices for May Wheat during month of March for the past thirty years, compared with the extreme range during March, April and May and the highest prices during May.

CHAPTER XXXI

Corn Tables

Table Showing Date of the First Killing Frost in Autumn

FALL OF	Chicago, Ill.	Spring-field, Ill.	Des Moines, Ia.	Dubuque, Ia.	Omaha, Neb.	Kansas City, Mo.	Yankton, S. D.	La Crosse, Wis.	St. Paul, Minn.
1932	Nov. 11	Oct. 11	Oct. 13	Oct. 6	Oct. 26	Oct. 26	Oct. 21	Oct. 6	Oct. 12
1931	Nov. 24	Nov. 6	Nov. 4	Nov. 6	Nov. 1	Nov. 6	Nov. 1	Oct. 17	Nov. 2
1930	Oct. 18	Oct. 18	Oct. 17	Oct. 17	Oct. 17	Oct. 17	Oct. 17	Oct. 17	Oct. 16
1929	Nov. 4	Oct. 25	Oct. 25	Oct. 23	Oct. 23	Nov. 15	Oct. 21	Sept. 18	Sept. 18
1928	Sept. 26	Sept. 26	Sept. 26	Oct. 26	Oct. 29	Nov. 3	Sept. 25	Sept. 26	Sept. 26
1927	Nov. 4	Oct. 14	Oct. 14	Oct. 14	Nov. 6	Oct. 6	Oct. 31	Oct. 14	Oct. 9
1926	Oct. 26	Oct. 25	Sept. 26	Sept. 26	Oct. 24	Oct. 24	Sept. 24	Sept. 26	Sept. 25
1925	Oct. 10	Oct. 10	Oct. 9	Oct. 10	Oct. 9	Oct. 10	Oct. 9	Oct. 10	Oct. 10
1924	Nov. 9	Oct. 23	Sept. 30	Oct. 22	Nov. 6	Nov. 8	Sept. 29	Sept. 30	Sept. 30
1923	Oct. 30	Oct. 21	Oct. 20	Oct. 20	Oct. 20	Oct. 21	Oct. 20	Sept. 13	Sept. 19
1922	Nov. 15	Oct. 18	Oct. 12	Oct. 18	Oct. 12	Oct. 17	Oct. 12	Oct. 12	Oct. 9
1921	Nov. 10	Nov. 2	Oct. 8	Nov. 2	Nov. 8	Rec. not filed	Nov. 1	Oct. 4	Nov. 1
1920	Oct. 29	Oct. 29	Oct. 1	Oct. 27	Oct. 28	Oct. 27	Sept. 30	Oct. 1	Oct. 25
1919	Oct. 29	Nov. 2	Oct. 17	Oct. 28	Oct. 11	Oct. 17	Oct. 10	Oct. 11	Oct. 11
1918	Nov. 2	Nov. 1	Oct. 20	Oct. 25	Oct. 28	Nov. 1	Sept. 19	Sept. 21	Oct. 3
1917	Oct. 8	Oct. 6	Sept. 6	Oct. 6	Oct. 8	Oct. 12	Oct. 8	Sept. 10	Oct. 6
1916	Oct. 22	Oct. 11	Sept. 29	Oct. 10	Sept. 8	Sept. 29	Sept. 8	Sept. 29	Oct. 10
1915	Oct. 9	Oct. 9	Oct. 9	Oct. 9	Sept. 9	Nov. 9	Oct. 5	Oct. 9	Oct. 9
1914	Oct. 27	Oct. 27	Oct. 25	Oct. 27	Oct. 27	Oct. 27	Oct. 15	Oct. 27	Oct. 27
1913	Oct. 21	Oct. 21	Sept. 22	Oct. 21	Oct. 20	Oct. 20	Sept. 22	Oct. 18	Sept. 18
1912	Oct. 24	Nov. 2	Sept. 26	Oct. 23	Oct. 22	Nov. 1	Sept. 27	Oct. 23	Sept. 27
1911	Oct. 24	Nov. 1	Oct. 22	Oct. 24	Oct. 23	Nov. 4	Oct. 20	Oct. 24	Oct. 22

Monthly Farm Marketing of Crops
10-Year Average 1918–1927 (Percent Monthly)

	Corn	Wheat	Oats	Barley	Rye	Flaxseed	Hay
July	5.9	14.3	9.9	12.2	6.8	2.2	7.6
August	6.4	17.9	18.9	17.1	17.2	7.2	8.8
September	6.6	16.9	13.2	16.9	18.7	23.0	8.4
October	6.0	12.9	10.1	12.1	14.6	27.0	10.0
November	9.2	8.9	6.6	7.8	9.8	14.7	10.3
December	12.9	6.4	6.8	6.6	8.1	7.5	9.4
January	13.5	5.1	7.1	5.5	6.4	4.2	9.0
February	11.0	4.2	6.3	4.4	5.0	3.3	7.9
March	8.4	3.4	5.5	4.4	4.5	3.0	8.4
April	6.0	3.1	4.7	3.4	3.3	2.1	7.7
May	7.1	3.4	5.4	4.0	2.8	2.3	6.4
June	7.0	3.5	5.5	5.6	2.8	3.5	6.1

Merchantable Corn Crop

The Department of Agriculture gave the following report of the yield of Corn and proportion merchantable in the years named:

Year Crop Grown	Crop, Bu.	Per Cent Merchantable	Merchantable, Bu.
1933	2,908,045,000	....	....
1932	2,556,900,000	84.3	2,165,466,000
1931	2,060,200,000	78.9	1,625,497,000
1930	2,614,100,000	77.0	2,019,094,000
1929	2,819,901,000	83.1	2,360,000,000
1928	2,786,000,000	78.0	2,090,340,000
1927	2,645,031,000	71.1	1,880,617,000
1926	2,916,961,000	78.8	2,278,565,000
1925	2,309,414,000	66.0	1,524,213,000
1924	3,053,557,000	80.8	2,462,000,000
1923	2,906,020,000	88.3	2,553,290,000
1922	3,068,569,000	87.5	2,684,634,000
1921	3,230,532,000	86.9	2,789,720,000
1920	2,816,318,000	87.1	2,448,204,000
1919	2,502,665,000	82.4	2,062,041,000
1918	3,065,233,000	60.0	1,837,728,000
1917	2,566,927,000	83.9	2,154,487,000
1916	2,994,793,000	71.1	2,127,965,000
1915	2,672,800,000	84.5	2,259,755,000
1914	2,446,988,000	80.1	1,961,058,000
1913	3,124,746,000	85.0	2,654,907,000
1912	2,531,488,000	80.1	2,027,922,000
1911	2,886,260,000	86.4	2,492,763,000
1910	2,552,190,000	82.5	2,104,775,000
1909	....	....	....

CHAPTER XXXII

Statistical Sources

THE farther a man goes in the analysis of price, the greater becomes his need for statistics.

In grain forecasting, I make frequent reference to "Wheat Studies" published by Stanford University, Cal.; Broomhall's "Corn Trade News" published in Liverpool, England; "Sanford Evans' Statistical Service" published in Winnipeg; Henri Bodenheimer's "Bulletin" published in Paris; "Bulletin de Halles" published in Paris; "Bennett's News"; Nat C. Murray's "Grain Review"; U. S. Department of Agricultural Economics, "Price Forecasts"; "Russell's Review"; Howard Bartel's "Daily Trade Bulletin"; Bartel's "Red Book Annuals" and Ainsworth's Financial Service Daily Price Range Wheat and Corn Charts.

The "Chicago Journal of Commerce" is used for stocks and bonds, as well as grain and other commodities. In cotton forecasting I refer more to "Commerce and Finance", 95 Broad Street, New York, than to any other publication. In determining real estate trends, I rely mostly on "The Economist" published in Chicago. Some books that have been of greatest help and interest in grain trading are "Commercial Commodities" by Matthews and "The Cotton Market" by Hubbard; "The Value of Organized Speculation" by Brace; "Risk and Risk Bearing" by Hardy; The Annual Reports of the Chicago Board of Trade, (large green bound volumes) ; "The Year Books of the U. S. Department of Agriculture" which are furnished by your congressman for the asking.

CHAPTER XXXIII

A Review of the World Wheat Situation

I AM giving this review just as it appeared at the close of 1933. This article is now out of date and is given only as an example of how a world wheat survey is covered. Much of this material was obtained from "Wheat Studies," Stanford University, California.

Wheat Price Lifting Legislation

All the major wheat exporting countries of the world are working on plans which they hope in due time will so reduce the supply and increase the demand as to bring about a price level that will be *not far below the five year average of 1912 to 1916 inclusive.* Such a price, when expressed in terms of gold dollars, would be $1.14 a bushel or $1.48 a bushel in United States inflated currency on the basis of 70 cent dollars. It may of course take several years to reach this objective.

International agreements which are working to reduce the world wheat supply were tentatively concluded late in August. About that same time the American press claimed an agreement had been reached by the twenty-two participating nations. The plan included:

1. A relaxing of import restrictions and control of uses of import, including tariffs as prices rise.
2. Encouraging domestic consumption.
3. It would discourage further expansion of domestic wheat acreage.

The United States and Canada favor a policy of acreage reduction, which is already being attempted in the United States. Argentina and Australia favor a plan of diverting surplus wheat to non-food uses such as the manufacture of motor fuel, etc. Tentative export quotas for year ending July 31, 1934 were allocated as follows:

1. Canada maximum exports not over 200,000,000 bushels.
2. Argentina maximum exports not over 110,000,000 bushels.
3. Australia maximum exports not over 105,000,000 bushels.
4. United States maximum exports not over 47,-000,000 bushels.
5. Danube countries maximum exports not over 52,-000,000 bushels.

This allocation of exports will be a powerful force for higher wheat prices in the coming winter months if it is rigorously enforced by all countries in a mutual effort to attain a higher price level. As it is there are so many "ifs" and "ands" in the plan that I doubt very much if the export quotas will be a major price lifting factor before July 1st of next year. Those who are enthusiastic over this plan to advance wheat prices, call attention to the actual exports from the four major wheat exporting countries in the year ending July, 1933, which were materially higher than the tentative quotas stated above. In the crop year that just closed, Canada exported 263,000,-000 bushels of wheat; Australia exported 105,000,000 bushels; Argentina exported 131,000,000 bushels, and the United States exported 36,000,000 bushels.

By making a comparison of past performances and contemplated allotments, it looks like the United States is favored, but the joker lies in the fact that the United States will do well to export 30,000,000 bushels of wheat unless we can get our prices more nearly in line with the prices of other countries.

I shall now cover in the briefest manner possible the wheat price supporting policies of some of the major wheat importing countries, which by encouraging home production, have resulted in raising the price in home markets. On the other hand, these same policies have been prime forces in curtailing the demand for imported wheat from the principal exporting nations.

The Wheat Policy of France

Governmental measures in France have been very effective in causing their native wheats to sell at a price far above the price of exporting countries. Not once in the past year has home-grown French wheat declined below one dollar in terms of United States currency and the average price of wheat for the month of July was $1.75 as compared to less than one dollar in the United States. The French legislation of July 10, 1933 provided for "fixation of a minimum wheat price" and for organization and defense of the wheat market. The minimum price to be paid to French farmers for the period of 1933 to 1934 is equivalent to $1.23 per bushel in terms of United States gold.

Not being satisfied with protective tariff walls against imported wheat, the French plan includes the payment of an export bounty on domestic wheat and flour as equivalent to the existing tariff duty on foreign wheat, which is eighty-five cents. It provides for the manufacture of motor fuel from low grade wheat and low grade flour. It furnishes financial aid for storage or orderly marketing or both. From the standpoint of world markets the French laws are, of course, detrimental, since without domestic price support, France would have continued to remain a major wheat importing nation; whereas, under the stimulant of high domestic prices, she has recently become a "now and then" net exporter.

The British Wheat Policy

The British plan of guaranteeing an average farm price of ten shillings per hundred weight on sales of millable wheat, has now entered its second year and has greatly stimulated British wheat growing. In the current season, 1933, the wheat acreage of England and Scotland is about thirty per cent larger than in the year of 1932.

The Policies of Other Countries

The Irish Free State is following plans similar to those employed in England.

Monopolies on wheat exports were instituted in Holland on August 14 in order to cut down imports and help to raise the domestic price.

Thus we see there is a tug of war being carried on between the major wheat exporting countries on the one hand and of wheat importing countries on the other hand. A slogan for wheat importing countries might be written as follows: "Grow our own food and live as well as possible; but, in any event, grow our own food."

Wheat Policy of the United States

President Roosevelt, the United States Department of Agriculture, and the Agricultural Adjustment Administration have all definitely committed themselves to a program of high farm prices. Through currency inflation, some part of this program to advance prices has already been achieved but there is still a great deal that remains to be accomplished. It is the general opinion of economic writers that higher prices for farm products will be achieved through legislation, but it is somewhat doubtful whether the advance will be permanent or whether it will be only temporary.

Those who have gone deeply into the subject admit that any plan that will permanently curtail production will likewise have a lasting effect in advancing grain prices. Yet when those of us who have made a careful study of the burdensome over-supply attempt to find a remedy for over-production we arrive at only one conclusion, and that is to put into effect a broad program of conservation of soil fertility in which it is made *mandatory to the farmer to keep at least one-third of his acreage in soil-building* legumes and to limit his grain and cotton production to not over two years out of five in any given crop. Such a plan would, of course, conserve and build up our soil fertility for future generations. It would cut the acreage in cash crops from one-fourth to one-third and at the same time increase the yield per acre in those acres that are cropped. The administration knows only too well that any plan that presents such strong arm methods and carries such dictatorial policies will be unpopular with farmers and therein lies the trouble.

I am of the opinion the Roosevelt administration marks the final abandonment of the rule of laissez-faire. The Roosevelt administration has the power to bring about a revolution in agriculture which will mark the end of that ruthless competition which is the result of over-supply. I have attempted to show that monopolistic and mandatory prices for farm products will be detrimental rather than beneficial. Acreage reduction should be compulsory and price should remain "free" and "natural." Cut production and let prices go where they please, which will be higher.

I am of the opinion that the efforts of the Roosevelt administration up to the present time to advance grain prices are of too temporary a nature to be of lasting benefit. In attempting to put forth plans that meet with the farmers' approval the results have been policies that have been too weak to bring about the desired objective, which is to advance permanently the level of farm prices by striking directly at the evil—over-supply.

U. S. Wheat Legislation

I shall now give a short review of the current wheat policy of the United States.

The Agricultural Adjustment Act was approved on May 12th. It confers wide powers upon the Secretary of Agriculture, permitting him to put through schemes for reduction in acreage of cotton, wheat, corn, and other agri-

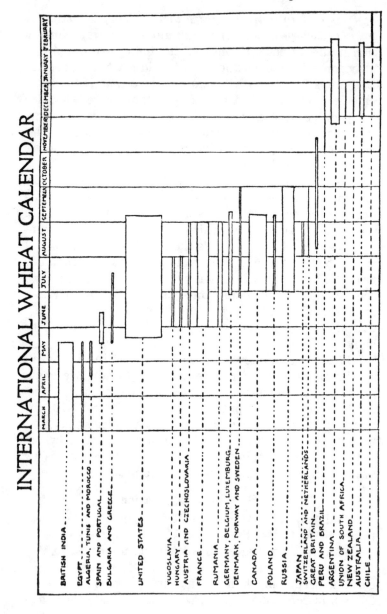

Showing the harvest season in wheat countries

cultural commodities. He is permitted to enter into marketing agreements and to issue and revoke licenses permitting processors, associations of producers, and others to engage in the handling of any agricultural product and to utilize funds for expansion of markets and removal of surplus agricultural products. An initial sum of $100,000,000 was appropriated to be available to the Secretary of Agriculture for use under this act.

A processing tax has been placed on certain agricultural commodities—notably wheat. The rate of the tax was specified as such rate as equals the difference between the current average farm price for the commodity and the fair average exchange value of the commodity.

On June 16 the main features of the wheat adjustment plan sponsored by the administration were made public. The Agricultural Adjustment Administration was formed with the suggestion that plans be put through which would result in the removal from the domestic market of certain types of wheat products in excess of domestic requirements in 1933–34. The funds for this purpose are to be obtained largely from the processing tax of 30 cents a bushel on wheat which is now in effect. Farmers have been given an opportunity to join county wheat production control associations. The definite contracts were made available to the farmers for signature on August 28th. The objective is a reduction of the 1934 crop approximately 15 per cent under the 1930–32 acreage.

It now seems probable that about 75 per cent of the wheat farmers in the United States either have signed or will sign these contracts. On the other hand, the 25 per cent that refuse to sign these contracts will probably greatly expand their acreage. The writer is of the opinion that the net reduction in wheat acreage, due to the efforts of the Agricultural Adjustment Administration, will result in a reduction in acreage of not less than 7 per cent and not more than 10 per cent for the crop season of 1933–34.

A credit of $50,000,000 has already been extended to the Chinese government in which $10,000,000 is available for the purchase of wheat in the United States. Up to the present time no purchases from China have been made; first because Chinese supplies are more than sufficient for current needs, and second, because United States wheat prices are too far out of line with other world markets.

In spite of all the legislation that has been enacted, the price of wheat in Chicago in terms of gold is still very low. A price of 95 cents for Chicago May Wheat in terms of inflated currency is only equivalent to about 66 cents a bushel in terms of gold dollars such as prevailed in February of this year.

World Wheat Supply and Demand

It is easier for me to present the subject of world wheat supply and demand by handling the subject under two heads. We shall first take up world supply, which is fairly definite, and will conclude with demand, which of course is a forecast.

World Wheat Supply

The following table is not only interesting, but it is impressive. It shows the world wheat supply, exclusive of Russia, at 4,410,000,000 bushels, which is 261,000,000 bushels under last year and compares very closely with the forecast which I made in July where I claimed that the world wheat crop will be approximately 250,000,000 bushels under last year.

Supplies in the United States and Canada are also the smallest in seven years, and this comes in spite of a record carryover for these two countries. This table includes the 1933 crop plus old stocks of about August 1st.

Clients who are interested in the 1933 crop by countries as arranged in groups will find it worthwhile to study the tables which follow. However, if you are interested only in world supply as a whole you may skip what immediately follows and take up the subject again under the title, "World Demand."

Year	World ex-Russia	European Importers	Principal Exporters	U. S. and Canada	Argentina and Australia
1926–27	4,000	1,145	2,282	1,387	485
1927–28	4,249	1,224	2,431	1,527	504
1928–29	4,649	1,279	2,827	1,707	640
1929–30	4,420	1,413	2,424	1,490	461
1930–31	4,635	1,254	2,764	1,713	563
1931–32	4,679	1,276	2,762	1,700	551
1932–33	4,671	1,418	2,612	1,689	161
1933–34	4,410	1,481	2,327	1,397	492

The European crop is one of record size and of good quality. This table shows the domestic crop of the principal European importing countries which is only ten million bushels below that of 1932.

Country	1927–31	Average 1932	1933
England, Wales	45	41	57
France	277	334	297
Germany	136	184	193
Italy	228	276	279
Belgium	15	16	14
Netherlands	6	13	14
Total	707	864	854

THE CROP OF CENTRAL EUROPE

Country	1927–31	Average 1932	1933
Poland	70	49	73
Czecho-Slovakia	49	54	66
Austria	12	13	14
Switzerland	4	4	5
Total	135	120	158

SCANDINAVIAN AND BALTIC COUNTRIES

Country	1927–31	Average 1932	1933
Scandinavia	30	38	33
Baltic States	13	18	17
Total	43	56	50

MINOR IMPORTING COUNTRIES

Country	1927–31	Average 1932	1933
Spain	141	184	129
Portugal	11	18	15
Greece	12	17	18
Total	164	219	162

EUROPEAN EXPORTING COUNTRIES

Country	1927–31	Average 1932	1933
Bulgaria	49	51	52
Hungary	82	64	87
Jugo-Slavia	87	53	90
Roumania	116	56	114
Total	334	224	343

A summary of the above tables indicates that the 1933
crop of European *importing countries* now appears to be
almost 175 million bushels above the 1927–31 average but
40 million bushels below last year's record crop. The crop
of the Danubian *exporting countries,* while by no means
a bumper crop, is much better than the short crop harvested in these countries in 1932. Exclusive of Russia,
Europe appears to have about 80 million bushels more
wheat than was produced last year, and furthermore the
crop is much better than it was a year ago. At the present writing we have no official indication of the Russian
wheat crop for 1933. The salient facts are Russian shipments from July 1 to date have been considerably smaller
than they were in 1930 or 1931 and are about equal to
the shipments in 1932 for this period. An attempt to
forecast the 1933 Russian crop by making a comparative
study of current exports compared to the last four years
indicates that the Russian crop is not a large one, although
it will probably be larger than the crop grown in 1932.

World Demand

The September issue of Wheat Studies makes the following statement: "Total net exports of wheat and flour
in 1933–34 may fall between 550 and 600 million bushels."

This forecast was made by M. K. Bennett and Helen S. Farnsworth, assisted by Joseph S. Davis, Alonzo E. Taylor, and Holbrook Working. These authorities call our attention to the fact that even the higher figure of 600 million bushels would represent the smallest export movement in more than a decade.

Estimates by Other Statisticians

Broomhall claimed on August 8th that probable total world shipments and import requirements in the crop year of 1933–34 would be approximately 552 million bushels as compared with 615 million bushels last year. The International Wheat Conference has placed import requirements at 560 million bushels.

I am convinced that the above forecasts on exports are not far wrong. The table on total world supplies as given on page 207 indicates that European wheat importing nations have 1,481,000,000 bushels of wheat, which is larger than any quantity they have had at any time in the past eight years. On the other hand, the principal exporters have only 2,327,000,000 bushels of wheat, which is the smallest supply of any year in the past seven years. With importing countries better supplied than they have been at any time in the last eight years and with exporting countries with the smallest supply they have had at any time in the past seven years, it is reasonable to assume that the international movement in wheat will be exceedingly small and probably smaller than at any time in the past twenty years.

A Long Range Price Forecast for Wheat

Under the subject "The Economics of Price" on page 128 I attempt to show that for the past 45 years $1.50 has been an exceedingly high price for wheat whereas 75 cents has been an exceedingly low price. These prices of course are expressed in terms of gold dollars and not in terms of inflated currency such as prevails at the present time.

Wheat Production in Principal Producing Areas and Countries, 1927–33

(Million bushels)

Year	World ex-Russia	Northern Hemisphere ex-Russia	Four Chief Exporters	United States Total	Winter	Spring	Canada	Australia	Argentina	USSR	Lower Danube	Other Europe	Northern Africa	India
1927	3,588	3,118	1,755	875	548	327	480	118	282	785	272	1,002	60	335
1928	3,924	3,350	2,002	926	591	335	567	160	349	807	367	1,042	69	291
1929	3,425	3,060	1,408	813	577	236	305	127	163	694	303	1,146	77	321
1930	3,686	3,182	1,728	857	599	258	421	214	236	989	353	1,006	64	391
1931	3,646	3,174	1,632	900	787	113	321	191	220	…	370	1,064	69	347
1932	3,652	3,140	1,607	727	462	265	429	216	235	…	224	1,256	66	337
1932	3,666	3,154	1,606	726	462	264	429	216	235	…	224	1,263	75	337
1933	3,297	2,875	1,141	515	340	166	283	152	200	…	343	1,226	64	353

Year	Hungary	Jugo-Slavia	Roumania	Bulgaria	Morocco	Algeria	Tunis	Egypt	British Isles	France	Germany	Italy	Belgium	Netherlands
1927	76.9	56.6	96.7	42.1	23.5	28.3	8.1	44.3	57.2	276.1	120.5	195.8	17.0	6.2
1928	99.2	103.3	115.5	49.2	24.7	30.3	13.7	37.3	50.9	281.3	141.6	228.6	17.9	7.3
1929	75.0	95.0	99.8	33.2	31.8	33.3	12.3	45.2	50.9	337.3	123.1	260.1	13.5	5.5
1930	84.3	80.3	130.8	57.3	29.8	32.4	10.4	39.8	43.4	228.1	139.2	210.1	13.7	6.1
1931	72.6	98.8	135.3	63.8	29.0	25.6	14.0	46.1	38.5	264.1	155.5	244.4	14.2	6.8
1932	64.4	53.5	55.5	50.6	22.0	29.2	14.7	52.6	43.7	331.4	183.8	276.1	15.6	13.7
1932	64.5	53.4	55.5	50.6	28.0	29.2	17.5	52.6	44.4	333.5	183.8	276.2	15.9	12.8
1933	87.4	90.0	113.9	52.1	25.7	28.1	10.3	39.9	57.0	297.1	192.7	279.2	13.6	14.2

Year	Scandinavia	Baltic States	Spain	Portugal	Switzerland	Austria	Czecho-Slovakia	Poland	Greece	Mexico	Japan, Chosen	South Africa	Chile, Uruguay	New Zealand
1927	25.3	10.0	144.8	11.4	4.34	12.0	47.2	61.1	13.0	11.9	38.3	5.7	46.0	9.54
1928	31.3	10.9	122.6	7.5	4.24	12.9	52.9	59.2	13.1	11.0	39.4	7.2	42.0	8.83
1929	31.5	13.7	154.2	10.6	4.21	11.6	52.9	65.9	11.4	11.3	38.6	10.6	46.7	7.24
1930	31.8	17.9	146.7	13.8	3.60	12.0	50.6	82.3	9.7	11.4	38.5	9.3	28.6	7.58
1931	27.7	14.6	134.4	13.0	4.04	11.0	41.2	83.2	17.0	16.2	39.2	13.7	32.4	6.58
1932	37.9	17.0	178.5	18.1	5.65	13.0	53.8	49.5	17.1	8.9	40.8	9.3	21.8	10.00
1932	38.3	18.0	184.2	18.1	4.18	13.0	53.7	49.5	17.1	9.7	39.9	9.3	31.3	10.00
1933	33.3	17.4	128.6	14.8	4.81	13.3	65.8	72.8	18.0	11.8	46.5	….	….	….

The above table was obtained from "Wheat Studies," Stanford University, California. Many of the 1933 figures were only estimates when this table was published in September. They have since been corrected. The year 1932 shows figures obtained from each of two sources.

If I can make my clients realize that 75 cents is a cheap gold dollar price for wheat and $1.50 is a high gold dollar price, then I shall be repaid ten times over for the efforts I put forth on October 2 in attempting to prove this assertion. Through all the range of wheat scarcity on the one hand and wheat over-supply on the other and through all the range of prosperity and full employment on the one hand and desperately hard times and unemployment on the other—wheat should move back and forth through a 75-cent price range. When wheat sells below 75 cents or above $1.50 we must assume that either price is absurd and can only be temporary. This condition should prevail through all time unless perchance some hitherto new type of gold mining machinery or chemical treatment should lower the cost of obtaining gold from the low grade ores. This is improbable although not impossible.

We sometimes hear the statement made that if some new gold fields were discovered as rich as the Rand Mines in South Africa we should have an over-supply of gold, a lower cost of production, and consequently higher prices. Such a possibility is extremely remote. When we think of gold, we should think of the supply as being adequate for at least ten thousand years. We must think of gold as being found in all parts of the world, but when it is found it is found in very minute particles that are mixed in with tons of earth, including the ores of the baser metals. The big cost of producing gold is a labor cost and not an equipment or engineering cost.

For the reasons I have just set forth, gold money is almost a perfect yardstick of measurement and therefore makes the ideal money by which the relative value of all commodities, services, and property is measured. When we think of the possibility of two-dollar-a-bushel wheat we must think of a hungry world that is willing to break its back to dig out gold to pay such a price.

In laying the foreground for values and a fair price for a bushel of wheat, we should never for one minute lose

sight of the fact that gold and wheat are bound tightly
together in a rather definite price relationship. When we
discuss the price of wheat we must also discuss the price
of gold.

Chapter XXXIV

Good Selling by Country Cash Buyers

THERE is no subject I would rather discuss than that of selling cash grain at a profit. Eighteen years of my life have been spent in the cash grain business in which I specialized in selling seed corn to the wholesale and retail trade.

While I cannot claim that I got rid of all the grain I purchased on the "hard spots" I do claim that my record of making profitable sales was far better than that of the average country elevator operator. I not only tried to find the daily tops but I frequently sold corn to feed dealers in Memphis, Tennessee and points in New York state at prices that netted me three to ten cents over what I would have realized in the Chicago or St. Louis market. In looking for the hardest way to sell grain and not the easiest way, I got a better price. On only one occasion was a loss taken on a bad account, and that loss was very small.

What I have to say in the following paragraphs refers more to the day to day selling that must be done by the day to day buyer in order to play safe.

Here is the plan I followed that never failed to get me a better price over a twelve month period than selling on a hit or miss bid basis. In August or September I would sell about what I thought would be one week's receipts of corn in November. I would do this by selling the May future short in August at the highest price reached in July, and failing to get the July high I would sell in September at the high in August and so on until I had sold some corn on a hard spot. When my cash corn was sold I bought in my contract. I sold only one week's receipts and nine years out of ten I was several hundred dollars ahead by my short sale. Sometimes I was several thousand dollars to the good.

I would sell December or May wheat short on any 15 per cent advance in July or August and it worked and made me money. The sale should amount to about one week's receipts of wheat in July if you want to be conservative. After having made this short sale I recommend the following day to day practice for the country buyer who must sell a little grain each week in order not to take too great a speculative risk. I would follow Trading Rule Eleven on the selling side only and price my cash grain each day at the high of the previous day. Then if I got behind on a gradually falling market, my short sale of the future would take care of a week's lag in the making of sales. If there is any better way of making sales two to four times a week on the hard spots, I have yet to hear of the plan. As a matter of fact, Trading Rule Eleven was used by the cash grain trade long before it was ever used by speculators in grain futures.

Don't forget, country cash buyer and seller, that July is a high corn and wheat month, whereas October and November are often months of low prices. Remember the low prices of the year should come weeks after the peak of receipts is past. It should come after mills have bought what they wanted of the cream of the wheat crop and when the off-grade odds and ends of weevil and weather damaged wheat are being pressed on the market.

By following this plan I sold the wheat grown on my farms this summer at $1.00 and $1.01, missing the year's high by only one cent. This wheat was sold on July 18, 1933 to the Farmers Elevator Co. of Mason City, Illinois and the Farmers Elevator Co. of San Jose, Illinois. The same plan gave me practically the season's high on my total corn crop sold from my farms in the fall of 1931.

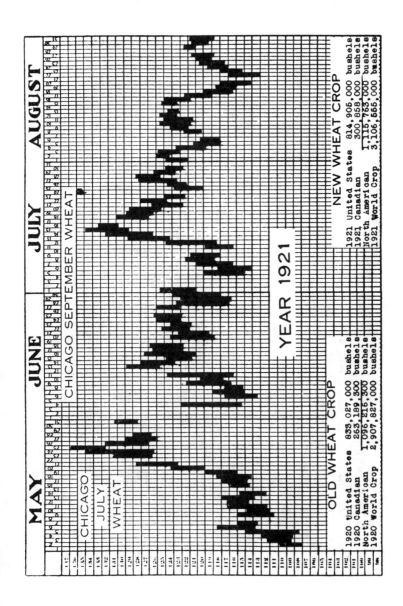

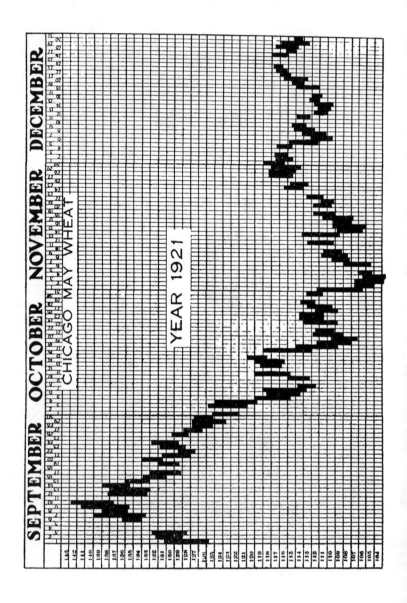

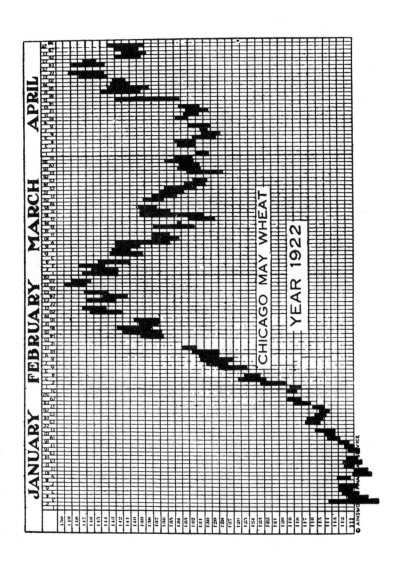

CHICAGO MAY WHEAT

YEAR 1922

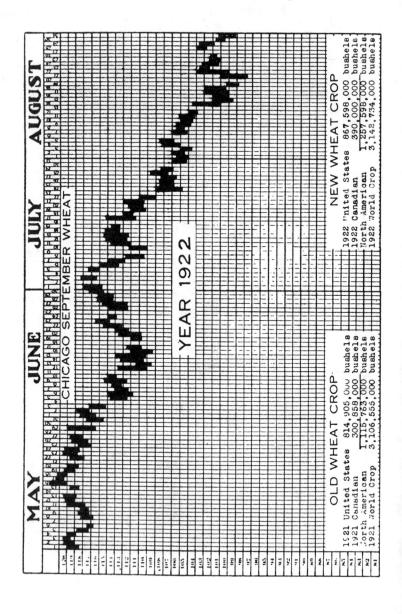

CHICAGO SEPTEMBER WHEAT

YEAR 1922

MAY   JUNE   JULY   AUGUST

OLD WHEAT CROP

1921 United States	814,905,000 bushels
1921 Canadian	300,858,000 bushels
North American	1,115,763,000 bushels
1921 World Crop	3,106,555,000 bushels

NEW WHEAT CROP

1922 United States	867,598,000 bushels
1922 Canadian	390,000,000 bushels
North American	1,257,598,000 bushels
1922 World Crop	3,142,734,000 bushels

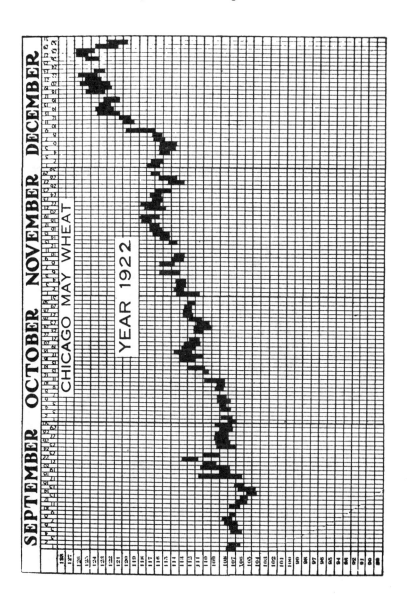

CHICAGO MAY WHEAT

YEAR 1922

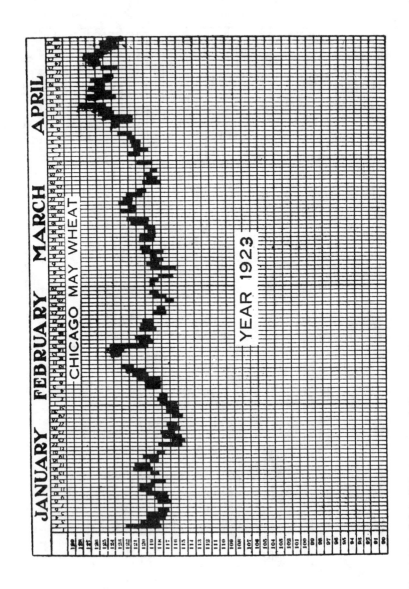

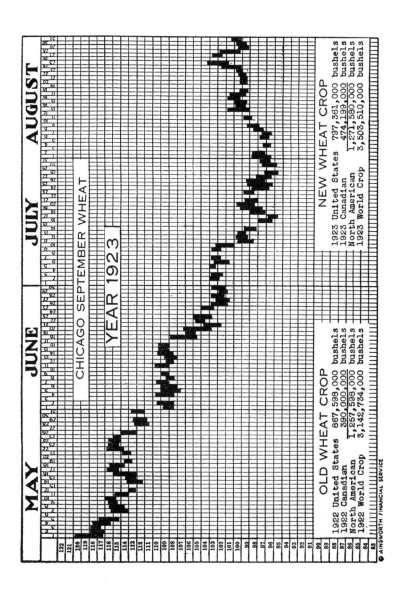

CHICAGO SEPTEMBER WHEAT

YEAR 1923

OLD WHEAT CROP

1922 United States	867,595,000	bushels
1922 Canadian	390,000,000	bushels
North American	1,257,598,000	bushels
1922 World Crop	3,142,734,000	bushels

NEW WHEAT CROP

1923 United States	797,361,000	bushels
1923 Canadian	474,199,000	bushels
North American	1,271,580,000	bushels
1923 World Crop	3,503,510,000	bushels

© AINSWORTH FINANCIAL SERVICE

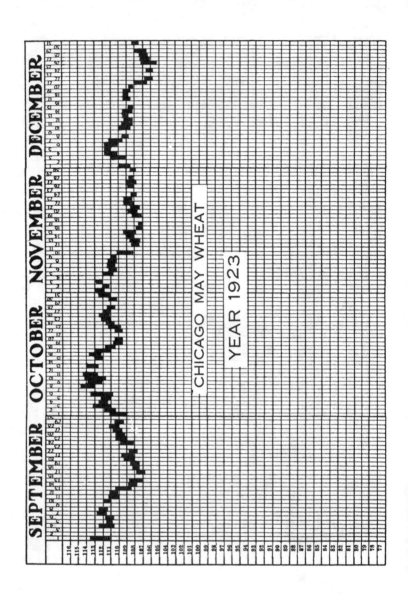

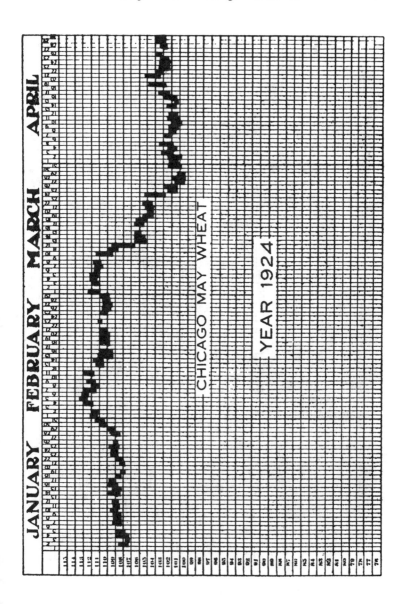

CHICAGO MAY WHEAT

YEAR 1924

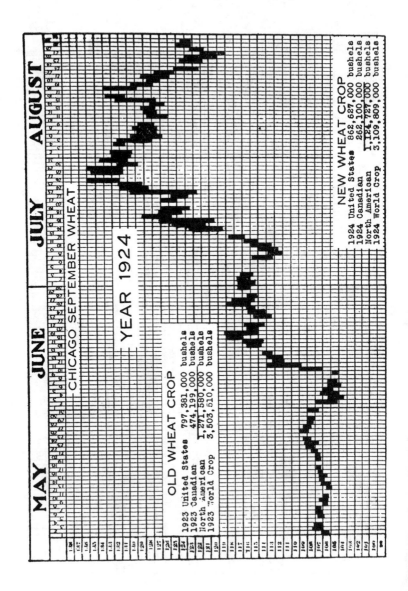

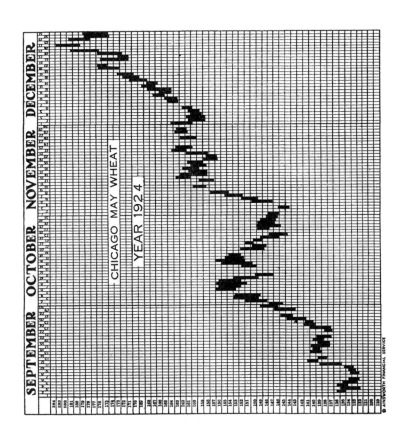

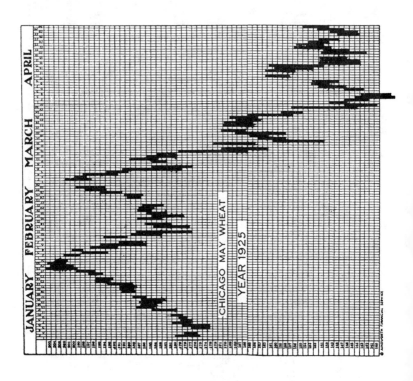

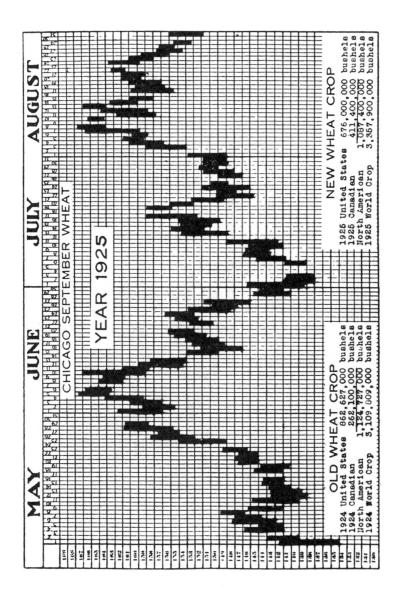

MAY   JUNE   JULY   AUGUST

CHICAGO SEPTEMBER WHEAT

YEAR 1925

OLD WHEAT CROP

1924 United States	862,627,000	bushels
1924 Canadian	262,100,000	bushels
North American	1,124,727,000	bushels
1924 World Crop	3,109,809,000	bushels

NEW WHEAT CROP

1925 United States	676,000,000	bushels
1925 Canadian	411,400,000	bushels
North American	1,087,400,000	bushels
1925 World Crop	3,357,900,000	bushels

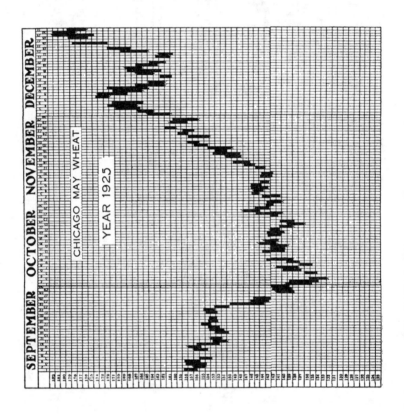

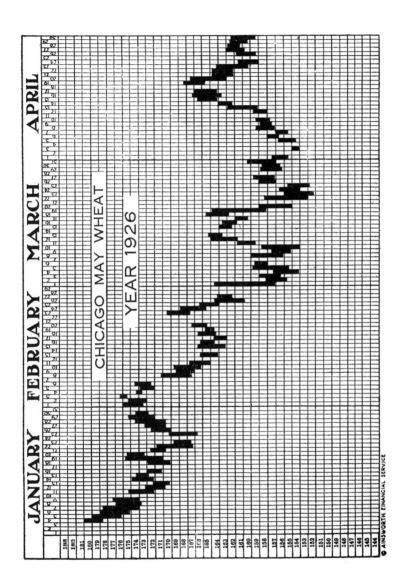

CHICAGO MAY WHEAT

YEAR 1926

© AINSWORTH FINANCIAL SERVICE

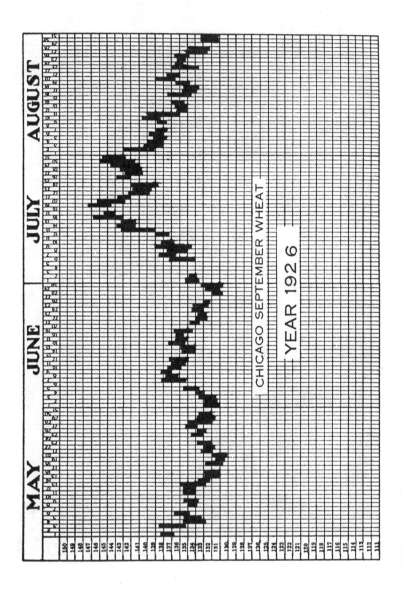

CHICAGO SEPTEMBER WHEAT

YEAR 1926

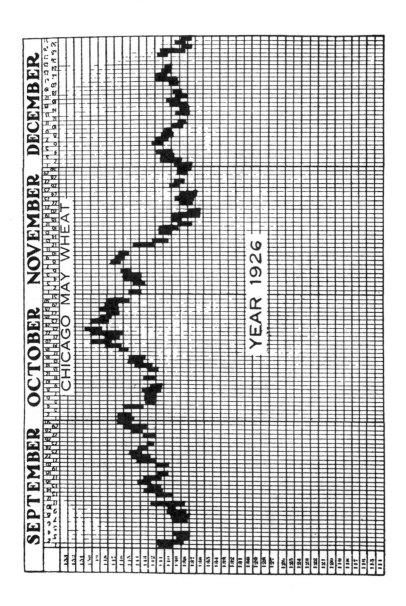

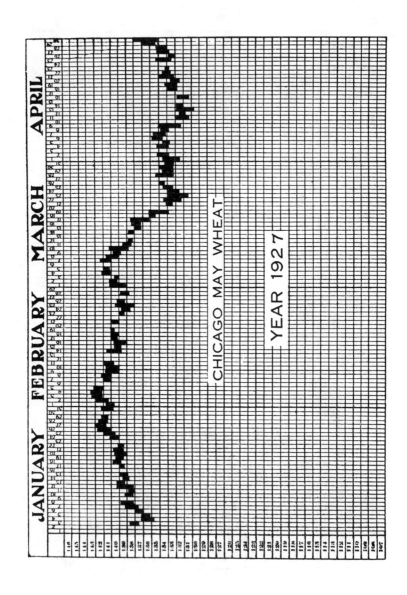

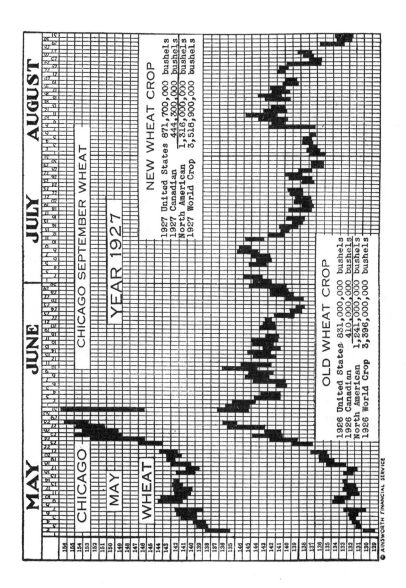

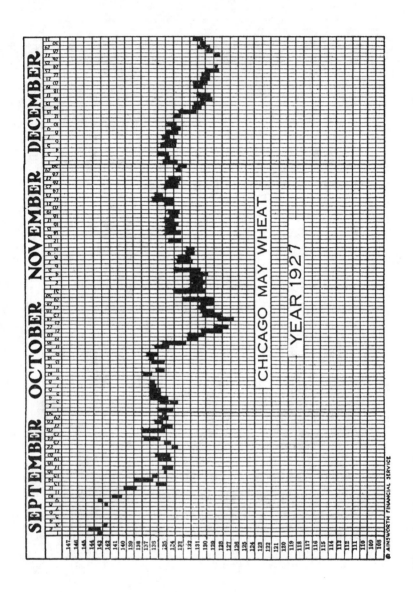

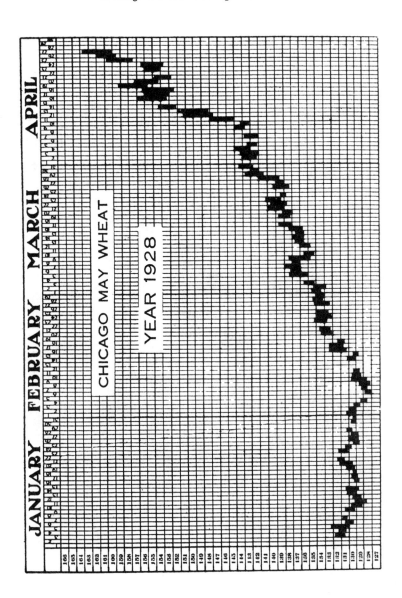

CHICAGO MAY WHEAT

YEAR 1928

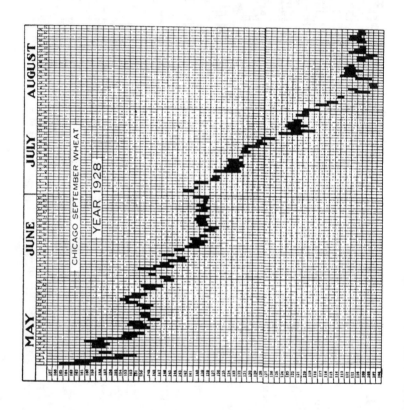

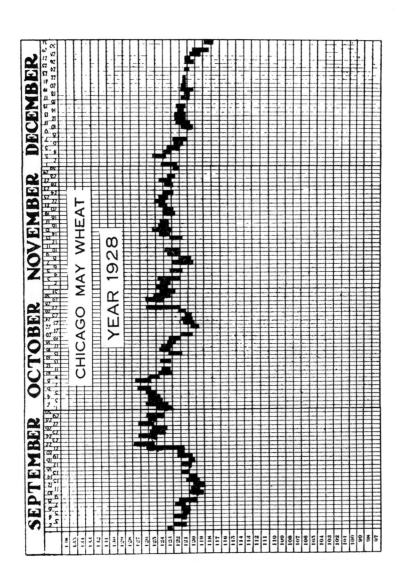

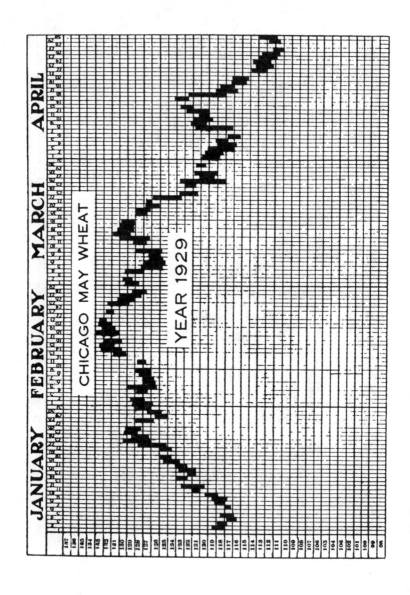

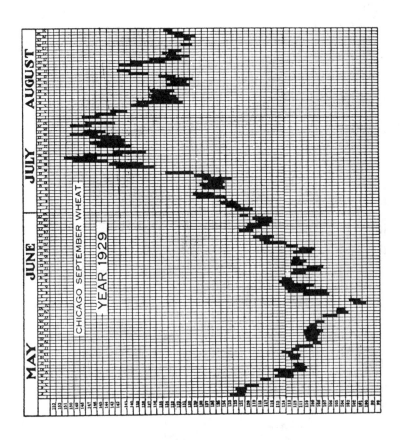

CHICAGO SEPTEMBER WHEAT

YEAR 1929

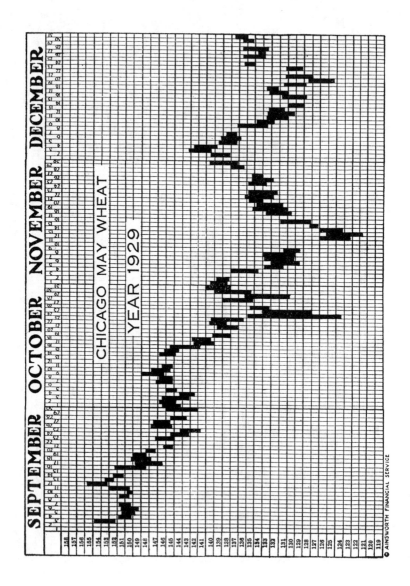

CHICAGO MAY WHEAT

YEAR 1929

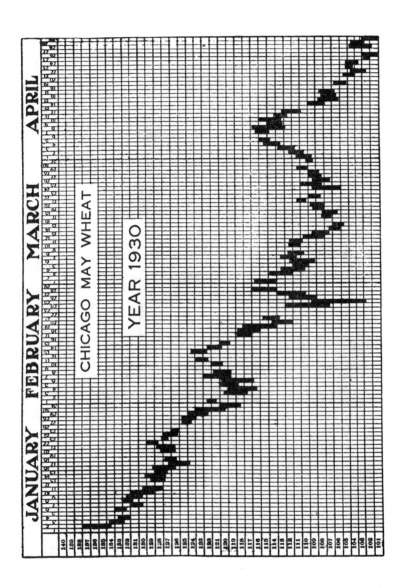

CHICAGO MAY WHEAT

YEAR 1930

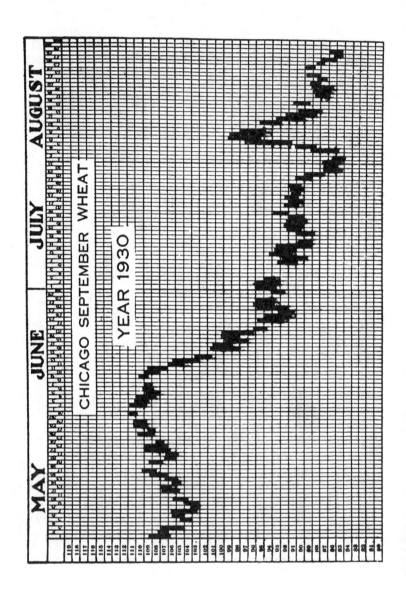

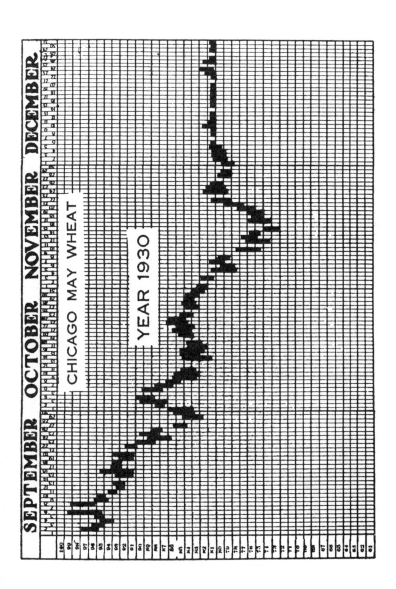

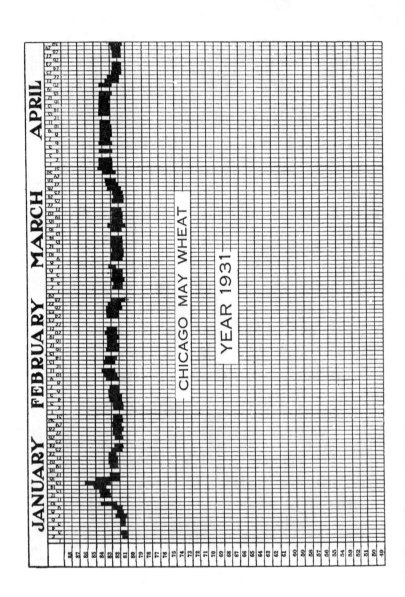

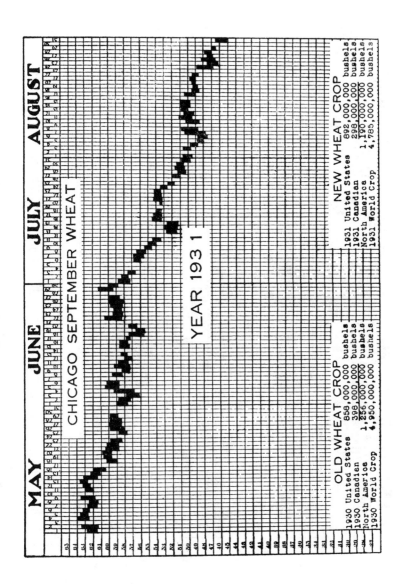

CHICAGO SEPTEMBER WHEAT

YEAR 1931

OLD WHEAT CROP
1930 United States 858,000,000 bushels
1930 Canadian 398,000,000 bushels
North America 1,256,000,000 bushels
1930 World Crop 4,950,000,000 bushels

NEW WHEAT CROP
1931 United States 892,000,000 bushels
1931 Canadian 298,000,000 bushels
North America 1,190,000,000 bushels
1931 World Crop 4,785,000,000 bushels

MAY   JUNE   JULY   AUGUST

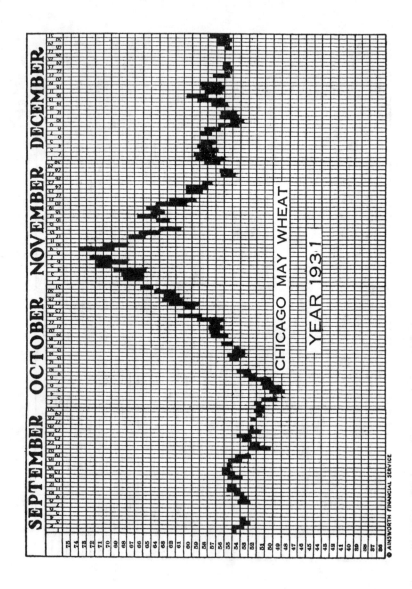

CHICAGO MAY WHEAT

YEAR 1931

Ainsworth's Financial Service

Statistical Advice on Grain Futures

COTTON , STOCKS , BONDS

ACCURACY OF FORECAST IS NOT GUARANTEED	FOR CLIENTS ONLY MASON CITY, ILLINOIS	REGULAR WEEKLY MARKET LETTER

October 7, 1940   *Number 732*

SPECIFIC ADVICE FOR THIS WEEK ONLY

CHICAGO WHEAT

I am short 5,000 bushels of December wheat at 83½. The sale was made last Tuesday as advised in my bulletin of September 30. This is my only position in the wheat market. I have entered an order to go short 5,000 bushels of May wheat at 85½ in the event we have a further advance.

I am placing an order to buy 10,000 bushels of December wheat at 75⅜. If filled, this will make me long 5,000 bushels. I am also placing an order to buy 5,000 bushels of May wheat at 75. If the order to go short at 85½ is filled before the buying order, my buying order in May wheat will be increased to 10,000 bushels in order to put me long 5,000 bushels of this future.

I rather expect the above buying objectives to be reached before the selling objectives. After the government estimated the U. S. wheat crop at 1,068,000,000 bushels in September, the private reports added nine million bushels to the spring wheat crop which now places the U. S. wheat supply at 1,077,000,000 bushels, or 70 million more than it was a year ago at this time.

According to the Bureau of Agricultural Economics the domestic disappearance for the year beginning July 1, 1940 will be about 700 million bushels which would leave 377 million bushels for export and carryover. If we export 48 million bushels of wheat in the current crop year (which was what we exported last year), our carryover on next July 1 will be 329 million bushels or 45 million bushels more than it was out July 1.

The Canadian crop at 561 million bushels (second largest on record) is 71 million bushels larger than last year and the current supply in Canada is the largest ever known.

Some of the private crop reporters place the condition of the 1941 winter wheat crop in the southwest at the best in several years and far ahead of where it was last year.

With the North American supply at least 140 million bushels larger than last year, and with new crop winter wheat prospects better, it is logical to expect U. S. wheat futures to sell lower in the fall of 1940 than in the fall of 1939. Let us now see just how much lower these prices should be.

December wheat had a "wartime" price range of 79½ to 87 cents in October of last year. In November the price range was 86 to 90. In December the price went zooming up to 112, but that was because the crop failed to come up to a stand in the southwest. This year the stand of wheat is so good in the southwest that it will furnish considerable fall grazing in less than 30 days. Therefore, I prefer to leave the high winter prices out of the price comparison I am making.

If December wheat could advance to only 90 cents in November of 1939, I believe 80 cents is a logical **top** for November, 1940. The fact that the December future declined from 83⅞ cents made in the past week, strengthens the point I have just made that 80 cents is about as high as December wheat can go next month, unless the market is helped by crop damage.

Because of the supporting force of wheat loans, I feel that December or May wheat will not decline below 75 cents during the life of either of the futures.

We are in a period of narrow-price-range (stabilized) markets, which are relatively easy to forecast, as I shall show in my mid-week bulletin.

CORN

I haven't recommended a trade in corn since I closed out my September corn on May 6 with a loss of one-half cent. I am frank to admit I considered the market too much of a stabilized affair to be worth fooling with. Notwithstanding what I have just said, I prefer to take my chances with almost any type of stabilized market rather than to risk my money with markets such as we had in the old days. Prior to 1930 the markets were at the mercy of the big speculators who were able to make prices go where they wanted them to go rather than where they should go. I have done twice as well in semi-stabilized markets such as we have had in the past five years as I did in markets prior to 1930 and I believe other traders have had a similar experience. When it comes to corn, this market has been virtually pegged because, unlike wheat, it wanted to go below the loan price but the loan kept it from declining.

OATS

Advise leaving this market alone

BEANS

I am short May beans at 78¾ as recommended in market order advice of last Monday. This is my only position in the market. I have entered an order to take profits at 66½ cents. I consider beans an outstanding short sale at the market.

Private reporters place the 1940 bean crop at 87 million bushels, or substantially the same as last year. Except that this year's crop and last year's crop were the two largest on record, the comparison ends here.

The carryover of old beans, if we include bean meal and oil, is many times larger than it was a year ago. Last fall, and early winter, we exported 10 million bushels of beans. This year we may do well to export a half-million bushels. This year linseed meal from a bumper flax crop will offer stiff competition to soy bean meal. If old crop beans could make a low of 75⅝ in June after we exported over 11 million bushels of the crop, new crop beans should not find it difficult to reach 65 cents on the bottom side unless helped by export demand.

COMMON STOCKS

I look for the investment type of common stocks to sell much higher as low interest rates continue and as corporation earnings increase due to the government preparedness program.

A number of clients have asked me for recommendations of specific stocks. I purchased several months ago, as a long-pull investment: Anaconda, Coca Cola, Corn Products and Refining, Reynolds Tobacco, Swift and Company, and Texas Corporation. I consider this a rather well-diversified list. If I were out of the market I do not know that I would substitute any other stocks for those I have just named.

FORECASTING AN ADVANCE
IN WHEAT, FOLLOWED BY A DECLINE

For the past three months I have been confident that a fair-sized advance would occur in wheat prices before October 5, after which a decline would get under way. I looked for the advance to come because I have claimed right along that there would not be enough "free" wheat to supply the mills. I have further claimed that the advance would bring out an abundance of "free" wheat and that a U. S. supply of 1,077,000,000 together with a poor export outlet, is too much wheat to justify prices remaining above 80 cents a bushel for the May future unless unusual fall damage occurs to the newly-seeded winter wheat crop.

In order to show clients that I not only anticipated the advance but that I have felt right along that it would be followed by a decline, I will quote from recent bulletins.

I made the following statement on July 17: "This desire to get in early on the long side . . . should place the top at 90 cents, **and this top should be reached before October 5.**"

I made the following statement on August 5: "The point I wish to stress in this bulletin, if we do have price advances such as I am forecasting, **I will look for most of the advance to be lost in the late fall and early winter months.**"

I made the following statement on August 12: "It is still my opinion (as stated for three weeks) that December wheat has one chance in two of selling up to 90 cents, **and if this price is reached it will be made before October 15** and with fair-sized declines coming in November or December."

After the sharp break to August 17, I said in my bulletin of August 19: "I cannot see any line of approach that indicates, or which justifies, any further decline in wheat prices." We took a long position in May wheat on August 19.

I made the following statement on September 2: "I am still of the opinion, however, that the **highs,** made between now and the close of the year, will come in the last two weeks of this month or in the first week of October."

I think I have made it clear in the above quotations from past bulletins that I have been just as confident in the last three months that **a decline would follow the advance** as I have been that the advance itself would occur. As this bulletin goes to press I feel just as confident of a decline from current levels as I felt confident of an advance on August 19 when I took a long position in May wheat.

OUR BEAN TRADES CLOSED OUT IN 1940

I want all my new subscribers to know that I took a loss of 24 cents a bushel on May beans closed out on April 22. This is one of the few heavy losses I have been required to take on any individual trade in commodity futures in the past eight years. On the other hand, it is the only loss I have ever had on a trade in bean futures. See bulletin of July 15.

The above-mentioned loss was more than offset by a profit of 26½ cents which was taken on July beans sold short at 108 on December 13 and closed out on July 8 at 81½ cents.

Our next profit was the October bean invoice shown below on which we took a profit of 20¾ cents.

On the same day I took this profit on October beans I went short the May future at 78¾. I feel confident this short sale of May beans will be good for at least 12 cents profit unless in the meantime the European war comes to a quick ending. I like to trade in beans because it is a crop where I can easily obtain first-hand information. Over half the crop is produced in Illinois and during the crop season I can look at thousands of acres in a short drive of not over one-half day. Illinois also has the largest processing plants in the world.

MID-WEEK BULLETIN

A mid-week bulletin will be issued on Tuesday or Wednesday of this week which will feature the condition of the 1941 winter wheat crop which has just been seeded; and the condition and quality of the 1940 corn and bean crops.

A REWARD FOR ACCOMPLISHMENT

On dozens of occasions in the past I have offered to refund the full price paid for my service to any client who can send us complete back files of a competing service that has shown a better ratio of profits to losses for the

same period. So far we have never had any claims for a refund. The above offer is now extended to include all trades made from January 1, 1939, to November 1, 1940. Details of this offer were published in our bulletin of July 15, a copy of which will be sent on request.

We are now offering a reward for market accomplishment on **single trades** which is the second time we have ever done such a thing. We will give our service complimentary for three months to any past or present subscriber who can send us complete back files of any service from the time the trade was recommended until it was closed out that shows the following accomplishment:

1. For a recommended **long position** in grains or beans made and closed out between May 1 and October 1 and showing a profit on a single trade of as much as 8⅞ cents. This was our profit on long May wheat closed out on September 23.

2. For a recommended **short position** in grains or beans made and closed out between April 22 and October 1, and showing a profit on a single trade of as much as 20¾ cents. This was our profit on short October beans closed out on September 30. A profit of as much as 43 cents was possible on the short side of September wheat from May 10 to August 17.

NOTE: If more than one buying or selling price was recommended by a competing service on a trade in any one future, we will take the average of the buying and selling prices. If a switch is made from one future to another, we will count only the profits shown in one future and not the combined profits on two trades. These two offers will be held open until November 4, at which time the names of those who are entitled to a reward will be published in our bulletin of that date.

MY RECENT TRADES

The following tabulation is a complete list of all commodity trades I have recommended to my clients and made for my own account since July 8 of this year. Ever since this service was started in 1927, I have made every trade for my own account that I have recommended to my clients. Furthermore, I have made no trades that I did not recommend. If I do not see fit to risk my own money on a trade, I do not consider it worth recommending to others.

New clients who would like to have an itemized list of all trades made between January 1, 1939, and July 8, 1940, should ask for our bulletin of July 17. If you want to see a list for a longer period, ask for our bulletin of October 31, 1938, and also our bulletin of July 17.

The two bulletins just mentioned, together with this bulletin, itemize every trade recommended to clients and made for my own account from April 17, 1937, to date.

Date		Loss Trades	Gain Trades
		(cents per bu.)	
6-17-40 Bot. 5 Sept. wheat at 75			
8-20-40 Sold 5 Sept. wheat at 70			
(A long position) Loss		5	
7-14-40 Bot. 5 Dec. wheat at 75¼			
9-21-40 Sold 5 Dec. wheat at 78¼			
(A long position) Gain			3
8-19-40 Bot. 5 May wheat at 71⅛			
9-23-40 Sold 5 May wheat at 80			
(A long position) Gain			8⅞
4-22-40 Sold 5 Oct. beans at 96			
9-30-40 Bot. 5 Oct. beans at 75¼			
(A short position) Gain			20¾
Gain on all Gain trades			32⅝
Loss on all Loss trades		5	
Net Gain since July 8, 1940			27⅝

RALPH M. AINSWORTH.

Ainsworth's Financial Service

Statistical Advice on Grain Futures
COTTON , STOCKS , BONDS

ACCURACY OF FORECAST
IS NOT GUARANTEED

FOR CLIENTS ONLY
MASON CITY, ILLINOIS

REGULAR WEEKLY
MARKET LETTER

October 28, 1940   *Number 736*

SPECIFIC ADVICE FOR THIS WEEK ONLY

WHEAT

If I were out of the market I would place an order to sell Chicago May wheat short at the opening today.

I am short 5,060 bushels of December wheat at 83½ cents which order was filled on October 1. I am also short 5,000 bushels of Chicago May wheat at 85½ which order was filled on October 23 as per advice given in our bulletin of October 21.

I am entering an order to buy 10,000 bushels of December wheat at 77¼, which, if filled, will place me long 5,000 bushels in this future. I am entering an order to buy 10,000 bushels of May wheat at 75¾, which, if filled, will place me long 5,000 bushels in this future.

It is my opinion that the excitement over the election has been a factor in advancing farm commodity prices in the past two weeks although I would find it difficult to explain just why this would occur. I do not believe the outcome of the election will have any influence on the market. Willkie has promised to continue the farm program for an indefinite period, or until something better can be found, if he is elected President. Roosevelt, of course, wants to continue the program as it is.

Unless we find an important export outlet for our surplus wheat and corn, I will expect a decline to get under way immediately after the election is over. The only important export outlet would be continental Europe.

There is a bare possibility that the United States may decide to donate wheat and other foods to the conquered nations of Europe. Before such a plan can be carried out we will first have to have the consent of Great Britain and it appears very improbable that Great Britain will agree to lift her blockade.

CORN AND OATS

Although I look for a decline in both corn and oats futures I would be afraid to take a position on the short side unless there is an increase in "direct from the field" marketing of corn by farmers.

SOY BEANS

I am short May soy beans at 83½ cents which order was filled on October 21 as per advice in our bulletin of that date.

I am placing an order to close out this short position on any decline to 75. If this order is filled I will stand aside unless a later advance offers what I consider a good opportunity for another short sale.

THE STOCK MARKET

I feel that so-called peacetime stocks offer a relatively safe opportunity for the investment of idle funds in these uncertain times. I prefer so-called peacetime stocks because I believe war stocks have largely discounted anticipated increased earnings. The earnings of individuals are bound to be high in the next few years notwithstanding the fact that taxes will also be high.

Therefore, idle funds will continue to pile up. With interest rates very low on government bonds, high grade industrial bonds, and savings accounts, common stocks appear to me to offer the best investment income that can be had at the present time.

If I were to make an investment in common stocks now, I am sure I would include American Telephone and Telegraph, American Tobacco, General Electric, General Motors, Swift and Company, and Texas Corporation.

THE CORN MARKET

Although I consider corn prices too high to hold, I feel that a short position taken at this time carries with it too much risk, especially since this is the season of the year when corn futures frequently make their lows for the year.

The quality of the 1940 crop is fully as good as the 10-year average and possibly better. The general use of hybrid corn has been a factor in improving the quality in the past three years. The quality, however, is not as good as it was last year. Some corn that was gathered early with pickers contained so much moisture that there is considerable risk of it going out of condition in the cribs. The risk of damage has been increased due to unseasonably warm weather.

Country stations in central Illinois are paying approximately 56 cents for new corn and 61 cents for old corn, which prices are too high to yield a good return when fed to hogs that net the farmer 5¼ to 5¾ cents a pound on the farm. Notwithstanding the poor feeding margin, most farmers who have will of course finish them out to market weights although it is probable that these weights will be lighter than usual and will result in a corresponding saving in corn.

In considering the trend of corn prices it seems to me that there are two factors which should be kept in mind. One is that due to the sealing program the price is far above what one would normally expect for better than average supplies. The other factor is that supplies of free corn will probably be more than enough to meet all market needs.

THE BEAN MARKET

I consider soy beans an unusually attractive short sale at the market. Traders who are now short May beans at 83½, or those who contemplate taking a short position at the better opportunity that now exists, should keep in mind that this is a rather hazardous market because of the limited amount of trading compared to grain markets.

Judging from local observations I would say that the bean crop is now all harvested under ideal conditions.

The advance in the past week can be accounted for largely because of smaller receipts compared to last year. On the other hand, shipments are far below what they were a year ago. We note that on Thursday shipments were 137,000 against 701,000 last year. On Wednesday they were only 71,000 against 304,000 a year ago.

It is still my opinion that processors are buying very cautiously and that this limited buying will continue as long as hogs remain at low price levels and as long as there is an abundant supply of linseed and cottonseed meal.

THE COTTON MARKET

I am afraid to take a short position in the cotton market due to cotton loans as well as the fact that this commodity is currently quoted at less than average cost of production. Experience shows that it is usually unsafe to sell a stable commodity short regardless of how large may be the supplies when the cost is less than the average cost of production.

On the other hand, I am afraid to take a long position in cotton futures because I feel that the demand from England for American cotton will be limited due to a shortage of ships for importing the staple as well as exporting the finished product. It is also my opinion that the people of the British Isles will effect unusual economies in their purchases of cotton wearing apparel until the war is over.

After the war is over Great Britain will naturally place all the business she can with the cotton-growing countries within her own empire. I am assuming that, regardless of how the war ends, England will be permitted to keep her empire unless perchance India on her own account demands and obtains her independence.

NATIONAL PROSPERITY
AND THE STOCK MARKET

Business activity is now at high ebb which to me is inevitable under the circumstances of the big government spending program which is now under way and which will probably continue for several years to come regardless of which administration comes into power.

The weekly payroll for wages is now the biggest ever known and while we still have several millions of unemployed, those of us who live in the center of farming areas have experienced the greatest shortage of labor in the past two weeks that has been witnessed since the stock market collapse of 1929.

Not only is labor scarce but non-union labor is demanding and receiving the highest wage per hour that it has received in ten years. There is no question but that this prosperity is of an artificial nature and that it cannot continue indefinitely, but it can continue for many years to come and it probably will continue for the next five years.

THE APPRAISAL METHOD
OF TRADING IN GRAIN FUTURES

I have written on this subject more often than any other subject pertaining to grain speculation for the reason I consider it one of the most important as well as one of the least understood.

Almost without exception I take my initial short positions in strong markets, which means that I take them as the market moves up to my selling objectives. (Note our short sale of May beans and May wheat made in the past week.) My initial long positions are invariably taken in weak markets as the market moves down to meet my buying objectives.

This is called the appraisal method of grain speculation. It is a method that is used by most of the veteran grain traders, and now that we have semi-stabilized markets, it is rapidly gaining in popular favor.

I believe the appraisal method is used in fully 90 per cent of the long positions taken in the stock market and in fully 99 per cent of the purchases and sales of farm lands and city real estate. The prospective purchaser of a farm would hardly say, "I can buy this farm at $80 an acre, but I am not interested unless it demonstrates its ability to command a price of $85. Then I will buy it, or one that is similar."

The appraisal method is nothing more nor less than finding a price, for the commodity in question, that seems to be in line with the facts. The price where the trader is willing to go short may be 5 to 25 per cent above the appraisal price. He also selects a price 5 to 25 per cent below what he considers a logical price and this becomes the buying objective. He will buy there because he considers the lower price too low to hold. The distance he moves away from the pivotal (appraisal) price depends on market activity, season of the year, and many factors that have been discussed in past bulletins.

Like the Dow Theory and trend-trading, the objective of the man who trades on pre-determined values is to find a price that he considers too high to hold or one that he considers too low to hold.

The methods of finding these buying and selling objectives are of course quite different. The trend trader invariably undertakes to sell in a **down** market that has followed immediately after an advance or he tries to buy in an **up** market that has followed immediately after a decline. Thus the trend trader, in theory at least, buys on a day when the market is strong whereas the appraisal trader buys on a day when the market is weak. Contrariwise, the trend trader sells on a day when the market is weak whereas the appraisal trader sells on a day when the market is strong. The appraisal trader hopes the trend will change after he takes his position and the trend trader hopes it will continue. Sometimes half or all of an advance is lost before the trend trader gets into the market on the long side or a decline may all be lost before he can find his short sale signal.

I am frank to admit that each method has its good points as well as its weak points; but I challenge any one to combine the strong points of both methods because, if he were to do so he might find himself in the ridiculous position of undertaking to buy and sell at the same time.

The outstanding weakness of the appraisal method of grain speculation is that when a short sale is made in a strong market following a fair-sized advance, the trader has no assurance that the advance will not continue much further, thereby making it necessary to ride the trade through a heavy paper loss and on occasions he will be required to take a fair-sized loss. The same situation applies on the bottom side.

These occasional heavy losses are the result of faulty appraisals of what grains are actually worth, inability to recognize the force behind a trend, or unknown factors that suddenly develop that really change values.

In theory, the trend trader is supposed to overcome these hazards and to a large extent he does succeed in overcoming these hazards. On the other hand, the trend trader is occasionally forced to take five to ten small losses in succession, ranging from two to six cents a bushel, before he gets a trade placed on the right side of a major trend.

In these times of semi-stabilized markets several years may elapse before the trend trader is able to secure the greater part of the profits that are possible in a major price swing.

It is, of course, impossible for any one to accurately measure the comparative merits of the two systems. In past bulletins I have frequently shown the market accomplishment of trend traders who used the Minor Trend Rule, the Seven-Day Moving Average Rule, or Trading Rule 19. The reason that the comparative merits of trend-trading methods (which are mechanical) cannot be compared with appraisal methods is that the latter cannot be reduced to a formula because it is a matter of market judgment. This judgment may be very good or it may be very poor.

All I can do is to compare the accomplishment of trend-trading methods with my own past results. This I have often done by offering rewards for the market accomplishment of competing services regardless of what method has been used.

In our bulletin of October 7 I offered to refund the full price paid for my service to any client who had taken a competing service that had shown better results over a period of two years or longer. I also offered to send my service complimentary for three months to any past or present subscriber who could show us a recommended long position in grains or beans that yielded a profit of as much as $8\frac{7}{8}$ cents, which was our profit on long May wheat closed out on September 23, or a profit of as much as $20\frac{3}{4}$ cents on a single short position, which was our profit on the short sale of October beans closed out on September 30. So far we have had no claims for any rewards under the above offers.

Although I grant that losses on individual trades under the appraisal method will exceed probable losses on individual trades under trend-trading, I am also firmly convinced that the appraisal method shows no greater risks over a period of years and also that the trades that do show a loss are much fewer in number. If I make ten trades that show a loss of two cents each, I am no better off than if I make two trades that show a profit of 10 cents each and end up with a trade that loses me 40 cents. The total margin put up for the period is exactly the same in the two unfortunate examples I have given.

Ever since Ainsworth's Financial Service was started in 1927, it has used the appraisal method in grain trading in which the amount of force behind a price swing is taken into consideration.

RALPH M. AINSWORTH.